Classics In
Child Development

Classics In
Child Development

Advisory Editors

JUDITH KRIEGER GARDNER
HOWARD GARDNER

Editorial Board

GROWTH

A Study of Johnny and Jimmy

BY

MYRTLE B. McGRAW

With a New Introduction
by
Myrtle McGraw

ARNO PRESS
A New York Times Company
New York – 1975

Reprint Edition 1975 by Arno Press Inc.

Copyright © 1935, By D. Appleton-Century Company, Inc.

Reprinted by permission of Prentice-Hall, Inc.

Reprinted from a copy in
  The Newark Public Library

Classics in Child Development
ISBN for complete set: 0-405-06450-0
See last pages of this volume for titles.

Manufactured in the United States of America

Library of Congress Cataloging in Publication Data

McGraw, Myrtle Byram, 1899-
    Growth; a study of Johnny and Jimmy.

    (Classics in child development)
    Reprint of the ed. published by D. Appleton-Century,
New York, in series: The Century psychology series.
    Bibliography: p.
    1. Infant psychology. 2. Infants--Growth.
3. Twins. I. Title. II. Series.
BF723.I6M32 1975   155.4'22   74-21422
ISBN 0-405-06471-3

40 YEARS REFLECTIONS
OF THE AUTHOR
1974
Myrtle B. McGraw

During the 1920s and early 1930s the study of INFANCY AND EARLY CHILDHOOD blossomed as an academic discipline and as an area for experimental research. Current evaluation of those early investigations can best be attained against a backdrop of the concepts, theories, and research strategies extant at the time. Studies of behavior or performance were for the most part under the direction of psychologists. Psychology as a discipline was young and struggling diligently to establish scientific methods. Graduate students preparing themselves for research in the area were admonished to cleanse their minds of "arm chair philosophy and folk lore", to be objective, to measure, to assemble the data and let the data speak for itself. These lofty methodological goals presented insurmountable hurdles for the budding genetic psychologists, using infants as subjects. Nonetheless, a legacy of ideas or concepts — cultural concepts, theories derived from other disciplines and from general psychology — did have an impact in the design of early experimental procedures.

A brief discussion of the commingling or intertwining of these residual concepts and theories may reveal their influence upon both investigative procedures and, in the long run, on some ideas about the rearing of young children. Consider, for a moment, the theory of evolution. It led to the assumption that generalizations derived from animal experiments could be applied to the interpretation of human behavior. Secondly, it sparked the dichotomy of classifying behavior into "hereditary and acquired traits". Pavlov, experimenting with dogs, articulated the "conditioning" theory. John B. Watson, one of the first to use newborn infants as experimental subjects, was searching to ascertain what traits were innate and which were acquired. The hypothesis was that all behaviors present at birth were inborn, and others were acquired. The number of inborn traits he considered to be few. Watson thereupon extended his experiments to demonstrate that the conditioning process was operative with infants as well as with dogs. Complex behavior was the product of environmental stimuli acting on the reacting organism, animals or human infants. Emphasis on the environment flourished. At the time that child development was emerging as an academic system BE-HAVIORISM (now referred to as S-R psychology) was espoused by many psychologists as the predominant frame of reference of interpreting behavior.* Clearly the emphasis on the environment as a determinant of behavior had considerable influence on experimental procedures and cultural ideas about child upbringing.

There were other forces in general psychology which set the stage for the study of infancy and early childhood. One of the most powerful forces was the standardized testing technique. The Stanford Revision of the Binet had established itself as a useful measuring tool for evaluating classroom achievements of school children. In the beginning some psychologists considered the I.Q. as an indicator of general intelligence.

Naturally, with this model, early researchers of infant development set about designing developmental scales for use in testing infants. The Gesell tests were among the first and remained the best established. Gesell did another study which became more theoretically challenging. Using the co-twin technique he vociferously challenged the enviromental-

---

*Indeed, it was Behaviorism and Psychoanalytic theories which drew attention to the significance of the early years. Psychoanalytical theory is not brought into this discussion because the book, "Growth, A Study of Johnny and Jimmy" is not concerned with pathology of behavior.

ists, notably Watson. In so doing he set up another dichotomy — MATURATION versus LEARNING. The theoretical battle was on!

In the foregoing paragraphs I have wanted merely to highlight some of the prevailing thoughtways at the time I embarked on a program of infant study. The study of Johnny and Jimmy was only an adjunct to a larger program designed to determine the relationship between the maturing nervous system and infant behavior. At the onset I was incredibly naive, essentially ignorant of the maturing nervous system and of genetics.*

In any event I felt that merely ticking off achievements and plotting them against chronological age would not yield the kind of information I was seeking. I was more concerned with *how* a trait or skill develops than with *when*.

But the Johnny-Jimmy study was sparked by another thought, equally naive. If Gesell was right that infant development could not be accelerated by experience — and I had no reason to doubt it — then I thought if I took an infant at birth and exercised him daily in any activity of which he was capable I would discover some kind of behavioral syndrome which would indicate the nervous system had ripened sufficiently for the child to improve by practice or training. Of course, it didn't turn out to be that simple!

When at a professional meeting I made my first presentation of the study, illustrated with movies of the infant swimming with his face under water and scooting around on roller skates, Gesell and practically everyone else jumped to the conclusion that the study negated Gesell's famous maturational theory. Of course I knew it didn't; it merely modified it. But no one paid any attention to my report that at the same time and for nearly nine months thereafter we had pushed the baby up and down the corridor five days a week on a tricycle, and he just couldn't master it until he was nearly 19 months old. Waiting for the appropriate nerve cells to mature?

The skillful feats of a swimming and skating infant of

*Perhaps that is why now I find so much redundancy in my 1935 publication.

about a year of age attracted the attention of the newspaper and magazine media. As a result the theoretical significance of growth and development during infancy was clouded. Even more amazingly, for years, my own colleagues, the textbook writers, would continue to cite magazine articles as references even though GROWTH had been published. Even unto this day scant attention is paid to the tricycling aspect of the study. Yet, as was pointed out both in GROWTH and the follow-up study[1], the tricycling was just as informative to the experimenter as was the more spectacular achievements of the infant.

During the ensuing years great conceptual and methodological strides have been made in allied sciences — neurology, genetics, communications, etc. — which serve to liberate the student of growth and development from some of the rigidities and constraints imposed by Behavioristic theories. We are beginning to think systemically, that is, the interfluence of differing systems in a constant state of flux or change interacting with each other. We are beginning to recognize that static concepts like stimulus-response, normative data, dichotomies, true-false, etc. — actually obscure or stultify our perceptions of a constantly changing phenomena like growth and development. Many modern writers, Jerome Bruner et al., are beginning to beam in on "process" rather than end-results, or achievements. Terms like "consciousness, intuition, and sensitivity", which were taboo during the early decades because they couldn't be objectively measured are becoming respectable again. Even so, those nomenclatural taboos had an effect upon the procedures and interpretations of young researchers during the 1930s. For example, to this day, forty years later, I experience an emotional excitement when I recall the moment when that tricycling baby looked up at me with wonderment in his face, a glint in the eye, as if he had just discovered the meaning of the universe. What he had discovered, after more than eight months of practice on the tricycle, was that it was the rotary movement of his own two legs which made the vehicle move. The emotional communication between me and the baby at that time is indelible; a recording of the experience was in my original notes. The reason for my telling it here is that on rereading the original publication of GROWTH, I noted that this incident in the tricycling experience was definitely deleted. Why? Because I was afraid I might be accused of being subjective, sentimental, and unscientific. That kind of criticism was difficult for a young researcher to face in the scientific milieu of those days.

To gain clarity and precision of meaning, scientists sometimes coin new words or restrict definition to familiar nomenclature. With the passing of time those definitions may become distorted primarily because the Zeitgeist of the culture changes. Borrowing from Genetics, I applied the term "critical periods" to indicate that there were occasions most favorable for expansion of modification of a particular function during infancy. But since the term "critical periods" attained great specificity in connection with the imprinting process of goslings, and since the more recent studies of deprived infants imply serious loss which cannot be overcome, the term has acquired connations which were not intended in my original publication. As long as there is growth, there is hope! If a function doesn't develop at a particular time, it may still be achieved, but the methods of development or instruction may, of course, be different. Although we haven't the techniques of measurement it is well to remember that the Zeitgeist, the milieu, will influence the design of investigations and the concepts and theories derived therefrom.

In view of the current trend for joint or interdiscipline studies of early child development, there is justification for optimism.

(1)McGraw: Later Development of Children Specially Trained During Infancy, CHILD DEVELOPMENT, Vol. 10, No. 1, March 1939

GROWTH
A Study of Johnny and Jimmy

THE CENTURY
PSYCHOLOGY SERIES

EDITED BY

RICHARD M. ELLIOTT, PH.D., *University of Minnesota*

---

* Published
August, 1935.

The Century Psychology Series
Richard M. Elliott, Editor

GROWTH

A Study of Johnny and Jimmy

BY

MYRTLE B. McGRAW, Ph.D.

RESEARCH PSYCHOLOGIST AND ASSISTANT DIRECTOR OF THE NORMAL CHILD
DEVELOPMENT CLINIC
NEUROLOGICAL INSTITUTE, COLUMBIA MEDICAL CENTER

*With a Preface by Dr. Frederick Tilney
and an Introduction by John Dewey*

Drawings by Kenneth W. Breeze

D. APPLETON – CENTURY COMPANY
INCORPORATED

NEW YORK   LONDON

TO

J. D.

PREFACE

In the course of our studies of behavior at the Neurological Institute of New York our attention was at first devoted almost exclusively to the growth and development of certain lower mammals. It was felt necessary to acquire a phylogenetic conception of behavior before approaching our ultimate objective, namely, the genesis of adaptive reactions in man. The study of human behavior in early life requires a technical set-up differing in many details from that used in studying lower animals. It was for this reason that the Normal Child Development Clinic was established in March, 1931. Since that time Dr. McGraw with a staff of trained assistants has devoted herself to systematic observation of behavior of infants during the first two years of life.

The underlying plan of our investigation is based upon the obvious fact that all structures of the body must attain adequate differentiation before they are capable of highly specialized reactions. This fact of essential specialization is particularly clear in the nervous system. Individual nerve cells acquire adequate differentiation in their bodies, in their cell processes (axones, dendrites) and in their intercellular connections. Adequate differentiation of this kind in nerve cells is a result of the gradual process of maturing. The process advances more rapidly in some parts of the nervous system than in others. Cells in the segmental portion (spinal cord and brain stem) mature at an earlier period than in the supra-segmental portion, especially the cerebral cortex. Certain series of nerve cells related to definite specialized reactions mature more rapidly than other series of this kind. In general, those series which are phylogenetically the oldest acquire adequate differentiation at an earlier period, while those which are of later acquisition in the brain are relatively late in attaining structural maturity.

On the basis of this ripening process it is possible to establish correlation between the time of development in the several different systems of nerve cells and the reactions in the animal depending upon the maturing of these systems. Schedules of the ripening

process have already been established in several different species
of mammals. In these schedules a definite correlation is apparent
between behavior and development of the brain.

Similar correlation between cerebral structures and human behavior is being undertaken. The analysis of behavior-patterns as
reported in this volume lays the foundation of this correlation.
The structural investigation in man, as well as in other species,
has been carried on by the reconstruction of wax models from
serial sections of the brain. This reconstruction technique offers
the nearest approach to an experimental method at present
available.

Dr. McGraw's work offers more than the material upon which
to base the structural correlation. It has been my privilege to
have intimate contact with her studies, so that I have gained much
first-hand knowledge of her methods and observations. It is probable that no other study of the human infant from the time of
birth through the second year has been made with such thorough-
ness and attention to detail.

The complexity of each pattern of behavior is so great that but
a few patterns can be considered at a time. For this reason future
investigations of the Clinic staff will embrace a number of other
patterns of behavior which it has been impossible to more than
touch upon in this book. A large number of somatic behavior-
patterns still remain to be elucidated. To these must be added the
still more intricate group which enters into and forms the basis
of splanchnic behavior. These latter reactions, upon which the
essence of life depends, have been almost wholly neglected not
only in the genesis of behavior but in its ultimate portrayal and
expressions as witnessed in the adult.

The studies reported in *Growth: a Study of Johnny and Jimmy*
and in all of the work being undertaken at the Clinic open a new
and illuminating path for those interested in the interpretation and
significance of behavior, especially to those interested, as more and
more should be, in *human* behavior.

Dr. Frederick Tilney,
Neurological Institute.

INTRODUCTION

The report that follows is so complete that it is unnecessary for me to attempt a summary. A few words may be said, however, about the method followed in the study that yielded the findings set forth in the volume—a method evolved in the course of the study itself. The nature of the method may be brought out by contrasting it with two other methods which I shall call, respectively, the inventory and the "whole child" method. If in my description of these two methods I ascribe to them a fixity that does not belong to them in actual use, it should be understood that my characterization is for the sake of making clear by contrast the method that underlies the present study.

Of recent years there have been many carefully conducted investigations that determine the successive ages at which infants acquire various forms of skill, such as grasping, reaching, sitting, erect posture and bodily balance, locomotion, etc. By means of controlled laboratory tests, the record of the succession of these gross forms of behavior has been extended and refined. As a result, "norms" have been established, and the comparative state of the development of a given baby can be measured against the norms for a large number of abilities. More important scientifically is the fact that the temporal sequence of the appearance of a large number of modes of behavior has been determined. This result justifies, within limits to be shortly stated, treating the conclusions that have been reached as a study of development. Since the various items for which norms are established follow one another in a regular temporal succession, there is reason to suppose that the acquisition of the earlier abilities conditions in some manner the appearance of the later ones.

A slight amount of attention discloses, however, that the conclusions of this method (which is what I mean by the "inventory" method) set forth an order of *achievements* in development. They do not lay bare the developing process, or tell *how* it occurs. They serve, as far as the developmental process is concerned, to refine and elaborate the *problem* of the ways in which growth* occurs. It is a matter of common knowledge that an infant learns to creep before it walks, to sit up before it stands. The investigations to which I have referred enormously extend and refine this common knowledge, thereby defining the problem of discovering the processes of change by which the results in question are achieved. The inventory method supplies us with a detailed scheme of cross-sectional achievements. It does not of itself show how the transitions from one stage to another are effected. It marks out mile-stones but does not show the road. The study reported in this volume deals with precisely the latter problem. It considers development longitudinally, so to speak, instead of cross-sectionally. To refer by way of illustration to one behavior-pattern dealt with in the following study: At a certain age a given child *has* learned to walk. But "stepping" movements show themselves almost at birth, and the study of the developmental process follows in detail the interactions with other forms of behavior and with environing conditions by which these movements finally pass into what is properly termed walking.

In connection with the "field" concept in physical science, the "organismic" concept in biology and *Gestaltism* in psychology, there has occurred of late a growing dissatisfaction with the conclusions of any *merely* analytic study of change. With respect to child development, this discontent has taken the form of a demand that the "whole child" be studied; that is, that an individual be studied in his total and unique individuality, instead of being split up into independent elements and then each part compared with a "norm" that exhibits only what is found, upon comparison, to be common with what is found in a large number of other children. The ambition to deal with each aspect and phase of a human in its connection with the entire individual instead of as an independent element is laudable. But it only throws us back upon the question of the *method* by which it shall be accomplished.

We seem to be in a dilemma. We cannot study everything at once; anything as complex as a human organism and its behavior,

---

* Traditionally, *growth* has been a term employed to designate changes in mass and size; but it is now so evident that spatial and temporal changes are only inseparable aspects of one and the same process that there is sufficient justification for using *growth* and *development* interchangeably, leaving it to the context to make clear which aspect is particularly denoted at the time.

even in an infant, has after all to be studied piecemeal, one aspect at a time. The organismic concept is valuable as a directive principle. But of itself it reveals nothing and solves nothing. It also is the statement of a *problem*, not of a solution. Moreover, as some of the results of the present study show, there is danger in erecting the organismic concept into a fixed preconception that will determine all observations, just as there is in holding fixedly to the idea of the whole as simply an aggregate of independent parts. Actual experimental observation seems to show that in some respects there is growth from the part to the whole as well as progressive individuation and specialization within the whole.

Since after all the whole child can be studied only with respect to this and that activity at this and that time under such and such conditions, those who have the ambition to study the whole child are faced in the end with a mass of multiple data. No one set of data discloses of itself its connection with other sets of data in constituting the total individuality. The way out, according to those who set up the end of attaining understanding of the total organism, must be that of correlation of these independent sets. But unless something is known about the way in which changes go on to produce development, what assurance can there be that the correlations set up are more than external? Moreover, there are so many variables in anything as complex as the organism of even an infant that the problem of adequate correlation with reference to the whole child is too complex for solution.

It seems clear to me, accordingly (and largely as an outcome of the present study) that there can be no assurance of an internal as distinct from an external correlation save as a base-line is established through discovery of the principles that characterize development as such. The institution of such a base-line is the distinguishing feature of present study. The basic idea is that all development is a matter of interaction of organism and environing conditions; the latter including both other organic processes with which a given organic structure is interacting and the extra-pellicular conditions included in the particular behavior that is taking place. More especially, the study has tentatively established the following *principles of the developmental process:* (1) With respect to various forms of behavior (conditioned by various organic structures) there is no such thing as uniform or homogeneous age. As far as some activities are concerned, the infant at birth is as old as an old man; with respect to others, it is truly an infant. This fact alone necessitates a study of the growth of different behavior-patterns one at a time, although of course the principle of interaction with the environment protects the observer from undue isolation of the particular pattern under study. (2) It follows from this first principle that at a given time some particular behavior-pattern tends to be dominant—that is, to be the pacemaker in the general process of development. One marked feature of the present study is the care with which dominant forms of growth are detected within an earlier state of diffuse activity—compare, for example, the tracing of locomotion from original stepping movements, and the connection of reaching with the Moro reflex. (3) The early stage of each dominant behavior-pattern is marked by overdoing, by exaggeration. An infant cannot do it too much or too often—a fact which, I remark in passing, sheds needed light upon the relation of repetition to habit-formation. (4) When another behavior-pattern becomes dominant, there is a period of interference, even in the case of an activity that has passed out of its stage of exaggeration and become relatively perfected. This phase is marked by growing hesitation and seeming regression in the performance of the activity that had reached its relatively mature state. (5) Gradually the behavior-patterns that had previously matured are coördinated and integrated with the new dominant behavior-pattern and it is coördinated and integrated with them. The occurrence of such phases of coming together constitutes those spurts in general behavior, including intelligent behavior, that are matters of common observation in the growth of an infant—and an adult.*

These general principles of growth, set forth at length in the concluding chapter, are significant because of the wealth of concrete experimental data set forth in the previous chapters; they grew out of the study and were not antecedent conceptions. The concrete materials and the conclusions derived from them show that the study here reported is a study not primarily of Johnny and Jimmy

---

*The incidental light thrown upon the comparative irrelevance of well-formed reflexes to the process of development, upon the difference between conditioned reflexes and development, and upon the temporary inhibition of certain achieved forms of skill by appearance of more complex activities, instead of merely by association with a prior painful experience, is worthy of note.

but of the principles of development manifested in the course of their first two years of life. The author would be the last to claim that these principles give a complete account of the process of development or that they do not need to be checked by further studies.* But the general principles set forth indicate of themselves the further more detailed studies that need to be executed in order to make the picture of the process of developing more complete, so as to fill in gaps and to refine details. But as they stand, they mark at least the definite and assured beginning of what I have termed a base-line for the study of the whole child. The author's belief that the general process of development is the same everywhere, in cells, plants, ideas, and cultures, provides both a check upon results already attained and a stimulus to further inquiries in fields outside that which has been directly studied. Many further problems of infant development have naturally come to light in the process of the survey of development that has already been made. Since these problems have grown directly out of the study of growth and are intrinsically related to it, it seems highly probable that an approximation to the ideal of understanding the "whole child" as an individual, instead of merely a specimen case of a homogeneous class, will be best attained by following out these leads rather than by a large number of independent studies undertaken in the hope that the data they yield will later lend themselves to proper correlation. For one great advantage of the genuinely genetic method that is represented in the present study is that every accomplished result reveals more specialized aspects and phases of the developmental process, while without such a frame of reference special studies have to be instituted without adequate control or understanding of the processes of change into which they fit and to which they contribute.

JOHN DEWEY.

---

* To a considerable extent they have been checked, however, by observations upon sixty-eight other babies carried on from birth simultaneously with the intensive study of Johnny and Jimmy, and also by the intensive study of another pair of twins.

ACKNOWLEDGMENTS

In 1930 Dr. Frederick Tilney desired to extend to the human level his work on the correlation of behavior with the structural development of the nervous system. For that purpose he organized the Normal Child Development Clinic, whose specific obligations have been to study the overt manifestations of behavioral growth in the infant and young child. The work of the clinic was made possible by grants from The Commonwealth Fund, The Josiah Macy Jr. Foundation, the Carnegie Foundation, The General Education Board, and Miss Margaret Ellwanger. A systematic study of a small group of children from birth through the first few years has been realized only through the generous coöperation of the Sloane Hospital for Women and the Babies Hospital.

Dr. Tilney has, of course, been the inspiration and guiding influence of all the work we have undertaken. We have profited materially from the suggestions and criticisms of an Advisory Council not only in the production of this book but in the formulation and management of our general research program. The manuscript has been read and criticized by the following: Dr. Frederick Tilney, Dr. John Dewey, Dr. L. Beverley Chaney, Dr. Rustin McIntosh, Dr. E. L. Thorndike, Dr. R. S. Woodworth, Dr. C. B. Davenport, and Mr. L. K. Frank. For any fallacies of judgment or production the writer is, of course, entirely responsible.

The writer is personally indebted to members of the clinic staff who worked diligently for long hours during the writing of this book. Our indebtedness to the mothers of the babies for their coöperation is obvious. I am also grateful to Mrs. Letty Lehmann-Haupt who read the manuscript for English construction.

To Dr. John Dewey who has read the manuscript not only once but during its several stages of writing, and who has watched its creation as sympathetically as I looked upon the first steps of Johnny and Jimmy, this volume is affectionately dedicated.

MYRTLE B. McGRAW.

CONTENTS

FIGURES

PLATES

GROWTH

A Study of Johnny and Jimmy

Chapter I

BEHAVIOR DEVELOPMENT

THE essence of childhood is growth. Growth of children is so ubiquitous that for thousands and thousands of years it failed to arouse curiosity or stimulate inquiry as to the nature of its development.

Recently that unconcern has given way before a wave of intense interest in the development of childhood. The technical scientific interest of the experimentalist, the practical interest of the clinician, and the curious eager concern of the layman are well represented in the vast array of publications on the subject. Elaborate research centers have been established for the sole purpose of studying the development of the child, and the physical, mental, emotional, motor, personality, and behavior development of the child have received both intensive and extensive analysis during the past quarter of a century. The infant and young child are now recognized as useful laboratory animals. They have served as subjects for innumerable types of studies: studies in the development of skeletal and muscular structures, the development of lymphatic systems, the nature of perceptions and sensations, and growth in social behavior.

Wherever children are used as subjects in investigations the study is automatically listed as one in "child development." The term seems to suggest that child development is unique, or different from any other kind of development. Emphasis upon development during a particular chronological period—childhood—implies furthermore that growth during childhood is in some way distinctive from growth at any other time. Classification of the literature pertaining to child development in terms of chronological periods —for example, fetal development, infant development, development of the pre-school, the pubescent, and the adolescent child— lends support to the implication that development during each chronological period is distinct in itself.

Although the literature is replete with studies of physical,

3

mental, emotional, motor, and personality development at these several chronological periods, there has at the same time been considerable stress upon the need of studying "the whole child." So far as the writer is able to perceive, a study of the whole child has meant primarily an aggregation of these items. The child has been considered more or less as a composition of compartments. When the status of each compartment is determined for each chronological period, and the aggregation of these various ratings computed, it has been assumed that the development of the child would thereby be revealed. That is, inventories of the developmental status at these several chronological periods, when pieced together, would presumably yield the story of development during childhood.

Not only has there been a tendency to break childhood up into convenient chronological periods, but the method of studying development during a given period has been largely that of cross-sectional analysis. This tendency persisted despite the loud praise which has been awarded to the genetic method. With the exception of a few instances those studies which purport to be genetic in method are in fact little more than inventories of the same child-subjects at different chronological periods. While these inventories represent increments of growth and are highly useful for certain purposes, they do not afford an analysis or understanding of the *process* of development. The student of development in behavior must focus attention upon the movements which give rise to an organized behavior-pattern, as well as the chronological sequence in which behavior-patterns reach maturity.

Wherever there is development there must be a period of preparation, consummation, and decline. It seems that many apparently controversial theories of behavior development are not really controversial but appear to be so because they have been derived from different stages of maturation. The experimentalist has too often undertaken to establish principles of behavior development from data which represent only a phase or a section of the developing process. The tendency to study the child in cross-sectional periods has undoubtedly provoked polemics on the nature of behavior and development, polemics which might not have arisen had the principle been derived from the entire developmental process rather than from a section thereof.

It would be well to consider here some of the more recent theories of behavior, especially as they have reference to the behavior of infancy and childhood. The development of a theory is in principle fundamentally akin to the development of behavior. If it were possible to recapitulate the processes involved in the development of theories and concepts of behavioral growth, we should probably find that the stages and characteristics of such growth in knowledge are similar to those of the infant in learning a new performance such as, for example, erect locomotion. In the beginning he is capable of reflex stepping movements only, and these he makes with little if any awareness or control on his part. As he becomes actively engaged in the developmental process he manifests a tendency to swing from one extreme to another, as, for instance, from an unusually narrow base to an extremely wide one, a tendency to exaggerate or overwork any new aspect of development, a decided dyssynergia, and a display of excess or overflow of activity. Gradually the excess activity is eliminated, the exaggerations are narrowed down, and an ever increasing specificity of pattern is by degrees manifested until a well-coördinated and integrated gait is achieved. Analogously, for generation upon generation whatever body of knowledge adults had concerning the behavior development of children was obtained through no direct conscious effort to study child development. Fortunately, children continued to grow despite the general unconcern over their manner of growth, and fortunately adults actually learned a good deal about development although they were not deliberately trying to do so. We have now, however, arrived at the stage of making conscious effort to determine principles of behavioral growth. Sometimes it even seems that too much effort is being exerted. Too much motion is being wasted without actually stepping forward. An idea or new theory emerges and shows the characteristic tendency to exaggerations in its claims; then in time the growth of that particular theory is checked as a new, counteracting one crops out. The new one in turn also becomes excessively ambitious and exaggerated. Finally the essence of the two may become crystallized into an unchallengeable truth, a specific, well-determined principle which can stand alone and walk through the universe of ideas full-grown. The study of infant behavior development is young, and such theoretical fluctuations are the signs of youth.

Theories of Behavior Development

One of the earliest theories of development having reference to infant behavior did not arise from studies of infants, nor was it concerned primarily with development. It essayed to explain behavior. Early psychologists, being inclined to think of all behavior as either inherited or acquired, were accustomed to classify behavior into reflexes, instincts, and acquired traits. According to this theory an infant was born equipped with a system of reflexes and instincts which were inherent in the germ plasm and presumably not subject to appreciable modification through experience. It was customary for the psychology textbooks at that time to include long lists of reflexes and instincts. All other types of behavior were considered as acquired traits. Although some *instincts* were delayed in making their appearance until the latter part of childhood, experience or environmental factors were of no consequence in determining their appearance. The disconcerting feature of this classification of behavior was that the list of instincts became very elastic. No two textbooks agreed, so that the term came to embrace a large share of human behavior. Obviously, the usefulness of such a classification of behavior was lost on account of its elasticity.

This theory implied that the process by which reflexes and instincts were developed was distinctly different from the process by which acquired traits were developed. Reflexes and instincts, being passed from generation to generation through the chromosomal genes, presumably developed in one way whereas individual attainments developed in another. Having attributed reflexes and instincts to organic inheritance, having placed their locus of origin somewhere within the genes, the psychologists made no further attempt to explain the way in which they did develop. The burden of explanation as to the process by which reflexes and instincts developed rested with the biologists and geneticists. The psychologists were content to recognize that they did exist and that their manner of development was different from that of acquired traits. Acquired traits were primarily a product of experience. In the development of individual attainments environmental factors were paramount. This theory might have lived longer and served a more useful purpose if the psychologists could have agreed upon a classification of instincts. Since they could not the theory had to give way to another.

It is in line with the typical process of development that the succeeding theory should have proclaimed the significance of environmental factors in the determination of behavior and development, since the instinct theory had attributed so much weight to original endowment. It is the contention of the early Behaviorists that the infant is born into the world equipped with a limited number of reflexes, or simple reaction mechanisms. By a process of *conditioning* these simple reflexes are concatenated into reactions of increasing complexity. In the conditioning process the environmental factors are of prime importance. Every one is familiar with the celebrated statement of Dr. Watson (*63*),* the chief protagonist of Behaviorism, in which he proclaims the relative influence of environment in the development of the child. "Give me," he says, "a dozen healthy infants, well-formed, and my own specified world to bring them up in and I'll guarantee to take any one at random and train him to become any type of specialist I might select—doctor, lawyer, artist, merchant, chief, and, yes, even beggar-man and thief." While many Behaviorists may not go as far as Dr. Watson in stressing environmental factors as opposed to innate endowment, there has been an undeniable tendency of this school to emphasize the extrinsic influences in behavior and to accept the conditioning theory as adequate explanation of behavior development. The term *conditioning* has therefore expanded far beyond its original meaning, so that it is now often used loosely to indicate any associational behavior. However, since the Behaviorists admit that the infant is endowed with a few simple reaction mechanisms, they imply that the way in which these few reflexes are developed is in some manner different from the way in which conditioned reflexes or learned activities are developed. As long as they refer to *learned* and *unlearned* behavior, they suggest two different processes of behavior development. So far as a theory of development is concerned, the difference between the Behaviorists' point of view and that of the earlier reflex-instinct theory is primarily one of emphasis. The Behaviorists, restricting innate endowment to the minimum, emphasize environmental factors.

---

* Italic figures in parentheses refer to the numbered list of references at the back of the book.

8 Growth: A Study of Johnny and Jimmy

It is not surprising that there was a reaction against this highly mechanistic doctrine of development. In the field of infant behavior Gesell (21) has most actively voiced opposition to the environmentalists and revived the significance of innate endowment. He has dressed it in a coat of a different color and called it "maturation." He defines maturation as "the intrinsic component of development (or of growth) which determines the primary morphogenesis and variabilities of the life-cycle." Gesell has repeatedly asserted the priority of the ripening process of neural structures preparatory to function. The neural ripening, he contends, is uninfluenced by environmental factors. He claims, "The nervous system grows according to its own intrinsic pattern and thereby establishes the primary forms of behavior. These forms are not determined by stimulation from the outside world. Experience has nothing specifically to do with them . . . the extreme versions of the environmentalists and conditioning theories suffer because they explain too much. They suggest that the individual is fabricated out of the conditioning patterns. They do not give due recognition to the inner checks which set metes and bounds to the area of conditioning and which happily prevent abnormal and grotesque consequences which the theories themselves would make too easily possible."

In drawing the distinction between *maturation* and *learning* Gesell implies that there are two distinct processes of development and that development during infancy is chiefly of the maturational type. A large portion of the studies of infant behavior which have emanated from the Yale Psycho-Clinic lend support to his thesis that behavior development during infancy is relatively uninfluenced by individual experience.

Another theory of development in opposition to the conditioning theory has been concerned not so much with intrinsic and extrinsic factors in behavior as with the mode of development. While this theory did not originate from studies of infant behavior, many of the more recent investigations concerning infancy have been interpreted in terms of *individuation*. The theory of individuation emanated from a laboratory in the Wistar Institute where Coghill has been for many years patiently and unostentatiously watching the first embryonic movements of *amblystoma*. He has followed these movements systematically through every stage of development until the animal and its behavior reach maturity. Coghill has correlated the developmental changes in the somatic behavior of *amblystoma* with progressive changes in the structure of the nervous system until he is convinced that the process of development is not one of synthesis or compilation of increasingly complex patterns, but one of *analysis* or individuation. He explains (*9*, pp. 431, 434-435), "It has been generally assumed that larger patterns of behavior are formed in the development of the individual by the integration or synthesis of smaller or elementary patterns. Conversely, the thesis of this paper is that smaller or partial patterns arise by a process of individuation or analysis within a larger pattern, and that the primary pattern is a total reaction which normally expands from the first as an integrated process. . . . Conditioned reflexes, which are generally accepted as the units out of which behavior develops synthetically in post-natal life, are generally regarded as differing in their genesis from the unconditioned reflexes of fetal life. It is probable, however, that this hypothesis is not well founded. Pavlov's dogs which condition their reflexes in an orderly way do so by progressive reduction of the field of adequate stimulation for the particular reflex and by progressive restriction of the motor field of action. These characteristics the conditioned reflex has in common with the unconditioned reflex. The conditioned reflex, like the unconditioned, is acquired by analysis of a total pattern which under normal conditions is from the beginning perfectly integrated." Coghill sounded a note in advance when he ascribed the same fundamental processes to the development of localized discrete reflexes as to conditioned reflexes and learning by trial and error. "The conditioned reflex is conventionally regarded as differing essentially from the unconditioned reflex, but this is contradicted by evidence drawn from the development of behavior. Like unconditioned reflexes, the conditioned reaction emerges on the motor side from a field of general activity and on the sensory side the specific stimulus emerges from a general or wide zone of adequate stimulation. . . . On the motor side of the conditioning, reaction is at first general, approximately a total reaction, at least of a postural nature, and only later does it become specific. Conditioning of reactions accordingly is accomplished by restriction (narrowing) of the zone of adequate stimulation and concomitant restriction in the field of action. The primary structural basis for this is in the mechanisms of the total pattern. The same interpretation can be applied also to learning by trial and error. The immediate response of an animal when placed in an utterly strange problem box or cage is general activity; and the stimulus to this action appears to be the situation as a whole. But within this general situation there eventually emerge particular features as relatively localized stimuli, and concomitantly out of the general field of action there emerges the particular act that is appropriate to the situation. Here again the mechanism of the total action pattern is the key to the process of learning."

Coghill has presented a theory of development which applies to any level of activity. He has shown that infracortical and cortical behavior-patterns manifest the same underlying principles in their course of development. Furthermore he has emphasized that the principles of growth are general whether the factors involved are organic or functional. That is, the principle of individuation applies in the structural development of the nervous system and in the overt behavior of the animal. Studies in experimental embryology and genetic psychology have been knit by Coghill's suggestion of a fundamental principle of development into a closer relationship than has ever before been conceived.

It is sometimes claimed that the Gestalt school of psychology is the one whose theories on behavior most closely parallel the work of Coghill. While the Gestaltists have not been concerned primarily with development and their theses do not constitute a theory of development, the general contentions of this school and their supporting experimentation oppose the notion that complex "wholes" are constructed out of simple elementary processes. To this extent they may be identified with the theory of individuation. Among the students of infant behavior Irwin (26, pp. 128-146) has most enthusiastically espoused the theory of individuation in depicting growth of specific reactions out of a general mass matrix as indicated in the activities of the newborn infant.

But it is the experimental embryologists and not the psychologists who deserve credit for formulating the most adequate theory of behavior development. It is they who are revealing the process of morphogenesis, and it is they who are bringing the most convincing experimental evidence to bear upon an evaluation of intrinsic and extrinsic factors in the process of growth. Let us examine some of the principles which have been educed from studies of embryological development.

In many ways development as manifest in the early metamorphosis of the germ cell is extraordinarily similar in principle to that shown in the development of behavior in the infant and young child. Growth of the germ cell shows a primary stage of rapid development immediately after fertilization. This period of rapid development is followed by a static period when smaller and fewer changes take place. It has already been established that early in the period of cleavage particular cells or groups of cells become destined to develop into particular organs or systems. Even before the gastrula stage it is possible to determine the specific region of the embryo—barring mishap—which will develop into the epidermis, the notochord, or the mesoderm. To say that they are destined is a little misleading, for that would seem to imply that there is no other course for them. As a matter of fact, they are destined to develop into the particular organs *provided* there is no interference with their customary course of development. But there is a period of "indeterminateness," when their fate, though suggested by the position of the particular cells, is not finally settled.

Although it is possible to ascertain definitely the organs into which these cells are likely to develop, there is a period of indeterminateness in which it is possible, mechanically or otherwise, to change their course of development completely, so that for instance the germ region which would ordinarily give rise to viscera may develop into epidermis. It has been demonstrated experimentally that it is possible to implant a bit of embryonic region which would ordinarily give rise to the development of bone tissue in the region which is destined to become epidermis, and that the implant, assimilating its new surroundings, will develop into perfectly normal epidermal tissue. But the most interesting thing about it is that there is a critical period when the transplantation must occur in order to bring about these results. At a later stage such a transposition of embryonic cells will have strikingly different results. The cells will then develop in accordance with their origin and not in accordance with their position. That is, transplanted presumptive embryonic bone tissue will, at a later stage, develop into bone even if it has been placed in the environment of presumptive epidermis. At this later period these cells have reached a stage of specificity, their growth destiny is sufficiently determined, so that they are resistant to the influences of their new environment. To recapitulate, embryonic growth reveals a period of indeterminateness when the destiny of particular cell groups may be indicated to the extent of organ rudiments, but not so fixed that their development cannot be altered by placing these rudiments in a new environment. Then there follows a period of greater determination in growth when the cells, true to their early influences, resist modification even when placed in a new environment.

It has also been attested that once a region of cells has differentiated or attained specificity there pass out from it influences which govern the destiny or determination of other embryonic cell regions. That is, the differentiation of one group of cells constitutes an organization center which exercises an influence upon the developmental fate of other cell regions. For example, the development of the optic cup is indispensable to the lens. If the rudiment of the optic cup is extirpated before the formation of the lens, then the lens never becomes fully differentiated. Furthermore, if a bit of epidermis which normally would develop into a lens is replaced at an appropriate time by a piece of epidermis from the trunk, then the lens is formed from this foreign transplant. If the trunk epidermis is transplanted at a later stage the lens will not form. And if the primary optic cup is transplanted at an appropriate time under any other part of epidermis it will often stimulate the development of a lens from the epidermis in this foreign position. The development of the lens is contingent upon the relationship between optic cup and epidermal tissue at a favorable stage of immaturity.

From the above illustrations it is apparent that all regions of the embryonic cells are not developing at the same time nor at the same rate. There exist in the same germ side by side parts which are fully determined, others which are rudimentary but still somewhat indeterminate, and still others which have not even begun to differentiate or evidence signs of organ development. Not only do different regions of embryonic cells begin their development at different times, but the periods of indetermination or plasticity are of unequal lengths. Since different cell groups are in different stages of development at any particular time it would be impossible to express the degree of development of a particular embryo in chronological terms from the moment of fertilization. Both position and time, it must be remembered, are important in the development of the embryo.

The process of embryonic development is from the general to the particular, but the progress from one phase to another is extraordinarily gradual. In emphasizing the gradual, step-by-step process of development from an undifferentiated to a specific and determined stage, the writer cannot do better than quote Dürken (*15*, pp. 121-122), from whose scholarly work she has drawn materially in this presentation of embryological development. "This determination comes about by degrees, earlier or later according to the kind of animal in question, so that an indeterminate condition gradually gives place to a determinate one. Further, since all the parts are not determined at the same time there arise in the germ local and spatial differences in the state of determination. But determination in itself is a gradual process. Not only does it lead little by little from the general to the particular, but the rigidly determined condition is connected by intermediate stages with the indeterminate condition, beginning with the first appearance of determination—when it is still indefinite—and proceeding to its final complete establishment. In order to distinguish between these degrees of determination we may use for the introductory phase the term *institution*, and for the final phase—in which ontogeny no longer remains uncertain— the term *destination*."

Not only during the stages of cleavage and early embryonic development, but during the fetal stage—in fact throughout the entire ontogenetic cycle—these aspects of organic development are evident. It is established not only that all organs of the developing embryo and fetus are not formed at the same time, that the formation of one organ may have an influence in the determination of another or subsequently developing organ, but also that the new organ, when it arrives at its period of rapid growth, may have an arresting or inhibiting effect upon the development of the organ previously developing. There is, it appears, a sort of growth competition between the various organs during their periods of development. This competitive relationship operates to gain a proper functional balance. It is important that each organ should have its period of rapid growth at the normal time, for otherwise the formation of a new organ may have an inhibiting effect before the former has reached its full development. This would result in a stunted organ and thus destroy the functional balance of the organ interrelationship.

The theory of epigenesis is therefore the first to suggest that development is a *process* having fundamental principles which inhere despite the nature of the organism which is growing. Development is a process having a period of origin, incubation, consummation, and decline. Therefore in order to study development it is necessary to initiate study at the inception of the growing organism or function and to follow the process through all the succeeding changes until it attains maturity.

Purposes of Present Investigation

The present investigation purports to analyze the process of development as it is manifest in the behavior of the growing infant and young child. When one proposes to study behavior development of the human infant he is beset with dire problems, not the least of which is the determination of the origin of the organism to be studied. Since in studying the process of development it is necessary to begin study at the time of origin, the locus of origin must be established. To establish the point of origin of an individual child is a problem which transcends experimental procedures. Does the new individual begin with ovulation, fertilization, or respiration? If conception is arbitrarily selected as the origin of the individual, then it must be admitted that considerable preparatory development has gone forward during ovulation, before fertilization and cleavage occur. Furthermore, even if conception is accepted as the most logical period for designating the beginning of the individual, the difficulties involved in initiating study of human behavior during fetal development are almost insurmountable. While no one would question that cellular cleavage is a phase of behavior development, it does not easily lend itself to experimental observation in the human embryo. So for all practical purposes, in this country at any rate, human fetuses are not often available as experimental subjects until respiration is established. It is obvious, therefore, that the experimentalist cannot initiate analysis of all human behavior at the time of origin.

Moreover there are other problems involved in considering the individual child as a unit of investigation in studies of behavior growth. Since the behavior of the human infant has attained a high degree of complexity and organization by the time the baby becomes available to the experimentalist, a mere listing of all types of behavior of which he is capable is impractical, if not impossible. A systematic genetic study of his total behavior-repertoire is even less feasible. Even if it were possible to record all the behavior of which the average infant at a particular age is capable and then all the behavior of which a slightly older infant is capable, such listings would not reveal the process of growth. Inventories of behavior even if arranged in chronological series do not reveal the movements which give rise to a particular type of behavior. It is an interesting fact that the average baby sits alone at eight months and that he walks at fifteen, but these facts constitute neither a description nor an explanation of the process of growth. Walking is the *end result* of a process of development, whereas the study of *development* in behavior must be concerned with the process by which the end result was attained. In order to understand the development of behavior the genetic psychologist must ascertain the anlages out of which a particular behavior pattern arises and the phases through which it passes before attaining maturity as adequately and accurately as the embryologist determines the cells or groups of cells and the conditions in which those cells give rise to a particular organ.

Since it is impractical to study all the behavior-patterns of the growing child from their origin to maturity or fixity, a possible method consists of the selection of only a few characteristic behavior activities in order to follow the progressive changes manifested in the course of development of these patterns. For convenience we shall use the term *behavior-course* to designate an organized function, such as erect locomotion, during the process of development. *Behavior-pattern* refers to the terminal form of activity, the end-result of the course of development. We prefer the term *course* as representative of the growing period since the word suggests movement and change as against the boundaries and fixity which the term *pattern* connotes. There are many different aspects and phases involved in a behavior-course before it develops into the stability of a pattern. It is these changes and phases which are of moment to an analysis of behavior development.

Not only is it impractical to study all the behavior-patterns within the capacity of a given individual but it is equally impractical to analyze all the aspects or ingredients which enter into the development of a behavior-pattern. In the present investigation we have elected to restrict our analysis to overt-somatic changes which can be observed in a behavior-course as manifest in the activities of the growing infant and young child.

In proposing to make analyses of the development of particular behavior-patterns we must avoid the implication that a pattern of behavior can be isolated from the individual and studied as a unit. It is at all times an integral part of the total behavior of the individual and is constantly influenced by intrinsic and extrinsic factors which enter into the development process. Although the behavior-pattern is an integral part of the individual, from which it cannot be dissected, it nevertheless retains its own identity at all times. Fortunately, dissection is not necessary in order to analyze its course of growth. It is possible to focus attention upon a particular behavior-pattern, or certain aspects of the pattern, in order to follow its course of development from the time of origin until it attains maturity or fixity.

A second purpose of the present investigation was to study the modification of behavior development during infancy. Behavior development is a process of interchange of energies within an organism and energies within its environment. In order to bring about a modification of development it is necessary to alter the energy relationship between the organism and its environment. Actually, wherever there is development there is a constant change of energy relationship. But in this treatise we are using the term *modification* to indicate that the course of development is being altered from that which prevails under ordinary or customary conditions. Thus considered, modification may be either in the nature of (1) acceleration in the *rate* of growth, (2) retardation in the rate of growth, or (3) alteration or interruption of the serial sequence in the ordinary phases of development. Modification of development in the sense in which we have used it is not merely change but change from the usual to the unusual.

The interrelationship of intrinsic and extrinsic factors in development may be altered by an addition to or a subtraction from either the organic or the environmental factors which enter into the growth process. In general it is easier experimentally to manipulate the environmental factors than the organic. The environmental factors alone which influence a given growth process are multitudinous. Therefore, in order to study the effect of one or a particular environmental influence, it is necessary to select the particular extrinsic factor and increase or decrease its action upon the growing organism. We have seen how embryologists have determined the influence of heat, humidity, and light upon the growth of particular organs or organisms. Comparably, in a study of human behavior the experimental factor may be that of temperature, light, and so on. But in the present analysis we have endeavored to ascertain the effect of exercise or use upon the growth of particular action-systems.

We elected to study the influence of increased or restricted use of an activity upon its course of growth. Since we were using infants as subjects, study was further limited to an evaluation of the influence of exercise upon the development of particular behavior-patterns during the period of infancy.

Intrinsic and Extrinsic Factors

It has been said that behavior development is a process of interaction of organic and environmental factors. But actually the distinction between internal and external is an arbitrary one used solely for the purpose of convenience. That which is external or environmental from one aspect is internal from another. At one time the same factor is extrinsic and at another it is intrinsic. In popular parlance, and in much of the psychological literature, it is customary to speak of those things as internal which are contained within the epidermis. Yet the body is full of foreign substances at all times. Food at one stage of digestion is external and at another internal. A disease germ within the body is medically considered as a foreign substance within the body. In the study of behavior the same disease germ might be considered an intrinsic factor. Epidermis might serve as an adequate demarcation between intrinsic and extrinsic for one purpose but be completely out of bounds for another. In order to study the development of an individual it is necessary to decide arbitrarily where the individual ends and the environment begins. Such demarcations are defined by the experimentalist for his own convenience in analysis.

Likewise in a study of the growth of a behavior-pattern it is necessary arbitrarily to define the boundaries within which the behavior-action will be analyzed. The consecutive serial changes which occur within the limits defined are an indication of development. Of course, the whole organism is involved in any behavior activity, but there are centers or concentrates of action which constitute a pattern of behaving. It is no more unreasonable to focus attention upon these centers of action within an individual in order to observe their course of development than it is to concentrate upon the growth of an organ within the body or to fixate upon the development of an individual within a society.

While the whole organism is involved in any action of the individual, behavior is nevertheless the primary concern of the nervous system. Morphological changes of the nerve cells, cellular lamination, and myelinization of nerve fibers are just as much a matter of behavior development as are changes in the overt behavior-patterns of walking, fighting, or writing a book. In this investigation we have not been able to cover all of the aspects of development which enter into the growth of even one behavior-pattern, to say nothing of all the actions which comprise the development of an individual. Systematic analyses of the changes as indicated in overt-somatic activity in the development of a behavior-pattern from the time of origin until it attains maturity constitute both a feasible and a revealing method of studying the process of growth. We have, therefore, restricted our analysis to the development of a few select behavior-patterns as they can be seen in the somatic activity of the infant and young child.

Since in the human infant the inception of many activities has occurred before the birth of the baby, we have found it convenient to classify the behavior-patterns of the infant in terms of the degree of fixity which the behavior-course has achieved at birth or at the time the subject becomes experimentally available. While the infant is young in ontogeny he represents the terminus of a long phylogenetic series; therefore a classification of infant behavior-patterns in terms of both phylogenetic and ontogenetic significance is necessary in order to study growth of the activity.

Classification of Infant Behavior

There are certain types of behavior-patterns which have *in utero* attained a high degree of specificity. By the time the infant is born he is able to exercise these functions about as efficiently, and in essentially the same manner, as he does during adulthood. They are subject to very little modification during post-natal development, insofar as form or pattern of reaction is concerned, through post-natal external influences. The newborn baby yawns, coughs, sneezes, hiccoughs, stretches, cries, and sleeps about as well immediately after birth as he will ever be able to do. To be sure these patterns of behavior may be slightly modified or controlled as the child grows older, but it is impossible to take the pattern of coughing and make something completely different out of it, any more than the embryologists can, during the later stages of development, take a kidney or intestine and make it grow into epidermis. During the early stages of embryological development, as stated before, such as interchange is quite feasible by transplantation of germ regions. Whether it is possible to catch the presumptive coughing pattern at the time of origin, or before it has attained specificity or determination, and by altering influential factors, develop the presumptive pattern into something quite unlike coughing is not known. Traits such as these which are fully developed at birth have a long period of functional maturity, since they exist throughout the life of the individual. They are so characteristic of the behavior of mankind that any major deviations in their functioning are considered pathological.

A second group of behavior-patterns manifested in the activities of the newborn have also attained a high degree of specificity during pre-natal development, although they do not in the human infant retain their usefulness. In the absence of a better term these behavior-patterns have been called atavisms because of their apparent phylogenetic significance. To give them this classification is in a way objectionable since it involves an interpretation of their origin and development which our present data do not afford. Some behavior-patterns of the newborn appear to be residual rudiments of activities which, earlier in the phylogenetic scale, were functionally useful. In the infant they appear to be reminiscent of a primordial function which in ontogeny is comparatively unessential to the well-being of the individual. The distinctive feature about them is that the overt action-pattern tends toward a diminution or weakening as the child grows older. The persistence of these patterns or their recurrence after a given time is considered pathological. An outstanding example of behavior reactions of this type is the Moro reflex. It is sometimes known as the embrace or body startle reflex of the newborn. Any number of stimuli will elicit such a reaction in the newborn baby, but one of the most common methods is to slap upon the bed or table on which the infant is lying. The theory is that it is a hangover of the clinging reflex common to primates. The young simian immediately after birth will clutch the mother's fur on the abdomen and cling to her as she jumps about the cage. The reaction of the human infant is incomplete and merely suggestive of the primitive reaction. The developmental sequence of this behavior-pattern is reported in detail in Chapter III.

A similar atavistic behavior-pattern of the newborn infant is sometimes called the Darwinian or suspension grasp reflex. The newborn infant will grasp so tightly on a small rod, if it is placed in his hand, that he is able to raise his body above the surface on which he is lying and remain suspended for a few seconds by his grip on this rod. The progressive phases in the development of this trait and its pertinence to the process of growth will be discussed in a later chapter. Crawling movements, stepping movements, and swimming movements are similar residual patterns of a function of considerable phylogenetic import, but patterns whose manifestations in the human infant appear to be merely residua of their earlier usefulness. In the newborn infant, they are approaching the stage of decline, so that development is indicated by a gradual diminution of overt action. It is the evanescence and not the expansion of activities of this type which indicates development.

Behavior traits of a third order, which have not definitely emerged in the activities of the newborn, are nevertheless of phylogenetic significance and are indispensable to normal human functioning. Traits which would fall into this grouping are reaching-prehension, creeping, the assumption of a sitting posture, and erect locomotion. Certainly it is determined long before the baby makes his first step that, barring mishap, he should ultimately stand on two feet and walk erect. The infant who does not in time acquire erect locomotion is pathological. Rickets or even the prevention of exercise in this activity may within a measure delay the development of certain aspects of the pattern or alter to a slight degree the form of its development, but if any external influence is sufficient to prevent the child from walking on two feet then he becomes a subject for pathology. These traits thus stand in unquestioned distinction from specific skills or abilities which may or may not be acquired by an individual.

Thus the fourth classification of behavior-patterns would include the vast number of skills and abilities the development of which is not indispensable to the life and normal functioning of the individual. It is essential that all normal children learn to walk erect, but it is not essential to normal life that they learn to ride a bicycle or to roller-skate.

It is, however, extremely pertinent for an understanding of the process of development that we ascertain whether or not the same processes and principles are involved in the acrobat's walking a tight-rope as in the infant's acquisition of erect locomotion, or in the development of organs, or cellular cleavage.

Chapter II

PLAN OF INVESTIGATION

THE purpose of the present investigation, it will be recalled, is twofold: (1) to study the process of development as it is manifested in the growth of particular behavior-patterns of the human infant and (2) to evaluate the influence of exercise or use of an activity upon its development.

Studies in experimental embryology indicate that the fundamental principles of development are inherent in the growing process and therefore transcend the particulars wherein the growth occurs. A recapitulation of the general principles of growth which apply in organic development reveals that:

(1) Growth and development are a process resultant from a constant flux or interchange of energies within an organism and energies within its environment.

(2) Different environmental factors will activate essentially the same organic changes if introduced under proper conditions. That is, there is no one specific extrinsic factor which always produces the same reaction from a given organism. It is no more accurate to say that a given stimulus makes the organism respond in a particular way than it is to say, for instance, that hydrogen makes oxygen react as water.

(3) The influence of a particular extrinsic factor is contingent upon the time it is introduced into the growth situation. The same external factor will activate a particular process at one time but will have a quite different effect if its influence is brought to bear upon the growing organism at another time.

(4) There are critical periods in the development of an organism or of an organ, when it is most susceptible to modification.

(5) The tendency in all organic growth is toward fixity. As a growth process attains maturity it becomes resistant to external influences to which it would have responded in earlier stages of maturation.

(6) Within the same individual all organs do not begin to

develop at the same time, nor do they develop at the same rate. Furthermore, the developing period of different organs is not of uniform duration. Therefore, at any one time a cross-sectional view of an individual would reveal that certain parts were fully developed, that others were in a rapid stage of developing, and that still others had not begun to differentiate.

(7) Development of one organ definitely influences the emergence and growth of another whose period of optimum development occurs a little later. Reference in this connection has been made to the determining influence the optic vessel has upon the development of the lens.

(8) Not only may the development of one organ determine the emergence and manifestation of a subsequent one but the development of the later one may react in such a way as to check the growth of the former part whose rapid development preceded the manifestation of the new part. If this principle holds true in the development of behavior, any expression of behavior, such as S-R, which does not indicate the influence of both previous and succeeding activities is inadequate. Such expressions as *stimulus-response* fail to take account of the preceding actions as a determining factor, and also the retroactive effect the immediate action may have upon the preceding one.

(9) We also observed in organic and embryonic growth that the period of greatest susceptibility to modification generally appeared to be near the time of origin, since as the organ matured it began to establish resistance to modification.

(10) Moreover, not only the time at which a modifying agent is introduced into the growth complex, but also the duration of its action, is highly significant with respect both to the degree and the permanence of its influence upon the growing organism. Regeneration or restoration is an inherent characteristic of the growing organism. The degree of maturation of the organism at the time the modifying factor is introduced, the duration of the modifying influence, and the plasticity of the organism at the time the modifying factor is withdrawn are cardinal factors in directing the process of growth.

If general principles of development apply regardless of the particulars wherein the developing process occurs, then it is to be expected that these tenets would obtain in the growth of human behavior. Recognizing the infeasibility of studying the total behavior repertoire of any one child, we selected representative behavior-patterns whose course of development could be followed systematically through the various phases until the pattern achieved a reasonable degree of fixity. The purpose was to analyze the sequential phases and growth process of particular behavior-courses. Obviously, no course of behavior can be separated from the infant or child in whom it is developing, but records have been made of the same type of activity in the same infant at periodic intervals during the first two years. Study of each infant was initiated at the time of birth. These observations were concerned not so much with the end result of these performances as with the manner of behaving; they pertained not so much to individual differences in behavior as to similarities in mode of action.

Step by step the growth of each behavior-pattern has been followed from the time of origin, or, more specifically, from the time it was first available for observation, until it arrived at functional maturity. Our data have been drawn from 1,456 different examinations of sixty-eight different infants. Forty-two of these sixty-eight babies are still active subjects as the study is being pursued further. On some infants there have been as many as 103 different examination periods and the average number of examinations per child on the forty-two active subjects is thirty-eight. At regular intervals written protocols of examination of each infant are supplemented by cinema film on which progressive phases in the development of each behavior-pattern are portrayed. The total film record on these infants amounts to more than 40,000 feet.

The second aspect of development in this investigation involved the problem of deliberate modification of infant growth. Just as the embryologist may undertake to ascertain the effect of variations in temperature, light, and moisture upon the growth of particular organisms, we were interested in the influence of exercise or use of an activity upon its rate and mode of development. Use of an act is commonly considered to be one of the most powerful influences upon functional development. Disuse of an organ or disuse of a function is expected to result in atrophy. It is proverbial that we learn by doing. For that reason a study was undertaken of the effect of *use* of various activities upon (1) the development of the particular behavior-pattern involved; (2) the development of other action-patterns growing at the same time;

and (3) the emergence and growth of subsequent behavior-patterns.

There are many ways in which a study of an effect of exercise of activities upon behavior might be undertaken. A desirable method would be to select three equated groups of infants at the time of birth. The basis for equating such groups is not at the present time easily determined. But once the groups were selected and equated, one group should, during a period of one or two years, be subjected to intensive exercise of the functions being studied; the second group should be excluded from all activities of that sort; while the third group should be allowed to move along without special stimulation or deliberate inhibition of such activities. At the end of the training period a comparison of the performances of the three groups in new and challenging situations, as well as in the activities in which the one group had received special stimulation and exercise would unquestionably yield illuminating data on the influence of exercise of a function upon behavior development. Desirable as it may be, such an intensive study of groups of human subjects is quite impractical even if the experimenter were sufficiently inured to assume the risk. An intensive longitudinal practice program precludes the utilization of sufficient numbers to make the statistical approach possible. For that reason a more feasible program was selected in the pursuit of this aspect of our problem.

A more practical method adaptable to a study of human subjects in such problems is that which has come to be known as the co-twin method of investigation. It is a method which has in the past few years gained considerable popularity with students of behavior growth, since nature has in the form of identical twins provided the experimenter with excellent controls. The co-twin method is too familiar to warrant discussion of it as a technique here. Its merit rests upon the proposition that identical twins are equivalent in their generic endowment. This assumption embraces the dichotomy of heredity and environment. That is, traits or individual characteristics which are commonly called hereditary are considered to have developed in a distinctly different manner from traits which are acquired through experience of the individual. The former are presumably passed from generation to generation through the chromosomal genes, determiners of biological heredity. Such traits are considered to be impervious to modification through environmental influences during ontogeny. It is true that major modification of certain traits during the post-natal development of the individual involves vital damage to the organism. These traits are modifiable only through breeding and are resistant to modification through individual experience. The theory is that they are passed more or less as unit characters from parents to offspring.

The genes are ultra-microscopic bodies whose function it is to carry these hereditary characters from parent to child. This transfer of hereditary traits is accomplished during the process of cellular cleavage. When a cell divides it divides into equal parts. Not only the cell divides but each chromosome divides lengthwise into equal halves. Then half of the chromosomes collect at one end of the dividing cell and the other half collect at the opposite end of the cell. In this way each daughter cell receives half of the original chromosomes, and hence the two daughter cells are equivalent in chromosomal content. In mono-ovular twins the cellular division is carried to such an extent as to involve separation so that the daughter-germ cells develop into separate individuals. Therefore each twin of a pair would be equivalent in generic endowment. Such twins are commonly known as monozygotic or identical twins.

Being an ultra-microscopic body and its concrete existence never having been otherwise established the gene has itself been the center of an inordinate amount of controversy. According to Morgan (39, pp. 12-15), "The evidence that the genes are the ultimate units of heredity does not rest on direct observation, since the genes are beyond the limits of vision of our microscopes. . . . The most general idea concerning the gene is that it is an entity with two fundamental properties: first, its power to grow and divide; second, its power to bring about changes in the protoplasm outside the nucleus—changes that affect the chemical and physical activities of the protoplasm. The first of these attributes rests on the visible—division of the chromosomes which split lengthwise at each division—each half containing all the properties of the original chromosome."

Dürken (15), on the other hand, referring to the genetic theory as being built upon fiction, contends that "It is very important to settle the question as to whether the corpuscular genes assumed in genetics do, or do not, in fact exist as discrete material parts of the chromosomes. It is often taken as proved that they are actually present in the chromosomes, definitely arranged in linear series; but a critical examination shews that not only has this not been established, but that the grounds on which the opinion is based are insecure. . . . To place the genes exclusively in the chromosomes, and to assume that these chromosomal genes are the sole decisive causes of development, is allowable for the special purposes of genetic theory—if we bear in mind that this is only an assumption, necessary to the presentation of one particular theoretical system. . . . But it does not present a true picture of what really happens. . . . Taking into account all that is known, we can only affirm with certainty that a chromosome consists of a thick, gelatinous material, impregnated more or less equally throughout with thymonucleic acid. At the same time, it may be that the actual chromosome does not simply consist of one completely homogeneous substance, but that it is some sort of mixture. Observation alone produces no objective evidence that a chromosome is simply an aggregate of discrete corpuscles which may differ completely from one another. Even though, in the prophases and the regressive phases of the chromosome (that is to say, during its formation from the nuclear reticulum, and again, later, during the development from the chromosome of the parts of the nucleus corresponding to it), definite structures make their appearance, this does not prove the presence in the chromosome itself of numerous corpuscular genes. It proves only that important processes of transformation are at work, as we have previously insisted.

"In view of all this, it cannot be said that individual corpuscular genes can be demonstrated. The genes are no more than an assumption, invaluable in theoretical genetics, and legitimate for the special purposes of that science. But this is not an admission of their concrete existence." (Pp. 258-260.)

In the light of the recent work of Painter, Bridges, Muller, and Prokofyeva (3), the discrete existence of the genes appears to be passing beyond the realm of doubt. The essential problem then, in so far as development is concerned, is to ascertain the fixity of the gene. Many recent embryological and genetic studies have demonstrated that some specific traits which have commonly been considered as hereditary and unmodifiable are subject to extraordinary alteration if the modifying conditions are introduced into the growth process at a favorable time. For example, a rise in external temperature during the growth period will increase the relative length of the tail with respect to the growth of the body in young albino rats. Caterpillars placed upon different backgrounds just before the period of pupation will develop variations in their coloration unlike the coloration of their progenitors. Many cave-dwelling animals have only rudimentary eyes, but if exposed to light during the formative years will develop eyes which are normal both structurally and functionally. Different kinds of stimuli will activate cellular cleavage; entrance of the spermatozoön into the ripened germ cell is only one method of doing so, though it is the most common one. Sometimes a puncture in the egg with a needle, mechanical shaking, sudden rise in temperature, or certain chemicals will activate the same cellular process. Yet all of these are characteristics which are ordinarily regarded as hereditary and endogenous to the species.

Certainly it seems that the old notion of fixity of hereditary traits is due for revision. Indeed there is some reason to believe that the process of growth involved in the development of so-called hereditary traits and acquired characteristics is fundamentally the same, the distinction being primarily a difference in the ontogenetic time at which the particular trait attains fixity or determination. In order to vary the coloration of the caterpillars they must be placed against the chosen background at a particular time during ontogeny. Those traits which are subject to modification only through breeding are probably traits which can be influenced most effectively during the early stages of ontogeny. Once growth of these characteristics has acquired a fair degree of specificity, the organism becomes resistant to further metamorphosis of that nature. Furthermore, resistance to external influences on the part of structures which have a high degree of specificity may be a matter of degree. For example, the color of the iris is a trait highly specific in animals at the time of birth and for which breeding is necessary in order to bring about any marked alteration. Yet it is a well-known fact that the color of the iris undergoes definite post-natal changes in the human subject. It is not inconceivable that the color of the iris might be modified in such a way as to differ from the familiar pattern provided certain post-natal influences were experienced before the coloration attained fixity. Organs differ in the ontogenetic period at which they attain maximum resistance to modification.

If genes are the fixed unmodifiable bodies they have been supposed to be in determining biological inheritance, it would seem that only a complete germ cell, or an equal division thereof, would develop into a normal individual. In some species that apparently is not the case, since even a tiny fragment of the original germ cell will develop into a normal individual. It has been demonstrated with eggs of sea-urchins that a fragment of the germ cell may give rise to the development of an individual as well as the whole cell. Eggs of sea-urchins were shaken in a test-tube so that they were broken into fragments. Only one fragment contained the nucleus, the others being enucleate. Yet when these fragments of the egg, fragments as small as 1/20 of the original cell, were inseminated, development set in and small but normal larvæ resulted. It is easy enough to see that equal parts of a fertilized egg which have developed during normal cleavage would contain the same number and kind of genes, but the instance of sea-urchin larvæ demonstrates the possibility of several individuals developing from a single ovum, though their endowment was obviously different in generic content.

It may be that two individuals who have developed from a single ovum are identical in their generic content, but they are thus equivalent only at the time of fission and not at the time of birth or during post-natal growth. Theoretically as well as actually, their subsequent development would not be identical. It therefore should not be expected that monozygotic twins would be identical in endowment at the time of birth, when they first become available for experimentation. The advantage of monozygotic twins as subjects of investigation lies in the fact that the *degree* of similarity between them is greater than is ordinarily found among siblings.

Aside from establishing the generic comparability of monoovular twins, the investigator who utilizes the co-twin technique is confronted with another perplexing and more practical problem. He must determine the ovular origin of the subjects. In human infants the absolute determination of zygosity is not an easy matter. There are, grossly speaking, two methods of ascertaining the ovular conception of twins. The first is based upon an examination of the placenta and fetal membranes, and the second is based upon the degree of physical correspondence of the two individuals, as manifested during their later childhood and adult life. Neither of these methods is adequate for indubitable diagnosis of all like-sexed twins.

There are certain conditions which, if prevailing, constitute fairly reliable standards in diagnosing monozygotic twins, but even these circumstances do not provide an all-or-none basis for judging the origin of all twins. Most writers seem to agree as to the two kinds of twins—mono-ovular and bi-ovular. There is no general agreement as to whether or not examination of membranes yields more reliable diagnosis than that based upon physical similarities of the individual. Evidence based upon an examination of the membranes indicates that:

(1) Fetuses developing in a single amnion are beyond doubt mono-ovular; but it is extremely rare that even monozygotic twins are in the same amnion.

(2) Monochorionic twins are, beyond reasonable question, of single-ovum origin. But in the opinion of some of the best authorities on the subject it is quite possible, and sometimes happens, that dichorionic twins are mono-ovular. The chorionic status is apparently dependent upon the stage in embryonal development at which fission takes place. A fusion of choria in the case of dizygotic twins may give the impression of a monochorionic condition. Adequate determination of chorionic conditions can be made only by a microscopic examination of the membranous septum dividing the two amniotic sacs. This is a detail which is disregarded in most maternity hospitals, and therefore a hospital record or diagnosis based on gross examination of the membranes is inadequate in judging the zygosity of twins.

(3) All monozygotic twins are attached to a single placenta, and for that reason persons less informed in the biology of twinning have assumed that the single placenta was an adequate criterion of monozygosity. Monozygosity is ruled out if two placentæ are unquestionably present. But two placentæ of dizygotic twins not infrequently fuse to such an extent that the placenta alone is not an adequate basis of diagnosis. An examination of the placenta for evidence of venous and arterial anastomoses, or villous transfusion at the placental attachment of the umbilical

cords is of greater use in diagnosing zygosity of twins than the number of placentæ or the fact of a single placenta.

The second method commonly practised in diagnosing identical twins is that of weighing the similarities and dissimilarities of physical traits, especially those traits in which there are ordinarily great individual differences so far as the general run of mankind is concerned. The following items are the ones on which judgment of twins by this method is commonly based:

(1) Mono-ovular twins must be of the same sex. On this all writers on the subject are in agreement.

(2) They should be strikingly similar in general appearance. Relatives and others closely acquainted with them should frequently confuse them. Similarity in general appearance is obviously a subjective rating, and there is no definite measure as to how different in general appearance twins may be and at the same time be rated as monozygotic.

(3) Mono-ovular twins should have essentially the same color, texture, and form of hair; the same color and form of iris; and essentially the same texture and coloration of skin.

(4) If they possess marked eccentricities in feature such as may appear in ear configurations, position and form of teeth, freckles, moles, and furrowing of the tongue, these individual peculiarities should appear in both individuals of a pair.

(5) Anthropometric measurements should be approximate; the same size and type of feet and hands are to be expected.

(6) There should be a strong resemblance in features which are ordinarily highly variable in individuals, such as correspondence in finger, palm, and foot prints. Sometimes these resemblances appear as asymmetry reversals. When similarities appear as bilateral reversals the individuals of a twin set will mirror each other. Only a trained observer is in many instances efficient in making a diagnosis by this method, since many traits which are in reality correspondent would appear to be different to one who is not sensitive to the reversal nature of the pattern.

(7) Single-ovum twins should grow to look more alike after birth than they do at birth.

One disadvantage of the resemblance method of diagnosis, especially when it is a matter of selecting infant subjects for experimentation, is that the subjects cannot be diagnosed as uni-ovular or bi-ovular until they are beyond the period of infancy. Both dizygotic and monozygotic twins are noticeably different in size at birth and are also noticeably different in appearance. These differences in individuals of a pair seem to be about equal in the two types of twins at birth. It is the opinion of some authorities that during uterine growth there is a greater discrepancy in the development of monochorionic twins than in dichorionic twins. The presence of a twin *in utero* is always a disadvantage to one or the other, and this disadvantage is increased when both are supplied through the same placental connection. In mono-ovular twins these differences, which are most apparent in uterine development, begin to diminish after birth when the two babies have a more equal chance at the food supply. The diminution of differences continues during extra-uterine life so that mono-ovular twins grow to look more alike after birth than they did at birth. This recognized disparity in physical appearance of monozygotic twins at birth implies that generic endowment is not so fixed as to preclude marked variation in their uterine development. Environmental differences are apparently greater during uterine than during post-natal life for most monozygotic twins.

Another difficulty in determining the origin of like-sexed twins during the period of infancy by the resemblance method is due to the fact that many of the traits which comprise the basis of comparisons are still in a plastic state of development. For example, color of iris, permanent dentition, and hair form and color undergo definite post-natal developmental changes. Newman (*42*), who claims to be able "through a sixth sense," as it were, to diagnose monozygotic and dizygotic twins at sight, restricts his subjects to children over six or seven years of age. Other studies (*40, 41, 43, 44, 45*) which have attempted to correlate diagnoses by examination of membranes and by the resemblance method have been discouraging.

It is therefore evident that the diagnosis of identical twins during the period of infancy is difficult. Reichle (*51*) says in this connection, "Our present methods of diagnosing the type of twinning are either impractical or unreliable when applied to young children and infants." In selecting twin infants for experimental purposes it would be wise to depend upon membrane examination as a basis for judging the zygosity of the twins. Membrane examination should include a microscopic analysis of the septum dividing the two amniotic sacs. Gross inspection is inadequate.

If the infants are monochorionic then the chances are great that they are also mono-ovular. But when it comes to facing cold facts one cannot be perfectly confident of a diagnosis of twin types in all individual instances, nor can one be perfectly certain of the correspondence in generic make-up even if their zygosity is accurately diagnosed. However, the use of twins as experimental subjects is advantageous, as it constitutes one of the most efficient methods of equating experimental and control subjects. But in using it the limitations of the method as well as the advantages must be taken into account.

After evaluating the advantages and disadvantages of the co-twin method as an experimental device, the writer selected it as the most practical, though not the most desirable, method of studying the effect of exercise upon the development of particular performances.

Selection of Subjects

The twins for this study were selected at the time of birth. Because of the writer's inadequate information on the biology of twinning at the time, the desired care and precaution in the examination of the membranes was not observed. Because of the single placenta they were considered monozygotic. It was not until several months later that some doubt was cast upon this interpretation. After the twins were older, study by the resemblance method cast doubt upon their single-ovum origin.

Since they have already become known to the reading public as "Johnny" and "Jimmy," they will for the convenience of the reader hereinafter be referred to by these given names. Johnny was the first born. Although they are in many respects quite alike, their differences in physical appearances are obvious, and those familiar with the children have no difficulty in distinguishing one from the other. The differences in personal appearance have become more noticeable as the children have grown older than they were during the early months of life. Skin coloration, pigmentation, and texture are quite similar, but differences in the size, shape, and type of hands as well as ear configurations need no expert to detect them. The irises of both children are blue flecked with brown. Johnny occasionally gives the appearance of esotropia, but none has actually been demonstrated. Both children have blond curly hair, though Jimmy's hair is more curly than Johnny's. On superficial examination Jimmy's hair also appears to have more red in it, but this may be an illusion due to the fact that his hair is thicker. Scaled according to Emil Fischer's Scale of Hair Color, the hair of both children is like #14 of the Fischer scale. Crown whorl of both infants is clockwise. Their correspondence and differences in anthropometric measurements will be discussed in the chapter on physical development. Both infants are of the same blood-type—group B. An analysis of their fingerprints * yields no high degree of correspondence or tendency toward reversals.

		1	2	3	4	5	
Johnny:		W	U	A	U	U	Right
		U	U	U	U	U	Left
Jimmy:		U	U	U	U	U	Right
		U	U	U	U	U	Left

Fingerprints were also made of the mother and five siblings, and there is no greater correspondence between the twins than there is between the other siblings or between themselves and any one of the siblings.

In certain aspects of post-natal behavior development, especially during the first few months of life, the boys showed extraordinary correspondence. This correspondence was greater than that of any other two infants of the same chronological age, siblings or otherwise, under the observation of the experimenters.†

In view of the fact that the membranes were given only routine cursory examination and that in some respects the babies are quite similar and in others distinctly different, the writer feels that the ovular origin cannot be reliably determined.

When an experimenter selects human infants as subject material in an investigation he must be content with mixed breeds. It is doubtful whether pure-bred subjects would have made any real difference in this study, even if such had been humanly obtainable. However, an account of the family history indicates that there was nothing extraordinary in the familial background of the twins chosen for this study. They are highly representative of a wide-spread middle-class American family with no history of

* Courtesy of New York Police Department, Bureau of Criminal Identification.
† With the exception of the apparently identical twin girls with whom the writer is now checking the results of this experiment.

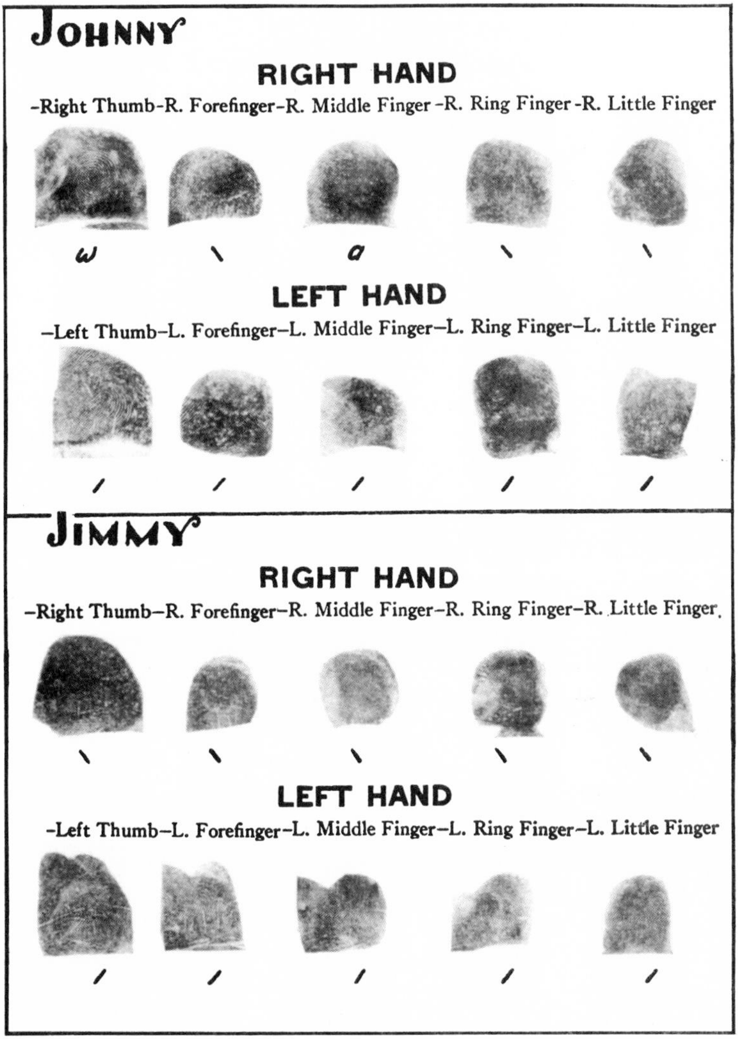

PLATE I. FINGERPRINTS

The prints show no high degree of correspondence between the twins. (Courtesy of New York Police Department, Bureau of Criminal Identification.)

fame or notoriety appearing in either the paternal or the maternal strain.

Johnny and Jimmy are the sixth and seventh offspring of American-born Irish-English parents. Both parental lines have been American-born for generations. These are the first twins born to these parents, though there is a history of twinning in both the paternal and the maternal family. The twinning tendency was stronger in the paternal strain, there being only one set of twins in the immediate maternal family and four in the paternal. Some authorities contend that only monozygotic twinning is inherited through the paternal strain, but since there is a history of twinning in both maternal and paternal families we are not thereby aided in determining the zygosity of these particular twins.

The family circumstances at the time these babies were born were the major factors which made it possible for them to serve as subjects for this investigation. The family lives in one of the familiar "railroad," walk-up, tenement flats. The parents and their seven children occupy five dark, poorly ventilated rooms. Because of the absence of a central heating system, the kitchen, heated by a coal range, serves as the center of all family activities during the winter months. The only playground for the children is the busy street below, which is a bustling local business center.

At the time of the birth of these babies the mother was only thirty-two years old, but their birth made her the mother of seven children. Before her marriage she had been employed as a telephone operator. The father was at one time a professional ball-player, but since his marriage he has been occupied at various times as a taxicab driver and as groundkeeper at the Yankee Stadium. The educational level of both parents is that of the elementary school. There is no record of any member of either maternal or paternal relatives going beyond the grade schools. All the maternal and paternal aunts are listed as housewives; and the occupations of the uncles include such activities as policeman, hotel detective, and sailor. There is no ascertained record of defectives or psychotics among either maternal or paternal relatives. The family has been listed with the social agencies for some years.

The record of their social-service contacts reveals the familiar picture of a losing battle against ever increasing family responsibilities, together with changing economic and industrial conditions. The social worker's comment on her visit to the family when there were only two children reveals that the six-room tenement apartment occupied by the family was nicely although plainly furnished; that it was clean and well kept. The two-year-old boy then appeared strong and healthy and was evidently getting excellent care, and no social problems existed at the time. Two years later when the mother was expecting her fourth baby the record shows that the family was beginning to experience financial difficulties. With each succeeding baby these problems were multiplied. It became more and more difficult for the father to maintain an adequate income, and during the period of this investigation they were rated with the social agencies as "dependents."

However, the family are observant Roman Catholics and the advent of twins was accepted as "the gift of God," notwithstanding the five older siblings ranging in age from three to ten years at the time these babies were born. All the children are living, and except for the customary childhood diseases there have been no serious illnesses. The fourth and fifth siblings have noticeable speech defects, but otherwise all appear to be normal and healthy. The oldest four attend parochial school regularly.

These statements may give a more drab picture of the family environs than is warranted or representative of the facts. Despite the handicaps of limited resources, a happy familial affection prevails, an atmosphere enriched by the proverbial Irish wit and humor. The parents enjoy each other and their children. There is no gross neglect of parental responsibilities, nor are these dutiful burdens which the parents grudgingly shoulder. It is quite impossible to give a picture of the family conditions, the *mêlée* of confusion and noise, without doing gross injustice to the rather fine inter-sibling and parental relationships.

In general intelligence, as measured on standardized tests, all of the immediate family rate normal or above. The father and mother rate in the 79 and 69 percentile respectively on the Army Alpha. The five siblings have I. Q. ratings on the Stanford Revision of the Binet as follows: 100, 127, 114, 125 and 103. It was the combination of a large family, restricted income, and intelligent parents which made possible this particular investigation.

The plan of study involved taking the babies out of the home and keeping them at the laboratory from nine o'clock in the morning until five o'clock in the afternoon for five days a week. The clinic assumed responsibility for the daily transportation. Each morning some member of the clinic staff called at the home and brought the babies to the hospital in the clinic car. On the whole they spent approximately thirty-five hours a week at the clinic. Their sleeping hours at home averaged approximately seventy hours. This would mean that they spent roughly sixty-three waking hours a week in the family environment. In consideration of the purely experimental aspect of the study, it is deplorable that the experimenters could not have had complete control of the infants during the twenty-four hours of each day, especially since many of the home influences obviously but unavoidably counteracted the purpose of the experiment. These home influences cannot be stated or measured in quantitative terms, since they are impressions derived from visits to the home from time to time by experimenter and assistants and those obtained from interviews with the parents.

Despite the disadvantage of conflicting influences at the home and in the laboratory, the present experimental set-up obviates some of the handicaps of working with completely institutionalized children. Furthermore, if this type of program should prove to be meritorious, it has greater possibilities of practical adaptation than would a scheme which involved taking the child entirely out of the home. The purpose of the experiment has, however, been strictly limited to a scientific study of certain factors in development and in no way purports to be a study in educational methods. Whatever educational implications it may have, they are purely incidental to the experiment.

Selection of Experimental Infant

The problem of selecting each child for his particular experimental rôle was easily solved, since there was an obvious difference in the size and responsiveness of the two babies at the time of birth. Study was initiated at birth, at which time the behavior of the infants during the first fifteen minutes of extra-uterine life, as well as the process of delivery, was recorded on motion-picture film. They were born after four hours of easy normal labor. The twin diagnosis had been made two months earlier by means of X-ray.

Johnny was born by spontaneous breech delivery. Jimmy, in normal vertex presentation, was expelled sixteen minutes and thirty seconds later. A stop-watch record was kept of the various aspects of the delivery from the time the presenting part could be first observed at the vulva. It is interesting, if not significant, that in point of time Jimmy responded vitally to the birth situation more quickly than did Johnny. It was one minute and twenty-one seconds after the entire body was delivered before Johnny uttered the birth cry. In the meanwhile he had been stimulated to the extent of having the mucus wiped out of his mouth and throat. Jimmy, on the other hand, uttered the birth cry in thirteen seconds after the body was born, before the mucus had been wiped from the mouth and throat. It was eight minutes and thirty-six seconds before Johnny opened his eyes, during which time he had been stimulated by a simple reflex examination and was being given an oil bath. In contrast, Jimmy opened his eyes in one minute and forty-three seconds after the body was delivered. There was a difference of 320 grams in favor of Jimmy in body weight at the time of birth. Johnny weighed 3,000 and Jimmy 3,320 grams at that time. Moreover, Johnny's birth weight is less than that of any of his siblings.

There was a noticeable difference in the behavior of the babies even during the first fifteen minutes of life. This is a difference in degree rather than in pattern or form of behavior. Johnny presented a picture of utmost flaccidity, being not only more flaccid than Jimmy but more flaccid than many infants whom the experimenter has had the occasion to examine immediately after birth. When he was raised from a supine to a sitting posture the head dropped back to such an extent that the occiput practically rested upon the interscapular spine. He showed no resistance or muscular tension whatever when brought forward into a sort of jack-knife position, so that his face lay on his feet. He did not turn his face to one side in order to free his mouth and nose for breathing. When supported by the experimenter's hands under the abdomen and held in a suspended prone position he showed a hyperflexion of the neck so that the chin rested on the chest. When supported under the arms in a vertical position so that his feet could touch the table surface, he made no response such as pressing against the table surface or making stepping movements—a reaction not uncommon in the newborn infant. If a small rod was placed in his hand there occurred a feeble reflex closure of the digits around the rod, but when the experimenter attempted to remove the rod there was no retention of the grasp. Some partunates * under these circumstances grasp sufficiently to raise the body entirely above the surface so as to hang suspended by the grasp of one hand. Johnny held his fingers around the rod for 0.6 of a second with the right hand and for two seconds with the left hand. He not only did not raise his body up by grasping with one hand, but when the experimenter held both hands around the rod until his body was raised above the surface, with no support beneath him, he still failed to retain the grasp even for a fraction of a second.

Jimmy, on the other hand, showed considerably more muscle tone and was not so flaccid as was Johnny immediately after birth. His head did not drop back quite so far when he was being raised from a supine to a sitting position, and when he was held in a vertical position so that his feet could touch the surface of the table he could be felt to tense the muscles of his body slightly and press his weight against the table surface for a second or so. He did not make stepping movements at this time, though he did so a few days later. Jimmy had a strong grasping reflex for a partunate. He grasped the rod tightly and held his fingers closed around the rod for 1.5 seconds with the right hand and 4.3 seconds with the left hand. His retention of the grasp was sufficiently strong for him to raise his head and shoulders off the examining table when the experimenter attempted to pull the rod away. When the rod was placed in both hands so that his body was suspended, he retained the grasp for 8.6 seconds.

The experimenter was of the opinion that Jimmy was better developed than Johnny at birth, in so far as behavior development is concerned. As a newborn infant he was undoubtedly more responsive to stimulation of various types than was his twin brother. These data have been presented as evidence of his superior development at birth and do not imply superior endowment. Since Jimmy appeared stronger and better developed at

* A word previously used by the writer to designate a baby only a few minutes old, as distinct from *neonate*.

birth, as well as during the first few weeks of post-natal life, he was selected for the passive rôle in this investigation. Johnny, the weaker and less responsive baby, was cast for the rôle which called for intensive special daily exercise in particular activities.

The exercise program was not initiated until the babies were twenty days old. From that time on they were brought to the clinic five days a week. They remained at the clinic about seven hours a day. During each day of the early months Johnny was stimulated at two-hour intervals, in order to evoke those activities which were within his scope at the time. As he grew older his exercise program became more extensive. The details will be reported in subsequent chapters.

Jimmy, on the other hand, was placed in a crib in the clinic nursery soon after his daily arrival at the hospital. At regular intervals—at first weekly, then biweekly, and finally monthly—Jimmy was taken into the laboratory so that his behavior under conditions similar to those wherein Johnny was experiencing daily exercise could be observed and recorded. Written and cinematographic accounts of the twins' performances were made on the same day by the experimenter. It is these records which comprise the basis of this report. Except for the periodic examination days, and the activities involved in his routine physical care, Jimmy's performances were definitely limited. He was allowed not more than two toys at a time and was left in his crib undisturbed. He was, however, by no means isolated, since his crib was merely behind a screen in a busy nursery.

It is safe to say that during the early part of the experiment Jimmy's activities were not restricted any more than would be customary for the average infant of corresponding chronological age. During the later months his opportunities for gross motor activities were considerably less than those of Johnny and probably less than would prevail for the average child of equivalent age.

This investigation does not purport to have studied the effect of special exercise of an activity versus absolute restriction. It is merely a question of more or less exercise of an activity and its influence upon development. Johnny's routine at the clinic called for considerably more exercise of particular acts than did that of Jimmy. Therefore their behavior development in the light of the performances of a larger group of sixty-eight infants whose activities were not artificially or experimentally tampered with yields illuminating data on the process of growth, the significance of which transcends the bare facts.

Chapter III

PHYLOGENETIC ACTIVITIES AND THE EFFECT OF EXERCISE UPON THEM

IN the preceding chapters the distinction has been drawn between those behavior-patterns of the human infant which are phylogenetically significant and those which are of ontogenetic origin. Phylogenetic activities are those which have functioned in the development of the species. On the whole they are indispensable to normal human development. Ontogenetic activities are those which an individual may or may not attain. While the origin and development of phylogenetic behavior-patterns is engendered in the phylum, in this investigation such activities have been observed only as they are manifested during ontogeny.

However, in analyzing the developmental sequence of behavior-patterns during infancy the phyletic origin as well as the ontogenetic manifestation must be taken into account. Some activities are more primitive in the phyletic series than others. It is reasonable to presume that swimming is one of the earliest phylogenetic activities of which there is a residuum in the behavior-repertoire of the human infant. The Moro and suspension-grasp reflexes are among the younger phylogenetic activities.

In observing these lower-level activities in the newborn infant it is apparent that the Moro and suspension-grasp reflexes are more specific and constant than are swimming, crawling, and stepping movements. That is, the frequency with which the Moro and suspension-grasp reflexes can be elicited is much greater than in the case of the other movements. Also the form of the action-pattern for the former types of reflexes is more consistent from one time to another than is true of the other types of actions. Nevertheless there can be no doubt that swimming, crawling, and stepping movements are definite and distinct patterns of behavior common to the newborn infant.

In studying the growth of these behavior-courses in the human infant, not only the phyletic origin but also the structural level at which the activities are controlled during the different phases of ontogenetic manifestation must be taken into account. Since the cortex is not functioning to any appreciable degree at the time of birth, all of the behavior activities of the newborn infant are governed at an infracortical level.

It appears that many of the residual activities of the newborn infant which never attain functional usefulness at an infracortical level are superseded by activities similar in function but governed at a higher structural level. Therefore, in studying the developmental process of these phylogenetic patterns of behavior it is necessary to bear in mind their state of maturation as an infracortical activity and the earliest sign of their emergence as actions under cortical control. These distinctions are indispensable to an adequate analysis of growth, as well as to a study of the effect of exercise upon the development of phylogenetic activities. Since the child is not uniform in his development at any one chronological age, there is considerable range in the degree of maturation in various activities of which he is at any one time capable.

Johnny and Jimmy were selected for the purpose of studying the effect of repeated use or exercise of particular activities upon their development. By stimulating one baby, namely Johnny, at frequent intervals in activities of which he was at the time capable and by deliberately restricting the stimulation Jimmy would receive in activities of the same order, a comparison of the development of the two children in these activities with respect to the developmental patterns of the larger group of infants, as well as each other, made it possible to judge:

(a) the effect of exercise of particular activities upon the development of action-patterns which had passed the period of greatest susceptibility before special stimulation was introduced into the growth process;

(b) the effect of repetition of activities which are controlled at lower structural levels as compared with those controlled at higher levels;

(c) the modification of behavior-patterns which are of different phyletic origin and also different in degrees of specificity at the time the factor of exercise is introduced; and

(d) the comparative effect of exercise upon activities which are indispensable to normal human development and upon those which may or may not be individually acquired.

The experimental program therefore involved stimulating Johnny at frequent intervals daily, so as to elicit those behavior-patterns which are characteristic of the normal infant at a given chronological age. As soon as new activities were observed, they were added to the daily practice schedule. During the first twenty-two months of life, Jimmy was given no special stimulation other than that which occurred during the daily routine handling in connection with his physical care, the stimulation he received during his hours away from the clinic, and that received during the weekly, bi-weekly, and finally monthly examination periods. Stimulation of specific behavior-patterns of Jimmy during this time being deliberately curtailed, the amount of exercise he received in any one activity at any time was considerably less than that which Johnny was getting.

The growth of these two infants during their first twenty-two months of life, when compared with each other and when individually compared with the growth of a larger group of infants comprising approximately sixty-eight children ranging in age from birth to three and a half years, yields a fair indication of the effect of use and exercise upon the development of particular functions in behavior.

Analysis of the progressive phases manifested in the development of particular behavior-patterns during infancy is constructed primarily from observations of the sixty-eight infants who constitute the major research program of the clinic. Since the data collected on these infants must await further growth of the babies before it is finally ready for publication, the phases as outlined here may be subject to revision, but in essence the sequence and phases, as presented here, are well substantiated by the unpublished protocols and cinematographic records already in the possession of the clinic. In the following account we shall present what we have found to be the essential phases of development in each behavior-pattern. Then we shall make a relative comparison of the development of Johnny and Jimmy in the same behavior-pattern, in order to show their deviations from the group and from each other during the time they were receiving different amounts of stimulation in these activities.

The Moro Reflex

This behavior-pattern will be recognized by those familiar with the behavior of the newborn infant as the body-startle reaction. Many different stimuli will set off the reaction, but one of the most common methods used, and that employed in the present investigation, was a sudden blow with a small stick upon the mattress on which the infant was lying in a supine position. In order to elicit an adequate or typical reaction it is essential that the infant should be quiet and that the stimulation should be sudden. It will be recalled that this reaction of the newborn was referred to in the first chapter as an atavism, a residuum from some primordial function; that it is rudimentary though highly specific in the newborn; and that its course of post-natal growth is toward a diminution of overt response rather than an expansion. There are, to be sure, individual differences in this type of reaction as well as all other reactions of the newborn. But, barring for the moment consideration of individual differences and concentrating upon the consistencies of the behavior-pattern, it may be said to consist of the following characteristics when observed as a reaction of the newborn infant.

A sudden stimulation will usually elicit from the newborn baby who is lying quietly in a supine position an extension of the spine from the cervical to the lumbar region. At times this extension of the spine is sufficient to roll the body laterally, or semi-laterally. Simultaneously with the extension of the spine there occurs extension and abduction of the upper extremities. This extension will usually include all the digits, except for the distal phalanx of the index finger which is flexed and the thumb which is flexed and adducted on the palm of the hand. This "C" position of the index finger and thumb can be observed at other times, but it is usually present as a part of the Moro pattern of the newborn. The extension and abduction of the upper extremities is followed by a slight bilateral flexion and adduction or "bowing" of the upper extremities in front of the thorax. The initial reaction in the lower extremities is most commonly extension, though not infrequently it is flexion. Whatever the movement may be, it is likely to be bilateral and simultaneous. The somatic reaction is usually accompanied or immediately followed by intense crying.

The literature on this reaction of the newborn baby is voluminous and includes many descriptions of the pattern as it is manifested in the behavior of the young infant. Many of the studies have quoted ages when the pattern normally "disappears" in the growing infant. At no time, however, has there been published an analysis of the process of evanescence or the changes manifested in the behavior-course as it proceeds toward a diminution of overt response. These changes are extremely gradual, and except for consecutive and frequent observations of the growing infant over a period of months the *process* would not be detected.

Although the pattern is a rudimentary one, it appears at birth not to have attained its maximum development. Ordinarily it is strongest during the second month. This observation on the general development of the pattern has been substantiated quantitatively by measuring the duration of the reaction as indicated by counting the frames of a 16-mm. cinema film from the first movement following the stimulus until repose had been resumed. About the ninth or tenth week, for most infants, the reaction begins to show a diminution of overt somatic response, that is, a decrease in the expansiveness of the reaction as well as in duration of response. These changes are shown by lessening the extension of the spine, diminution of the "bowing" of the upper extremities, a loss of the characteristic "C" posture of the index fingers and the thumbs, and a less intense reaction, whether flexion or extension, in the lower extremities.

Soon there is no "bowing" in the upper extremities at all. They are merely extended and abducted, the "C" posture of the index fingers and thumbs is completely gone; the infant remains in a dorsal position; the torso appears to be comparatively inactive, and there is no marked extension of the spine or rolling from a supine to a lateral or semi-lateral position. These changes we have considered as indicative of a *transition* phase from the newborn pattern to the mature reaction. There is, however, no sudden or complete change, at any particular time. Little by little and bit by bit this diminution of response is effected. Moreover, even when the transition pattern is the more common reaction, there will be reversions to the earlier phases of the pattern.

Ultimately, however, there comes a time when the infant never, or seldom, reverts to the typical newborn phase. Then the transition phase begins to merge with the mature response to this stimulation, and this merging shows the same tendency, a slow weaving of one phase of the pattern into another. This mature reaction consists of a blinking and a quick, fine body-jerk. Again the change from the transition reaction to the mature one occurs by gradual mingling of one phase with another, both in form and in time. That is, for a while there is a gross body-jerk merging with partial extension and abduction of the upper extremities; then the extension and abduction of the arms grow less and the jerk becomes finer. There are times, however, when the pattern may tend to be more like the transition phase and other days when it will tend to be more approaching the mature phase, but finally there comes a time when the mature reaction—blinking and a fine body-jerk—compose the dominant form of the behavior-pattern.

The duration and expansion of the pattern at any one time is contingent somewhat upon the degree of relaxation and quietude of the infant, as well as upon the strength of the stimulation. Variations in these respects were not subject to experimental control. Nevertheless, despite the variability of stimuli, there is a definite sequence in the phases of the behavior-course to such an extent that the typical infantile reflex pattern could not be elicited in the older infants. The body-jerk is essentially the same reaction as that of an adult to startle. Although the data have not been tabulated on all infants under observation at the clinic, it is safe to say that by the eighth chronological month in normal infants this trait has reached its mature form. It has attained a degree of specificity or fixity, so that any outstanding subsequent modification of the pattern of action becomes pathological. There may subsequently be modifications as to the type and intensity of stimuli which will elicit the response, but the form or pattern of action remains the same. The change in stimuli which may activate the response after the pattern has become fixed is a matter of *conditioning* or establishing *associations*.

Examinations for the Moro reflex were always made by the writer and dictated to a recorder, the only other person in the room at the time of the examination. At the time this experiment was begun the writer was unfamiliar with the progressive phases in the development of this pattern. For that reason records were made in terms of gross anatomical segments. That is, the experimenter gave the stimulus and then dictated what movements were made by the child in the region of the head and neck, the trunk, the upper and lower extremities. This method of recording obviated errors which might have occurred had we set about indicating the presence or absence of preconceived patterns. It is admitted that the accuracy of the analysis depends upon the judgment of the experimenter, but whatever errors or frailties of observation may have entered in, they are constant for all subjects. Further-

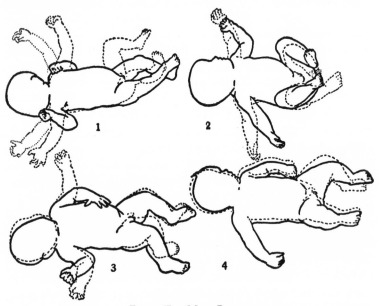

FIG. I. THE MORO REFLEX

I. Characteristic bowing posture of the newborn. 2. Reduction in activity, extension and abduction of upper extremities; bowing eliminated. 3. Greater reduction in the degree of action. 4. Characteristic response of quick body-jerk.

more, the analyses based upon the observation of the experimenter were supplemented by cinema records of the infant's reactions to the same stimulation at periodic intervals. During the examination periods reaction-time was taken by the recorder with a Meylan 1/10 second stop-watch.

Beginning when he was twenty days old, Johnny was stimulated in order to elicit this reaction at intervals of two hours, four different periods a day, twice during each period, for five days a week. This practice was continued until he was nine months old. During this period of nine months, Jimmy was examined once a week to test out his pattern of reaction to this particular stimulation.

A comparison of their development in this type of activity shows a very high degree of correspondence, and both infants passed through the essential phases as manifested by the other infants under observation.

For convenience of comparison we shall consider the development of this trait as consisting of three definite phases, though it must be borne in mind that there are no sharp lines of demarcation between one phase and the next. These phases we shall call (1) the newborn reaction pattern; (2) the transitional phase; and (3) the specific mature response. If we consider extension of the spine, bowing of the upper extremities, and the "C" posture of the digits as symptomatic of the newborn pattern, we find that this pattern persisted in both infants until the 108th day. Neither "bowing" nor "C" posture were recorded at any time subsequently, although extension of the spine was recorded in Jimmy's reaction on the 115th day and in Johnny's on the 129th day. There had been days previous to the 108th day when the transitional phase had been recorded. Strangely enough, these variations were reported for both infants on the same days. However, after the 108th day the typical newborn pattern did not reappear. It is easy to see that there was a period of forty-five days when the newborn pattern and the transitional phase were overlapping. The first indication of the transitional period was recorded on the 63d day in both infants, and it extended in both until the 140th day, or over a period of seventy-seven days. The first appearance of the "body-jerk" or mature response was recorded for Johnny on the 115th day and for Jimmy on the 122d day. It is possible that this difference might have been even less had the examinations of Jimmy been more frequent than a week apart. In any event there was an overlapping of roughly twenty-five days between the transitional phase and the mature response. Before the infants were five months old the "mature" response was the dominant pattern of reaction. After a period of time they became inured to this particular stimulation and frequently failed to show any overt response, so it was dropped both from the exercise period and from the examination schedule when the infants were about nine months old. It is most probable that other types of sudden stimulation would have educed the "body-jerk" reaction, though the babies had through association and experience become complacent to the striking of a stick on the bed.

There were only thirty-two different occasions when the reactions of Johnny and Jimmy were recorded in this situation. However, these thirty-two examinations spread over a chronological period of 231 days, and during that time Johnny had been receiving frequent daily stimulation. There was considerable correspondence in their reaction-time as well as in the pattern of their response. According to stop-watch account, Johnny's reaction-time varied from 0.6 of a second to 3.4 seconds, with an average of 1.5 seconds. Jimmy's reaction-time ranged from 0.9 of a second to four seconds, with an average of 1.4 seconds. It was not possible to have the same recorder at all times, and the wide range in reaction-time may be somewhat attributed to difference in the reactions of the recorder. This seems highly probable, since the range for both Johnny and Jimmy was great. It is interesting that, despite the variability, the average reaction-times for the two children showed a negligible difference of only 0.1 second. Furthermore, when reaction-time was calculated by counting the frames in the 16-mm. film recording this activity, Johnny averaged 0.062 second and Jimmy 0.078 second. The range in reaction-time when calculated in this way was much less, and the difference in their average reaction-time was only 0.01 second.

Since the response to this stimulation is variable with the degree of quietude of the infant at the moment of stimulation and with the force of the stimuli, and since these factors are not easily controlled, the consistency in the reaction patterns of the two babies is all the more striking.

The duration of the response is a better indication of the intensity of their individual reactions than is the reaction-time. Duration of the response also indicates the gradual increase in specificity and narrowing-down of the behavior-pattern. This measure was calculated by counting the 16-mm. frames of cinema film from the first indication of a somatic move following stimulation until the termination of that particular response. The duration of Johnny's responses ranged from 0.4 of a second to 2.7 seconds, with an average of 1.4 seconds. Jimmy ranged in duration of response from 0.5 to 3.1 seconds with an average of 1.8 seconds. These ranges in duration of response were in inverse ratio to the

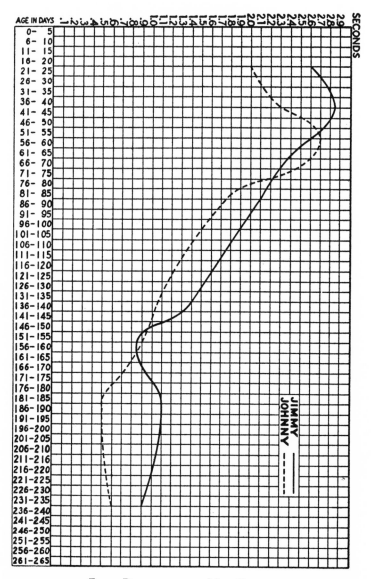

FIG. 2. DURATION OF THE MORO REFLEX

These curves show a gradual diminution of the amount of the activity involved in the reflex as well as the correspondence of the twins in this behavior-pattern.

chronological age of the child. The smoothed curves in Figure 2 show a definite tendency toward a shorter duration as the infants grew older. The reaction was strongest in both infants when they were about two months old and following that time there was a consistent tendency toward a diminution in the duration of response.

When consideration is given to the consistency in the pattern of action, the reaction-time, and the duration or intensity of the responses, the high degree of correspondence between the two babies in this activity is indicated. In this type of activity, therefore, the daily stimulation of Johnny was essentially ineffectual in so far as somatic response was concerned.

In another respect, however, there was a decided difference in the babies, and this difference grew progressively more noticeable as the babies grew older. It will be recalled that crying following the stimulation is a part of the general picture of the newborn pattern. Out of the twenty-four occasions on which the emotional reactions of Johnny to this situation were recorded, there were only eight times that he cried following the stimulation. Seven of these eight occasions occurred before he was 129 days old and therefore are true to the newborn reflex. Five of the eight occurred when "movies" were being made, when the lights introduced an element into the situation which was not ordinarily present during his practice periods. Jimmy, in contrast, cried on eighteen of the twenty-two occasions on which his emotional reactions are reported. On two occasions he cried so much during the examination period that he could not be tested for the somatic reaction.

Even from the beginning, in behavior-patterns which are definitely infracortical, as in this instance, repeated exercise or special stimulation of a function appeared to influence the baby's attitude toward the situation, though the somatic aspect of the reaction had already developed sufficiently to be resistant to noticeable change. In this activity the somatic and the attitudinal aspects are less interinfluential than prevails with cortical activity. That is, the change in attitude with increased familiarity in the situation did not appreciably alter the somatic form of the behavior-pattern.

Suspension-Grasp

One of the most spectacular behavior traits of the newborn infant is his ability to grasp a small rod sufficiently with one hand to support his body suspended for several seconds. It is erroneous to consider the course of growth in grasping behavior without taking into account the change in structural levels at which the behavior-course is governed during different phases of its development. At birth it is a reflex controlled at an infra-cortical level. At this level it is a rudimentary behavior-pattern of phyletic origin. As a reflex it is highly developed at birth of the infant, so that one would need to study fetal behavior in order to ascertain the movements which gave rise to the reflex.

In the present situation we propose to analyze the sequential changes in the overt behavior-pattern which accompany the change in structural control from a lower to a higher level. Our methods of testing growth in this type of behavior consisted of two situations. In the first situation a small round stick was placed in the infant's hand, and when he had grasped it, it was slowly raised in order to lift the baby by the strength of his own grasp above the surface on which he had been lying. It is well known that most newborn infants when at rest tend to hold their digits flexed and the thumb flexed and adducted. If an object is placed in the hand of a young infant he will immediately clutch it. His fingers close tightly in flexion, and the flexion is not pre-ceded by extensor movements. This digital flexion is about as automatic as any reflex action of which the newborn infant is capable. All infants are not equally able to sustain the grasp and hold themselves suspended from a rod by the grip of one hand, but despite the individual differences in the strength of the reflex it is safe to say the reflex is present in practically all newborn infants. It is improbable that a statistical study of a hundred or a thousand newborn infants, wherein each baby was tested for this reaction only once, would yield a 100 per cent record, but a consecutive study of a group of infants over a period of days, weeks, or months, wherein the same babies were tested at fre-quent intervals, would undoubtedly show that the activity is present in all normal newborn infants and can on occasion be demonstrated.

Although this reflex begins developing *in utero* and is a well-developed behavior-pattern at birth, it does not reach its peak of development as a reflex activity until about the second post-natal month. Soon after this peak is reached there is a rapid decrease in the strength of the reflex. It is changes in the pattern of the grasp more than the strength of it which best indicate the phases of growth from an infracortical to a higher-level activity. In order to bring out the process of development we shall consider certain aspects of the behavior-course in detail, and it will be seen that in the development of these details a conformity to the fundamental principles of growth is manifest.

The grasp of the newborn infant is decidedly digital; the thumb is ordinarily flexed and adducted on the palm just below the rod around which the fingers are flexed. This is a typical pattern of the reflex grasp of the newborn infant. With the grip of only the digits he clings tenaciously while his body is raised above the surface, and in this way he suspends himself with the grip of one hand. This type of grasp we have called the *reflex* phase. Soon, however, it is observed that the thumb begins to shift or turn slightly upward as if beginning to encircle the rod. It is apparent that the rod is also at this time being held a little more proximally or toward the center of the palm. These changes denote a transition period from the digital to the palmar grasp. About this time it is also observed that the infant grips less tightly on the rod, so that when one attempts to withdraw the rod the baby will frequently let it slip out of his fingers before he has raised his entire body above the surface. Furthermore, he is less and less likely to close his hand on the rod immediately it is placed in his palm. Most infants show a period when it is unlikely that they will immediately grasp the rod if it is placed in their hands. Instead they hold the fingers extended and resist, flexing them around the rod. These changes indicate the transition period from reflex to voluntary suspension.

When the behavior-pattern is fully developed under the dominance of higher neural centers, it is nearly always initially a palmar grasp, and the thumb actively encircles the rod. In grasping and in the matter of holding his body suspended the child is now able to exercise individual choice at this level. Although the growth process definitely moves from one level to another, it must be borne in mind that at no time is there a sudden change. The transition phase merges or overlaps the reflex pattern, and the voluntary grasping merges with the transitional. The infant may show the new or emerging phase only during the initial reaction, then slip back to the less mature pattern before he finally releases the rod; or perhaps there will be several weeks when it appears

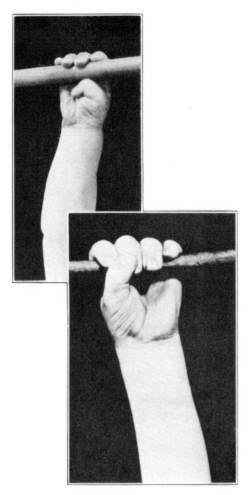

PLATE II. SUSPENSION GRASP

Above, digital grasp of the newborn; below, palmar
grasp characteristic of voluntary grasping.

as if the new phase is fully established, and then there will be occasional reversions to the more immature pattern. It is well known that the reflex pattern is not completely obliterated, since it recurs pathologically in adults. Any type of stress and strain is likely to bring out a less mature form of the pattern.

It is with some hesitation that we venture to offer periods in chronological development at which these various stages of the grasping reflex are most likely to be present, since the data on the larger group of infants are not sufficiently assembled to justify any norms whatever at this time. However, it is quite safe to say that, roughly estimated, the reflex grasp of the newborn extends from birth until somewhere around the third or fourth month. The identifying aspects of this reflex response are: (1) the digital grasp, (2) the thumb inactive and usually adducted on palm below the rod, (3) an ability to raise the body and hold it suspended above the surface. The transition phase emerges about the fourth chronological month and prevails until approximately the ninth or tenth month. The identifying features of the transition period are: (1) tendency toward palmar grasp, (2) tendency for the thumb to encircle the rod though it is not actively engaged in doing so, (3) probable failure to raise the body entirely off the surface (the head and shoulders may be raised but ordinarily the entire body is not), and (4) less spontaneity in closing the digits around the rod immediately it is placed in the infant's hand. This transition stage leads up to a brief period when it is quite likely that the infant will refuse to close the digits around the rod at all. He is quite capable of grasping and willingly does so if an object is handed to him, but he cannot be forced to grasp the rod when it is placed in his hands. Instead he holds the digits extended and withdraws his hand. This act is an illustration of an exaggeration in a developmental phase, since at a later period he is likely to grasp the rod when it is placed in his hand.

Voluntary * grasping definitely follows this interim of failure to grasp. In voluntary grasping the infant will from the first hold the rod definitely in the palm of the hand, and the thumb, around the rod, is actively engaged in the grasp. He frequently will grasp

---

* In using the term *voluntary* the author wishes merely to draw the distinction between the reflex, more or less automatic response of the new-born infant and the type of reaction over which the infant exercises some control. In doing so, there is no intention of entering into the general controversy of the function of volition and will in behavior.

sufficiently to pull himself to a standing position but refuse to hold on when suspended. Although he may hang on until suspended, he certainly exercises his own choice in this matter. At this stage he has as adequate neuro-muscular mechanisms for the performance as he ever had, but cortical powers of inhibition and facilitation have entered in to modify his behavior.

In the development of grasping behavior as judged under these conditions, the growth of Johnny and that of Jimmy were in many respects strikingly similar, although Johnny was during the first twenty-two months of his life given daily exercise in grasping a rod and holding his body suspended. Jimmy was stimulated in this activity at weekly intervals during the first twelve months, and at bi-weekly and finally at monthly intervals during the last ten months. It will be recalled that Jimmy had a much more pronounced grasping reflex at birth than did Johnny. In strength and duration of grasp he maintained during the first twenty-four months of life a definite superiority over Johnny, although, as the following analysis of their behavior reveals, new aspects of the pattern emerged and developed in both babies at approximately the same time.

Reflex Phase
Digital Grasp

	Left	Right
Johnny:	Birth to 78 days	Birth to 49 days
Jimmy:	Birth to 63 days	Birth to 78 days

Thumb Below the Rod

	Left	Right
Johnny:	Birth to 56 days	Birth to 49 days
Jimmy:	Birth to 56 days	Birth to 122 days

Raises Body and Suspends

	Left	Right
Johnny:	Birth to 108 days	Birth to 108 days
Jimmy:	Birth to 154 days	Birth to 129 days

Transitional Stage
Rod Held at Distal Margin of Palm

	Left	Right
Johnny:	56 days to 200 days	56 days to 122 days
Jimmy:	63 days to 261 days	84 days to 276 days

Thumb Inactively Around the Rod

	Left	Right
Johnny:	63 days to 200 days	56 days to 147 days
Jimmy:	63 days to 129 days	84 days to 276 days

Raises Body Partially

	Left	Right
Johnny:	115 days to 320 days	84 days to 320 days
Jimmy:	84 days to 337 days	84 days to 337 days

REGRESSIVE PHASE
No Grasp of Rod

	Left	Right
Johnny:	337 days to 413 days	337 days to 427 days
Jimmy:	337 days to 427 days	337 days to 427 days

VOLUNTARY PHASE
Palmar Grasp

	Left	Right
Johnny:	129 days to 780 days	115 days to 780 days
Jimmy:	129 days to 780 days	129 days to 780 days

Thumb Actively Engaged Around Rod

	Left	Right
Johnny:	129 days to 780 days	115 days to 780 days
Jimmy:	129 days to 780 days	129 days to 780 days

Voluntary Suspension

	Left	Right
Johnny:	337 days to 780 days	337 days to 780 days
Jimmy:	494 days to 780 days	456 days to 780 days

A comparison of their growth in this performance is better illustrated by Figure 4. It is easily seen that Johnny tended to be a little more constant in his patterns once a new phase emerged, whereas Jimmy was more given to reversions to a less mature pattern. Superficially this may appear to be a developmental difference and lead to the conclusion that once new patterns emerged with Johnny they were more likely to remain constant because of the daily exercise he was getting in this performance. But the significant fact is that the first appearance of a new phase in the behavior-course was observed in both infants most frequently on the same examination day, or within a short time of each other. This correspondence in development was much greater than that evidenced by other babies or even fraternal twins under the observation of the experimenters. Had the examination intervals been more frequent, it is likely that the time discrepancies in the appearance of different phases in the behavior-course would have been greatly reduced. The reason for Jimmy's greater variability in pattern is easily explained by the fatigue which must have ensued during his longer suspension, as well as to his more disturbed attitude under conditions which were less familiar to him.

Crying appears to be a part of the suspension-grasp pattern of the newborn. If the baby does not cry during suspension the fall will, in all probability, stimulate him to do so. This is true of practically all young babies, and crying during the reflex reaction may therefore be considered as part of the general pattern. Crying is not a characteristic feature of the subsequent voluntary stage. Record was kept at each examination period of any crying which occurred before, during, or following suspension. During the first seventy days both Johnny and Jimmy are reported to have cried during and immediately following all suspension-grasp reactions. After the appearance of the transitional phase of development and subsequently there was, however, a marked contrast. There are only five out of forty-two examination periods during the period from seventy to 780 days, or the twenty-three months following the evanescence of the reflex pattern, in which Johnny is reported to have cried either before, during, or following suspension. In contrast, there are only four times from birth to 780 days when Jimmy did not cry during this performance. Any intense feeling of perturbation is likely to stimulate a more infantile form of the behavior-course. In view of the enormous contrast in the attitudes of Johnny and Jimmy toward the situation, the fact that new patterns first appeared on approximately the same day is all the more significant. To what extent Jimmy's disturbed attitude strengthened his grip and the time of suspension we are not at the present time able to judge, but the fact that he did cling to the rod for a longer period than Johnny would also contribute to his greater inconstancy in pattern.

Johnny's duration of suspension, the time being recorded on a

stop-watch in tenths of a second from the time the foot was completely above the surface, ranged from 0.5 to 24.1 seconds with
the right hand. The average suspension time with this hand was
6.0± seconds. On the left hand his range was from 0.4 to 24.3
with an average of 5.2±. The longest period of suspension
occurred during the second month, as the accompanying smooth
curve illustrates well. To be specific, it occurred at the examination made on their 56th day.

Jimmy has a more erratic record in terms of duration of
grasp. His range with the right hand was from 0.8 to 19.5 seconds
with an average of 7.7± seconds. With the left hand the range
was from 0.2 to 62.1 seconds with an average of 13.2±. The high
point of 62.1 seconds occurred on his 63d day. The curve showing
the duration of suspension has the characteristic rise and rather
sudden drop during the second and third months. Although
Jimmy's suspension grasp in terms of time was much stronger
than Johnny's, the shape of the curves, their rises and falls, are
strikingly parallel.

The second situation used for testing the suspension-grasp
reflex in infants attempted to determine the character of the grasp
when all support was removed, rather than the infant's ability in
raising himself to a suspended position. In this situation the
experimenter placed both of the infant's hands securely around
the rod, and the hands of the examiner were held over those of
the infant until he was raised above the surface. Once he was
suspended, the hands of the examiner were removed and the time
of his suspension grasp was calculated from that moment until,
releasing his grip on the rod, he fell. In this situation an analysis
of the body posture during suspension is of greater developmental
significance than is the duration or fact of the grasping.

In the newborn infant the grasp is usually digital and the
thumb is adducted below the rod, as was the case in the single-
hand grasp. When suspended the baby's head drops back toward
the interscapular spine; the lower extremities are ordinarily flexed
at the knees and the hips; and not infrequently the upper extremities are flexed. But as the infant grows older the grasp becomes
palmar, especially at the initial stage of the grasp, and the thumb
becomes actively engaged in encircling the rod. These changes
show the same gradual aspects of development as the single-
handed grasping.

Furthermore, as the infant grows older, little by little there is noticeably less and less dorsal flexion of the neck, so that gradually the head is held more in a plane with the body, until finally the infant can sustain the head in this vertical position, unless fatigue or other disturbing factors set in. In this respect as in others, growth is not a constant and persistent stream of increments. Instead the baby holds his head a little more forward and then again drops it backward and then slightly more forward and less back, until finally he has sufficient control to do as he chooses in the matter. As a well-developed trait he ordinarily does hold the head in the body plane, though fatigue or any other type of strain may educe the less mature posture.

About the same time he is gaining in control over the head, it is observed that the lower extremities, and most likely the upper extremities as well, are tending toward extension rather than flexion as the most characteristic posture. There is also in most infants a very definite weakening of the grasp during the transition stage from reflex to voluntary grasping. At this period some infants fail to sustain the suspended position at all, but drop immediately the experimenter's hands are removed from covering their hands on the rod. The strength and duration of the grasp are again increased as voluntary grasping becomes established. Finally maintenance of the suspension position is under the individual control of the child.

Johnny and Jimmy showed a high degree of correspondence in their development of this type of grasping, in so far as the appearance of new phases of the pattern was concerned. The suspension grasp of both infants was digital during the first two months of life. When they were sixty-three days old both were showing a tendency to hold the rod more in the palm indicating a transition in the development of this aspect of the pattern. This transition stage continued with Johnny until he was 176 days and with Jimmy until he was 221 days, during which time there was less consistency in the mode of activity in each child. That is, definite palmar grasp was first recorded for both infants when they were examined on the 129th day, and *only* palmar grasping was recorded as the *initial reaction* for Johnny after the 176th day and for Jimmy after the 221st day. Even after the grasp had become definitely palmar as an initial reaction, it would slip down to the digital level if they remained suspended long, until fatigue set in.

Likewise there was high correspondence in the two babies in making use of the thumb for grasping. The thumb was inactive for both during the first two months. On the 78th day both began to encircle the rod with the thumb, denoting a transition phase. The transition period continued until the 122d day with Johnny and until the 200th day with Jimmy. Jimmy showed a greater tendency to revert on occasion to an early form of the pattern. Jimmy's greater frequency in reversion to less mature forms of behavior was probably due in large part to his perturbed attitude during the performance. Notwithstanding Jimmy's more frequent reversions to immature patterns, the first appearance of any new aspect of the pattern closely paralleled its first manifestation in Johnny. Subsequent to the reflex stage, daily exercise or familiarity with a situation altered the attitude of the child toward that situation. Johnny obviously enjoyed the performance. Attitude in turn modified the duration of the grasp. Moreover, in the case of Jimmy on occasions it stimulated a less mature type of grasp. Even though his grasping had developed to the voluntary level he would still hang suspended, although crying and complaining as he did so.

The suspension grasp thus has two outstanding phases, viz., the reflex and the voluntary. The reflex activity is governed at an infracortical level. Despite the fact that Johnny had been given exercise in this activity, the reflex pattern of reaction did not persist. In his behavior as well as in that of Jimmy and other infants in whom this activity has been studied by the experimenter, there occurred a period of inactivity between the reflex and voluntary phases. Johnny's daily exercise in this performance did not bridge the gap between these two phases.

Inverted Suspension

Postural adjustment of infants when held by the feet in an inverted position shows a definite developmental sequence. In fact it contains the key to physiological development in other behavior-patterns. The newborn baby when suspended in this fashion engages in frequent rotation of the head and bilateral torsion of the trunk. Often the lower extremities are alternately flexed and extended at the knees and at the hips so that the whole body is moved up and down as a unit. At this stage of development the head, trunk, and lower extremities are held in the same plane although there is usually considerable flexion in the lower extremities at all times. Flexion is the least expensive movement of the body. The tendency of the newborn is to maintain the flexed position. Gravity pulls him down, he again tries to get into the state of flexion. This flexion and extension continue so as to give an impression of a continuous up-and-down movement, the foci of action being at the knees and pelvis. The torsion and general body activity of the infant when in this position grow noticeably less during the ensuing months, as a slight spinal extension at the neck becomes apparent. This extension denotes the appearance of a transitional phase uniting the newborn phase with the second outstanding phase.

The latter consists of a hyperextension of the spine; the vertebral column, from the cervical to the lumbar region, forms an arch, the head being held considerably posterior to the pelvic girdle and lower extremities. Being unable to sustain the flexed position against the pull of gravity the infant begins to use the more costly movement of extension. Then he becomes extravagant and engages in hyperextension of the entire spine from head to tail. In this phase the lower extremities are usually extended at the knees and the upper extremities are most commonly extended and abducted.

The third outstanding phase in postural adjustment in an inverted position is in many respects just the opposite of the second. The baby attempts to hold the body in the reverse position of the hyperextended spine. This reaction consists of a ventral flexion at the hips and ventral flexion at the neck so that the head is held anterior to the pelvic girdle. It appears as if the infant is trying to right himself, since the head is brought upward toward the chest. While in this position the lower extremities are frequently extended at the knees, though they may be flexed. Ordinarily the infant shows great tension, the upper extremities are adducted and sometimes they clutch the baby's own knees, or thighs, or reach toward the experimenter. It is definitely an attitude of rejection of the position.

But the infant does not arrive at this righting position in a day, nor does he maintain it without variation even after it has become the dominating action-pattern. There is a period between the characteristic position of hyperextension and hyperflexion of the

spine when neither is quite dominant. There will be reversions to
the extended spine, ventral flexions which will not be maintained,
and sometimes a lateral flexion and rotation of the spine so it
appears as if the baby is trying to extend and flex his spine at the
same time. Distinct merging of the two patterns is evident. But
finally the ventral flexion comes to be the dominating and characteristic position.

The fourth phase we have called the mature one. At this level
the infant is most likely to hold himself straight, that is, the head,

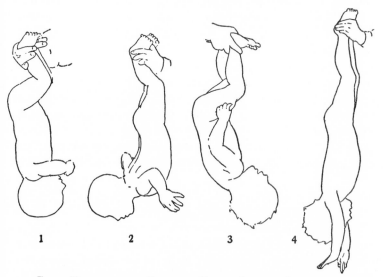

1   **2**   **3**   **4**

FIG. 5. DEVELOPMENTAL REACTIONS DURING INVERTED SUSPENSION
Characteristic postural adjustments: 1, extension and flexion primarily in
lower extremities; 2, spinal extension; 3, flexion at pelvis in attempt to right
position (note reversal features of positions 2 and 3); 4, acquiescent attitude
to the inverted position.

trunk, and lower extremities in the same plane. It is a state of
relaxation. The upper extremities are extended and hang down
beside the baby's head. He may flex or extend his spine, but
neither movement is likely to be sustained consistently as a
dominating posture during the period of suspension. The attitude
is one of acquiescence. Perhaps it is merely experience that brings
about this postural change, but the writer is inclined to believe
that it is the integration of other sensory mechanisms of recent
development. This opinion is based upon the observation that

most infants of two years or more gain this acquiescent postural attitude even though their experience in the situation has not been extensive. It is as if the child had adequate perceptive abilities to appreciate that the expenditure of energy in trying to correct the position was too costly, even though his crying indicated that he did not enjoy the situation. Crying most frequently accompanies the newborn reaction, whereas in the mature pattern it is likely not to do so.

In the present investigation the infants were held suspended by the feet for fifteen seconds and the pattern which was the most predominating one during those fifteen seconds was the one considered as representative of the baby's level of development at the time. The development of this behavior-pattern illustrates well the fundamental growth process. At first there was the generalized undifferentiated response of the newborn. This was followed by a gradual extension of the spine which in due course became exaggerated. Then there follows a period of tension and hyperflexion of the trunk—an excessive exertion in the opposite direction—before the pattern is fully matured. Roughly estimated this trait is matured in most infants when they are about twenty-four months old. An intense attitude at any time will provoke less mature phases of activity.

A comparison of the records of Johnny and Jimmy in the growth of this behavior-course indicates that the daily exercise of this performance did not appreciably alter the characteristic or identifying patterns, but the change in the attitude of Johnny during the experimental period definitely modified his retention of the patterns of bodily posture during suspension. We have for the purpose of convenience divided the development of this activity into six periods, as follows: (1) the newborn posture; (2) the first transition phase, denoting the shift to the extended-spine posture from that of the newborn infant; (3) hyperextension of the spine; (4) the second transition stage, indicating the shift from the hyperextended to the hyperflexed posture; (5) ventral flexion of the trunk; and (6) finally the fully matured posture. The typical newborn postural reaction persisted with Johnny until the 49th day and with Jimmy until the 56th day. On the 56th and 63d day respectively the first transition phase was indicated in both infants, and it continued persistently with Johnny until he was 108 days old. A reversion to this transitional pattern occurred when he was 176 days old. The first transition phase continued with Jimmy until he was 115 days old. Hyperextension of the spine was persistent with Johnny from the 115th day to the 147th. There was a recurrence of it on the 191st day. Extension of the spine was Jimmy's most characteristic reaction from the 78th day until the 191st, although there was an overlapping of a period of twenty-two days when the second transition phase was at times manifested. The second transition phase extended with Johnny from the 161st until the 396th day and with Jimmy from the 169th to the 221st day. During this time the reaction pattern was mixed. Sometimes within the fifteen-second period there appeared extension of the spine, then ventral flexion; and sometimes it looked as though the baby were trying to do both at the same time. This resulted in a strange lateral twisting of the body. But in time ventral flexion became the dominant form of action in both infants.

The third phase, the ventral flexion or righting posture, occurred frequently in the reactions of Johnny between the ages of 245 and 625 days, and it was the most pronounced reaction of Jimmy between the ages of 200 and 686 days. Johnny did not show this hyperflexed position as often as Jimmy. The fully developed or mature postural adjustment occurred with Johnny quite frequently between the ages of 269 and 780 days. In this instance experience or conditioning modified Johnny's retention of a particular phase of the pattern. He soon developed an acquiescent attitude which served somewhat to lengthen his transition periods.

In the matter of attitude there is sharp contrast in the behavior of the two babies. Jimmy was crying 77 per cent of the time during the examination of his reactions in this situation as contrasted with Johnny, who was crying only 21 per cent of the time. The majority of these crying reactions of Johnny occurred during the period when the newborn phase of the pattern was most characteristic, at which time crying was a part of the general form of behavior. It must be emphasized that while Johnny's adaptation to the situation tended to make him relaxed and therefore curtailed the periods of hyperflexion and hyperextension, the daily exercise or use of this performance did not alter the fundamental sequential phases in the development of this behavior-course. Although he did not retain the exaggerated reactions as long, in reality he showed all the developmental aspects in his reactions to this situation. Moreover, they occurred in customary sequence and in close approximation to the chronological age at which they were developed in Jimmy. Attitude, on the other hand, was considerably influenced by the daily exercise. This change in attitude in turn modified the persistence with which the newly emerged patterns were retained. In the development of this particular trait Jimmy's modes of behavior more closely resembled those of other infants in sequence and duration of phases than did Johnny's. Since, however, the difference in Johnny's reactions and those of other infants was not a difference in form or sequence, but merely a difference in the duration of a particular phase, this performance is another in which mere repetition of the act did not alter the essential phases of the behavior-pattern.

Crawling and Creeping

The age at which infants begin to creep and their various methods of creeping have been topics of general interest to persons concerned with problems of child development for some time. Although considerable literature on the subject of infant creeping has accumulated, none of it contains an adequate descriptive analysis of the movements, or the anlages, which give rise to the behavior-pattern of creeping.

For convenience of studying the development of this behavior trait we have grouped the reactions most characteristic of growing infants at this time into five phases or stages. It is impossible to study the growth of prone progression without taking into account the cephalo-caudal course of development. For this reason the upper and lower portions of the body are, at the same chronological age of the individual, in different stages of development. At the time of birth it is very apparent that the head and shoulder regions of the infants are in a more advanced stage of development, functionally, than the pelvic girdle and lower extremities. This is true even though the superior part of the body is less overtly active.

When one first views the crawling reactions of the newborn, he may be perplexed over the meaning of cephalo-caudal development. The newborn infant, certainly during the first month of post-natal life, gives the impression of being a little top-heavy. There is a great deal of activity in the lower extremities, such that the infant tends to push alternately, and more or less rhythmically, with the toes or knees against the surface on which he is lying in a prone position. Some infants are able to make progressive moves forward in this fashion. Most frequently the face rests on the surface, though occasionally the head may bob up for a second. The chest is resting on the surface in such a way that an observer is made to feel that except for the inactivity of the head and shoulder region, the infant could make considerable progress in this position. The pelvic girdle, specifically the crests of the ilia, do not come in contact with the surface at this stage. The upper extremities are flexed and abducted, and compared with the lower extremities they are noticeably inactive. The digits are usually closed. It is possible that at a certain stage in fetal development the upper extremities are more active than the lower, but by the time of birth, in the normal well-developed infant, they are approaching the transition phase. These activities of the newborn are of infracortical control and are considered as reflex crawling movements. They are less specific than the Moro or grasping reflexes, and there is considerably more individual variation in the pattern, but there is nevertheless reason to believe that these movements are atavistic rudiments of a well-developed ancestral trait, which in man have been relegated to higher levels of control for final development and functioning.

Following this early reflex crawling stage there is a transitional phase which is recognized by the less rhythmical activity of the lower extremities. The head and chest are held up for longer periods of time and a little higher above the surface, though there is still a great deal of dyssynergia in the head and shoulder girdle as the baby supports himself on the forearms. The activity of the lower extremities is more generalized, less specific, less rhythmical, and less of a definite pattern than in the reflex stage. The baby will kick simultaneously above the surface of the bed, usually arhythmically. He also displays excess or overflow of activity, especially in the lower extremities.

Except for the fact that the principal subjects in this particular investigation are boys, one might be tempted to call the third stage the mermaid posture. This stage of development is distinguished by marked individual control over the upper part of the body. The baby supports himself on the palms, the upper extremities extended, so as to sustain his head and chest raised well above the surface. The pelvic girdle at the height of this phase rests flatly on the surface to such an extent that often the crests of the ilia touch the underlying substratum. The lower extremities are extended and comparatively inactive. Now it is the inferior portion of the body which has become the dead weight. It appears that the level of control attained over activities of the pelvic girdle at this stage is comparable to that attained in the head and shoulder regions shortly after birth. It is a period of comparative inactivity, representing the transition from reflex activities to those under a higher level of control in so far as the pelvic girdle and lower extremities are concerned. The individual control over activities in the superior portion of the body indicates that the region has advanced beyond the transition phase.

The infant when placed in the prone position maintains this inactive posture with the pelvis resting flatly on the underlying surface for only a short while. Soon there follows, or rather merges with it, a second transition phase. This transition represents a shift from the non-progressive posture to definite creeping. During this period the conflict between the portion of the body above the umbilicus and the inferior portion is apparent. The infant may be able to flex and abduct his lower extremities so as to lift the pelvic girdle off the surface of the floor, but in so doing he throws the shoulder girdle down so that the chest and face may strike the surface. Although the infant will sometimes draw one leg up underneath him and then lunge forward rather helplessly, he does not succeed in making much progress. A little later this lunging activity becomes a definite technique which the baby uses in making progress forward. Although still unable to creep on hands and knees, he supports his abdomen off the surface for a moment, then thrusts his body forward and lands a little forward on his abdomen. This deliberate lunge for the purpose of moving forward is easily distinguished from the earlier phases when he lost control but lunged forward as he landed on his face.

Other times, although the infant remains with the abdomen on the surface of the floor, he is able by alternate pulling with the upper extremities to make considerable progress, dragging his abdomen on the floor and the lower extremities rather uselessly behind. Not infrequently an infant in this stage, or the latter part of this stage, will get up on his hands and knees, holding the abdomen above the surface, and in this position will rock back and forth before he is able to make actual progress forward. Scrutiny of the action reveals the importance of this rocking phase. It is obviously preparatory to the movement of thrusting his body forward in order to make progress. The rocking back and forth rather than the steady progression forward is denotative of the excessive, exaggerated movement which is so characteristic of an emerging aspect of a behavior-course. Although these different patterns are manifestations of development, we are, for the sake of convenience, grouping them all under the second transitional phase, or the period just before unmistakable creeping has developed. At this period it is difficult to tell just what will be the chosen method of creeping, but since the majority of infants creep on hands and knees or all fours, we shall in this treatise more or less avoid going into the phases manifest by the infants who assume a rather bizarre method of creeping, such as hitching on the buttocks.

The final stage is that of creeping. During the initial aspects of creeping the infant shows some lack of coördination. Perhaps he will move ipsilateral members rather than associated ones, and the movements are isolated separate actions which need knitting together. In a short time, however, well-integrated associated movements are established. It is the observation of the writer that most infants will at times creep on hands and feet, or if not on hands and feet they will, during the later part of the creeping period, move with one knee and one foot and both palms on the surface. This method or quadrupedal locomotion merges with, and is preparatory to, development in erect locomotion. Development of this activity will be discussed subsequently.

In calling attention to phases of development in this way, we feel impelled again to reëmphasize the gradual and continuous process involved. Never does the infant pass completely and irretrievably from one stage into another. There is always a merging of patterns and parts of patterns both in the degree of perfection of the action and in the frequency of occurrence. There are often regressions to the less mature response. Excessive interest in lures beyond reach and emotional stress and strain are likely to evoke greater variations in the actions of an infant at a given time.

In order to determine the effect of repetition and exercise in this type of activity upon development, the experimenters in this

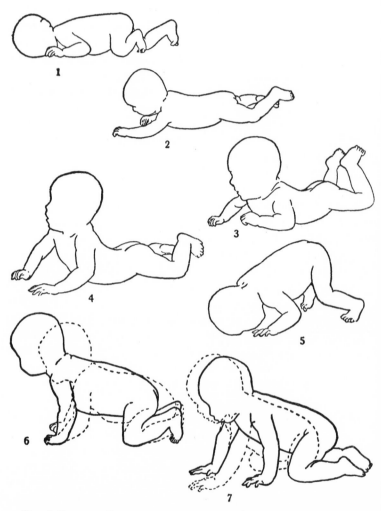

FIG. 6. POSTURAL PHASES IN DEVELOPMENT OF CRAWLING AND CREEPING

1. Newborn crawling movements. 2. Less activity in lower extremities; begins to hold head up. 3. Increased control over movements of head and shoulder girdle. 4. Marked development in upper part of body; pelvis rests on the surface. 5. Conflict in action of pelvic and shoulder regions; when pelvis is raised, head and shoulders are lowered. 6. Rocking movements; maintains abdomen above surface. 7. Associated creeping movements.

investigation placed Johnny four times a day during the early months of his life in a small jacket, attached to ball-bearing rollers and suspended from a rod above his head. He was placed in the jacket in such a way that his hands and knees could touch the underlying surface, although his abdomen was raised slightly above it. This situation would activate the reflex crawling movements ordinarily. We essayed to learn whether or not daily stimulation of these early reflex crawling movements would in any way modify—accelerate, retard, or alter the sequential phases of—the development of creeping. Jimmy was examined for his reactions in this situation at weekly intervals during the first nine months of life. As soon as Johnny began to show definite attempts at creeping he was given daily practice on the floor, without the support of the jacket, whereas Jimmy was kept in a crib. During the time spent at the clinic Jimmy was allowed on the floor only at the time of the weekly examination periods given to test his developmental behavior.

A comparison of their development in terms of the five phases mentioned above yields the following results:

Reflex Crawling
Johnny: Birth to 70 days
Jimmy: Birth to 56 days

First Transition Phase
Johnny: 78 days to 140 days
Jimmy: 63 days to 122 days

Period of Diminished Crawling
Johnny: 129 days to 200 days
Jimmy: 122 days to 169 days

Second Transition Phase
Johnny: 176 days to 238 days
Jimmy: 154 days to 261 days

Creeping Stage
Johnny: 232 days to 343 days
Jimmy: 200 days to 329 days

These figures might have been altered somewhat had the examination days been at shorter intervals, but that would not have altered the fact that on the whole Jimmy was slightly younger than Johnny in the development of creeping. An infant was considered to be in the reflex crawling stage as long as he pushed rather rhythmically and alternately with the lower extremities while the face and shoulder girdle were often resting on the surface. It appears as if there were, due to the daily exercise, a definite conditioning of the movements of the lower extremities on the part of Johnny, for when placed in the jacket he would, during the early months, start pushing with his feet against the surface. This performance was a conditioned response which, however, had no fundamental effect upon the development of the behavior-course. During the first transition period, when most infants are less active in a progressive fashion, Johnny began making very rapid progress when placed in the jacket. His progressive movements consisted of pushing simultaneously with his toes and pulling against the surface with his hands. In this way he was able to start the ball-bearing rollers moving. Repetition of this pushing and pulling was sufficient to carry him to the end of the table to gain the desired object. Abandon and an utterly care-free attitude characterized his actions. But these attributes did not appear to accelerate his actual growth in creeping.

Jimmy's behavior at this time denoted extreme caution. He moved slowly and deliberately, though his developmental posture was accelerated beyond that of Johnny. There is no doubt that Jimmy attained a creeping posture and associated creeping movements a week or ten days younger than Johnny. To what extent training or exercise might have delayed Johnny's development of these patterns we are not at the present time prepared to say. We are quite justified, however, in stating that although the daily exercise apparently *conditioned* Johnny to greater activity, it did not hasten the developmental process or the manifestation of a new phase of this behavior-course. It might be inferred that he gained so much satisfaction in moving about in the jacket that his normal urges to get up on his hands and knees to creep were checked. In that event exercise retarded his development. This interpretation would seem more plausible but for the fact that training in the jacket and on the floor without support overlapped in terms of time, so that he was thus given an incentive to creep unaided even more than Jimmy was at that time. Jimmy began making definite creeping movements on his hands and knees thirty-two days before Johnny did. The contrast in his extreme caution and Johnny's abandon was marked during the whole period. It is therefore all the more interesting that, during the later period of the creeping stage, it was, so far as the examination periods revealed, difficult to get Jimmy to creep, although he had done so quite readily earlier. It appears that restriction in use of this performance checked its maximum development, although use or disuse of the function did not materially alter the fundamental course of growth in the trait, nor did it appreciably affect subsequent development of erect locomotion.

Creeping merges with the development of erect locomotion, and for a while, although the infant engages in both activities, creeping is the preferred method of getting about the room. In a short while there comes a time when erect locomotion is preferred and creeping is resorted to only in play. At the initial phase of this aspect of development an infant's struggles to get into a standing position are among the most amusing of his performances. He falls down, gets up again, and so on interminably. He will insist on walking even though the objective is only a few feet away and he could have crept to it with ease.

Erect Locomotion

Probably no one infant behavior-pattern has been the subject of greater controversy than has the development of erect locomotion. This fact is not surprising, since it is a trait peculiar to the human species and therefore outstanding in distinguishing the human from other mammals. The earlier psychologists felt that in a study of walking there would be found the key to the problem of instincts and acquired traits or to the nature-nurture dispute. In 1896 William James (28) proposed that "if a baby were kept from getting on his feet for two or three weeks after the first impulse to walk had shown itself in him,—a small blister on each sole would do the business,—he might then be expected to walk about as well, through the mere ripening of his nerve-centres, as if the ordinary process of 'learning' had been allowed to occur during all the blistered time." (P. 407.) It is obvious that James failed to consider the phase of development of the behavior-course at the time he would have introduced the experimental factor. If the child was already beginning to show the "impulse to walk," the period of greatest susceptibility to external influences had probably been passed. To have kept him off his feet for two or three weeks at this time would probably have been negligible, but to have kept him off his feet for three or six months would have made an enormous difference both then and later. In the present investigation the control subject was not kept completely off his feet, but his chances of exercising the function of walking at the time independent walking began to develop were considerably reduced as against the opportunities of his twin brother, who was urged and stimulated to walk as young and as much as possible. Therefore, a comparison of the development of Johnny and Jimmy in this trait is a relative measure of the effect of use and disuse upon the growth of the function in question.

But before we can compare the development of these babies we must analyze some aspects of the trait which are of developmental signficance. Erect locomotion is a complicated performance subject to greater individual variation than any pattern of behavior so far discussed. Therefore, in the present analysis of the course of its development the writer can touch only the high spots and leave the finer details of the analysis to some later publication, after the individual records of the major group of our experimental infants have been sufficiently studied. These "high spots," however, are adequate for bringing out the comparative course of growth in the twins, Johnny and Jimmy, and to illustrate the fundamental processes of development in this particular behavior-pattern.

The procedure set for judging the infant's course of development in erect locomotion was for the experimenter to hold the baby at the axillæ so that his feet could barely touch the surface of a footprint board. This board measured fifty-two by twenty-four inches, thereby allowing the infant to take several steps. It was smeared with mimeographing ink and then covered with a strip of smooth paper. When the infant stepped upon the paper an imprint was made on the reverse side. The purpose of the footprints was not to record plantar epidermal ridges, but rather to record that part of the foot which touched the surface as the child stepped and to show upon what part of the foot the greatest amount of pressure was exerted.

Our analysis of the processes and phases involved in walking is based upon the study of approximately forty of the sixty-eight infants who have attained a fair degree of independent walking while under the observation of the experimenters, and of the twins who are the particular subjects of this report. Examination records were supplemented by routine cinematographic records of the same activity. Our cinema records of the twins during the first twenty-six months of life in this one pattern of behavior amount to approximately 500 feet of 16-mm. film. These films have been studied in detail, as well as the individual written protocols of the babies.

Most persons think walking begins when the child takes his first step alone, and previous studies of walking have ordinarily dated from that time. While such studies may bring out very interesting data on individual differences in time and methods of walking, they do not reveal the movements or anlages which give rise to the act of walking nor do they show the process of development involved. Shirley's study (57) is an exception. She conducted an intensive study of the development of walking from the earliest phases, and on the basis of her studies she points out four different stages in the growth of this behavior-pattern. These stages or phases are: (1) early stepping movements, (2) standing with help, (3) walking with help, and (4) walking alone. Shirley seemingly considers these stages as milestones and not necessarily intimately and functionally connected with one another. Although she insists that they follow an orderly sequence, and one stage cannot be hurdled by a precociously developing child, she does not show how one pattern gives rise to a subsequent one, nor in what way they are related.

Since erect locomotion is a complicated performance, and since each aspect introduces possibilities of variation the details of which are significant in the process of growth, an adequate analysis of the steps involved is not at this time available. In defining the major phases in the growth of this behavior-pattern we have based our analysis upon postural relations of the growing infant as observed at regular intervals. Grossly considered, the growth period of erect progression may be grouped conveniently into four periods, but it is by the details or identifying features of each period that the growth process is revealed. Since these stages are quite complex in themselves and no single name could identify them, we shall refer to them merely by the numbers 1, 2, 3, and 4. Then in our descriptive analysis we shall endeavor not only to point out the salient growing aspects in each stage but the steps by which one stage succeeds another.

The first period covers roughly the first three or four months of post-natal life. The posture of the newborn infant who is held supported under the arms so that his feet can touch the surface ordinarily shows the chin flexed on the chest and the upper extremities flexed and adducted and held close to the body; the lower extremities, usually flexed at the knees and at the pelvis, are often crossed. When the feet touch the surface, some infants will press against it so that the muscular tension is sufficiently palpable to indicate that the infant is partially supporting his weight on his feet. Quite often, however, the lower extremities simply double beneath the body weight. It is well known that frequently the newborn infant, when thus stimulated, will make rhythmical stepping movements. It is the alternate rhythm of these movements which distinguishes them from the random kicking movements so characteristic of newborn infants. These movements are segmental and so localized that the upper part of the body appears to be involved merely because it is attached to the lower extremities. One gains the impression in observing and feeling these actions of the newborn that the same response might be elicited even if the upper part of the body were severed from the lower. Ordinarily the infant does not take more than three or four rhythmical steps at a time, though the writer has records of occasions when the newborn infant thus stepped the length of a bed. These stepping movements are present in the behavior of most newborn infants, but they cannot be educed on any or every occasion that the baby is taken up and held under the arms. It is an act of phyletic origin reminiscent of a period when walking was a function controlled at a lower structural level than it is in the human. It does not in the human infant attain functional maturity as a segmental activity.

During the newborn period there is very little consistency in the contact of the foot on the surface. Sometimes this contact is made on the lateral aspect of the foot, again on the toes or the entire sole. As the baby begins to hold his head more in a plane with the body, the upper and lower extremities become less flexed and adducted; and as the contact of the feet upon the surface becomes more definite, the first stage merges with the second.

The second stage covers roughly the period from four to eight months. It is characterized by a tendency for the child to hold his head in the plane with the body, although the body is held forward from the pelvic level. Thus the head is anterior to the pelvis and about in line with the feet, which are also held anterior to the pelvis. In other words, the buttocks form the apex of a triangle of which the trunk and lower extremities constitute the two sides. Most frequently the lower extremities are extended at the knees, though they may be slightly flexed. The infant will ordinarily make some attempt to rest his weight upon his feet, though after a few moments, especially during the early part of this period, the lower extremities may give way beneath the weight of the body. The contact of the feet upon the surface is decidedly *digital*. The base is extremely narrow, the two feet usually being in juxtaposition. The upper extremities are more extended and held in front of the body. This position of the arms constitutes the inception of extension and abduction, which occur later and become indispensable as balancing mechanisms. It is easy to see that in this posture the stepping movements would have greatly diminished. In some infants it is practically impossible to elicit stepping movements at this stage. How much this posture is determined by the ratio of the trunk length to the length of the lower extremities we would not at the present time like to hazard a guess. But whatever may be the cause, this is a posture which characterizes a phase of behavior in all infants for a shorter or longer period during the early growth cycle of erect locomotion. For that reason alone it is of developmental import. It is, however, possible that the leaning angle of the torso and the digital position of the feet are of phylogenetic importance. There is resemblance in the posture of the infant at this stage to the posture commonly assumed by simians.

The third period denotes a sort of transition from the second stage to the time when the infant begins to walk independently. The writer hesitates to estimate the chronological period when this stage most frequently occurs, since the data on our larger group of infants have not been tabulated, and there is, to be sure, considerable individual variation. In the beginning of this stage it is observed that the infant now tends to hold himself in a more erect posture—that is, the head, trunk, pelvic girdle, and feet are in approximately the same plane. The lower extremities are often slightly flexed both at the knees and at the pelvis, and there is a greater tendency toward extension and abduction of the upper extremities. There is a great deal of dyssynergia, and during the early part of this stage the infant is more likely to stamp with his feet or "jump" up and down with his body while holding his feet in position than he is to take walking steps. During the later part of this period the infant is likely to take steps if held by the hand rather than under the arms. When held under the arms he seems to depend upon the experimenter and thus is stimulated to engage more vigorously in the stamping or jumping play. Also, during this stage the base changes from the narrow to a wider one, the foot contact with the surface becomes distinctly plantigrade rather than digital, and the upper extremities become extended and abducted. It is a period of incubation before the birth of independent walking.

Most writers, having assumed that the infant should be able to stand alone before he could walk alone, have placed standing alone and walking alone at different stages in the development of erect locomotion. It is the writer's observation that the two emerge simultaneously in most infants. Frequently an infant may be able to take a few steps alone before he can maintain independent balance. The fourth period extends from the time the child can maintain his balance or take a few consecutive steps alone until he has a well-developed gait. Actually this period should be broken up into three shorter phases in order to bring out the essential features of development. It is obvious that at this time the activity of walking has come under the dominance of a higher neuro-structural level. During the early part of this stage it is observed that the infant maintains an excessively wide base, that his upper extremities are extended and abducted, and that the lower extremities are slightly flexed at the knee and pelvis. There is a constant balancing movement of the upper extremities. If the infant loses balance he falls rather helplessly, usually to a sitting position. A great deal of dyssynergia is observed, and such walking steps as he may be able to take are either isolated movements or excessively hurried. That is, the child carefully places one foot down and gets it definitely set before picking up the other one, or, seemingly realizing his poor control, he may take several running steps before he topples over. His progression is plantigrade, but he puts his entire sole down at once.

During the later part of this period of growth we observe the base become gradually narrowed until finally it is quite normal as the infant steps one foot approximately in line with the other. His progression now is not only plantigrade; his movements are from heel to toe. The upper extremities during this period gradually lose their function as a balancing accessory and are dropped down by the sides. During the latter part of the second year or early part of the third, associated movements of the upper extremities become part of the child's gait. Also, during this period the slight flexion of the lower extremities at the knees and the hips becomes less and less; the isolated movements give way to well-integrated movements. The infant who, at first, would fall helplessly into a sitting position if he lost his balance soon begins to show signs of "catching himself," then of slowly and cautiously getting into a squatting position, and finally sitting down deliberately. Thus he gains control over the maintenance of balance and erect locomotion.

These constitute the essential aspects of the development of erect locomotion once the infant is in an erect position. We have made no attempt here to bring into the analysis an evaluation of other aspects of development such as rolling over and rising from a recumbent to a sitting and standing position which enter into this behavior-course. These obviously play a major rôle in the development of erect locomotion, but they will be discussed in this connection after their particular course of development has been analyzed. For the time being we may confine ourselves to the developmental patterns of locomotion as seen in the child after he has been placed in the erect position.

But it is not in the development of erect progression as such that the process of growth and development is most adequately revealed. Principles of development are better revealed when detailed aspects of the total behavior-course are considered. Let us for a moment consider merely the way in which the feet touch the surface when the child is held in an upright position. It is this contact of the foot upon the surface of the bed or table which ordinarily sets up the reflex stepping movements of the newborn. In the newborn infant this contact is undifferentiated and is likely to be on the lateral aspect of the foot, near the toes, or on the soles. During the second period the baby most commonly stands on his toes. There is, however, a good deal of overlapping of this stage with the undifferentiated type of contact. There also is over-

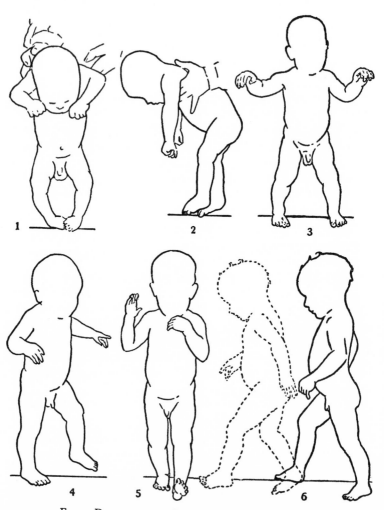

FIG. 7. DEVELOPMENTAL PHASES IN ERECT LOCOMOTION

1. Newborn posture: general flexion of upper extremities, lower extremities, and neck; note lateral contact of feet with underlying surface. 2. Trunk held forward, extension developing in upper extremities; digital progression and narrow base. 3, 4. First appearance of balancing and stepping alone: wide base, plantigrade, upper extremities extended and abducted. 5. Normal base, steps from heel to toe rather than on entire soles; upper extremities no longer needed for balancing. 6. Associated movements and well-controlled activity involved in walking.

lapping of the digital contact with the plantigrade contact which occurs later. Subsequently in the older infant plantar contact is the characteristic response, but the baby places the whole sole of the foot on the floor at once. The final development in the contact of the foot upon the surface is indicated when he steps from heel to toe. The process of development in this aspect is as follows: first, an undifferentiated contact; then a shift to digital; then a period when the contact of foot on floor is excessively plantar; and finally a mature state of progression in which contact is neither all digital nor all plantar, but a heel-toe movement. It is fairly obvious here that growth has been a movement from an undifferentiated state to extremes in opposite directions until finally maturity settles midway between the two, so that digital grade and plantar grade become integrated into one progressive movement.

The gradual growth process as the infant develops control in the function of walking is evident in the changing position of the upper extremities. It will be recalled that the upper extremities in the newborn infant are flexed and adducted and usually held close to the body. With development there is a diminution in this flexion and adduction until the infant begins to hold his arms extended in front of him. Perhaps at this time during a particular examination period it is difficult to tell which is the more predominating posture, adduction or abduction, since the infant engages in both, but little by little the abduction becomes much more decisive, until finally even the inexperienced observer can easily and accurately recount the characteristic position assumed by the upper extremities during an examination period. The extension and abduction of the arms at this stage are as much a part of walking as is the position of the feet. It is noted that the developmental change in the position of the arm has been from extreme flexion and adduction to equally extreme extension and abduction. But this extreme posture of the arms does not persist. Another period follows when there appears to be no consistent pattern in the arm movements as the infant walks. Sometimes he does one thing and sometimes another. Most often the arms are held down by the sides. Out of these movements there finally develops an associated swing of the arm as the feet alternately step forward. It is by no means, at the initial stage, the customary swing or associated movement common in the gait of the older child or adult. It is a partial reaction and often can be detected only in ultra-rapid motion pictures. However, it continues to become more definite until it can unquestionably be recognized as a typical associated movement. These changes in arm movements constitute an excellent illustration of the tendency for development to swing from one extreme to another before finally settling down to a well-integrated, fully matured pattern.

This same tendency is shown when we glance at the foot base assumed by the child at different levels of growth in erect locomotion. At first the base is extremely narrow, so much so that often the lower extremities are crossed. The base gradually widens until it becomes excessively wide. Later it narrows down again, but it is never so narrow as it was in the beginning. Time does not permit here a detailed analysis of all aspects of the developing pattern of erect locomotion. Those mentioned are sufficient to illustrate that the process of growth is gradual; that no aspect of a pattern emerges fully developed; and that there is often a tendency for development to swing from one extreme to another before it is finally settled into a well-integrated mature function.

There is another difficulty experienced in judging the several stages of the development of erect locomotion as here outlined. It is that all aspects of the pattern do not undergo a change of form at the same time. For example, a wide base and plantar contact with the surface are here considered as characteristic features of the third stage, yet the plantigrade contact may be observed weeks before a definitely wide base is noted. Nevertheless, when this stage of the development is most pronounced both of these aspects of the pattern will be present.

A comparison of Johnny and Jimmy in the development of erect locomotion reveals that in many respects metamorphoses in pattern occurred at approximately the same chronological age. The change from the first to the second stage occurred in both infants between seventy and eighty days of age. Until the 80th day the following characteristics were predominant in the reactions of both infants: flexion of the chin on the chest, flexion and adduction of the upper extremities, a lack of muscular tension in the lower extremities, a marked tendency to flex these members, and an undifferentiated contact of the foot on the surface. During this newborn period Jimmy showed a greater tendency to make the reflex stepping movements than did Johnny. As a matter of fact, such steps were not actually elicited from Johnny on regular examination days until he was seventy days old. Since they did occur during the daily practice period, it would be a misrepresentation to say that such reactions were not present, although his reactions during practice periods do not constitute a part of this report. The writer has repeatedly emphasized that had these examination periods been more frequent many of the apparent differences in the babies would have been diminished.

When approximately fifty days old both infants began holding their heads up so that the chin was not flexed on the chest. Although they did hold their heads in the body plane, for a period of three months they actually faced the floor. Facing the floor was indicative of their growing into the second stage, a noticeable feature of which is a marked flexion at the pelvic girdle so that the upper part of the body is bent forward, bringing the shoulder girdle anterior to the pelvis. The tendency to hold the body forward in this way was present in Johnny for a period of 200 days, from the 70th to the 270th day; and in Jimmy from the 60th to the 290th day. Although Jimmy began to bend the body forward a few days younger than Johnny, and the span of time during which he continued to show this postural reaction was longer than it was reported for his twin brother, Jimmy nevertheless attained a vertical posture about two and a half months earlier than did Johnny. In other words, there was greater variability in Jimmy's postural reactions as shown by the overlapping of four months of the forward posture and the vertical posture, although there was a period of three months when only the forward posture was noted. In contrast, Johnny's overlapping of the forward and vertical posture of the trunk was only thirty days, although the vertical posture emerged as a part of his action-pattern much later than it did in Jimmy. There was a period of two and a half months between the reflex stepping stage and voluntary walking when no stepping movements were educed in Johnny's reactions; and there was a similar period of three and a half months when no such reactions were elicited from Jimmy. Distinctly digital progression made its first appearance in both infants within the same week, and it continued as a characteristic phase of the behavior-course for the same period of time in both infants. Although plantigrade progression emerged earlier in the behavior of Jimmy, there was a greater period of overlapping in digital and plantigrade progression in the actions of Jimmy than in those of Johnny. There appeared to be a general tendency in Jimmy for the overlapping of one stage with another to last comparatively longer than it did in the case of his twin. Whether or not the repetition or exercise of the performance reduced the variability of the behavior-course in Johnny's performances we are not at this time prepared to say.

When Jimmy was 245 days old, seated on a bench so that his feet could touch the floor, he rose and took three steps alone. These steps were cross-legged and poorly controlled. Additional steps alone were not elicited from him until twenty-four days later. This action appears to be one of those fleeting spurts in development when a new activity is being tried. It is the proverbial "beginner's luck." Jimmy was at a period when structural control of erect locomotion was shifting from a lower to a higher level. To date his walking alone from that time would be erroneous, since his postural reactions were not characteristic of the infant who is beginning to walk alone.

When 269 days old both Jimmy and Johnny took a few steps alone. At that time they had acquired the typical wide base as well as the extended and abducted arms as balancing accessories. The incubation period of independent erect locomotion in both babies was roughly seven months. When Johnny was fifteen months old he ceased to make constant use of his upper extremities as balancing accessories and began stepping one foot in front of the other in a fairly mature fashion, and by the time he was eighteen months old associated movements of the upper extremities were beginning to appear. Associated movements of the upper extremities and stepping one foot in front of the other emerged in Jimmy when he was sixteen and a half months old. While Johnny developed a fairly mature walking step a little earlier than Jimmy, this factor is offset by Jimmy's developing a natural swing of the arms earlier than Johnny.

In summary, it is easily seen that so far as progression is concerned both infants present a period of reflex stepping movements; a period of comparative absence of such movements, indicating a shift from a lower to a higher level of structural control; and the appearance of voluntary stepping followed by a period of independent walking at approximately the same time, despite the daily exercise of Johnny.

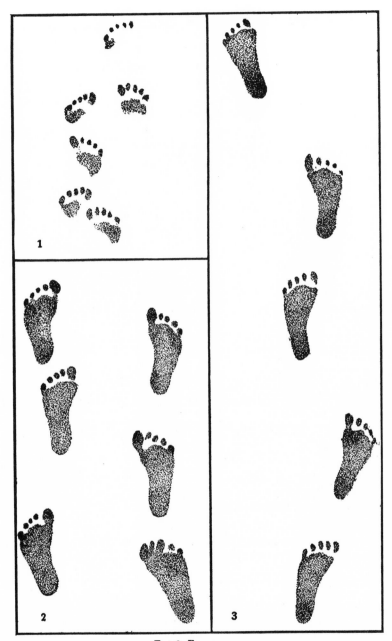

Fig. 8. Footprints

These prints illustrate developmental phases in the contact of the feet upon the surface during erect locomotion. 1. Digital progression, narrow base. 2. Plantigrade progression, wide base. 3. Heel-toe progression, normal base

But the daily practice in stepping movements from the time Johnny was twenty days old was not without some effect. There developed a conditioned response in the lower extremities, so that every time the experimenter placed hands underneath his arms he would start alternate and rhythmical kicking of his lower extremities. It was not necessary to have the soles of his feet touch the surface in order to elicit these reactions. He would make the same response when he was held in mid-air. It seems to the writer that this reaction is a definite conditioned response. It denotes the substitution of one stimulus for another (that is, substitution of experimenter's hands under baby's arms for the usual stimulus of having feet touch the surface) in eliciting essentially the same type of somatic response. The exercise did not, however, eliminate any of the characteristic metamorphoses of the developing pattern, and it did not apparently advance the day when Johnny was able to stand and walk alone. On the other hand, as soon as the babies began to balance and walk independently the daily exercise in the activity undoubtedly had a qualitative effect upon Johnny's locomotor style. This influence is such that it cannot be expressed quantitatively, but the moving picture records stand as indelible testimony of Johnny's greater agility and control in this performance. Likewise it appeared that Jimmy's restriction of activity checked his development of a normal stride during the latter part of his control period. Thus it appears that the fundamental sequence of pattern-phases in the development of erect locomotion was not altered either by repetition of the activity or relative restriction in frequency of performance. But the style of walking was influenced by the more extensive use or exercise of the activity.

The Assumption of a Sitting Posture

Development of the ability to sit erect, as well as to stand erect, is a peculiarly human trait. Other animals sit on the haunches and not on the ischii as the human species does. Development in a sitting posture as well as an erect posture is demonstrated by an increasing resistance to the force of gravity. While many newborn babies have sufficient muscle tone to maintain balance in a sitting posture for a second, there is no specific lower-level sitting reflex similar to the swimming and stepping movements. In our study of the progressive phases involved in the development of a sitting posture, we have considered bodily adjustments in the four different postures involved in bringing the body from a supine to a sitting position: (1) the rising posture, (2) the vertical posture, (3) the falling posture, and (4) the hyperflexed or jack-knife posture. These four postures really represent segments of an arc through which the trunk of the baby passes when raised from a supine to a sitting position. The rising posture is indicated from the time the trunk leaves the underlying surface until it has attained an approximate right-angle position with respect to the surface. In the illustration on page 91 the solid line drawings of figures A1, B1, C1, and D2 would represent the rising posture. The vertical posture, as the name suggests, refers to the actual sitting position, or that segment of the arc when the body is practically at a right angle to the floor or base. This posture is represented by the solid line drawings of figures A2, B2, C2, and D3. Young babies are not able to maintain the sitting position, consequently when support is released they fall forward on their faces. This falling posture is indicated by the dotted drawings in figures A2 and B3. After the baby has attained a certain degree of development he does not fall over completely on his face but maintains the position represented by the dotted line in B2. The newborn baby, however, being unable to resist the pull of gravity, his body falls completely forward so that his face rests upon his toes. This position we have called the jack-knife posture, and it is represented by the dotted line drawing of figure A3.

A better understanding of the phases and processes of development can be gained if we start our analysis with the fourth position and proceed backwards, so to speak, to the rising position. While the rising position is the initial step in the activity at a given time, it is not the first position over which the infant begins to gain control. The characteristic reaction of the newborn infant when his trunk is raised into a sitting posture consists of falling forward as soon as support is released, so that his face rests upon his feet or near them. In this position of hyperflexion most parturnates show very little, if any, sign of discomfort. It will be recalled in this connection that flexion is a less costly activity than extension. The newborn infant apparently prefers to remain in what appears to an adult a most uncomfortable position rather than to engage in the necessary extension to free his legs. Within a very short while, however, probably a week or ten days, the baby begins to engage in a sort of general movement of the pelvic girdle and lower extremities. This activity results in freeing the lower extremities from their flexed position beneath the body, and thus the infant assumes a typical newborn prone position. At this stage of development it is apparent that most of the activity in liberating his legs is restricted to the pelvic girdle and lower extremities. Subsequently, there is a brief period when the infant shows less agility in freeing his lower extremities from this hyperflexed position than he had previously shown, although he obviously finds the position more uncomfortable than he did earlier, as is indicated by his crying.

This phase merges with the following one when he is able to extricate himself from the uncomfortable position. He now, however, frees his lower extremities not by activity in the pelvic region so much as by pressing against the surface of the bed slightly with the upper extremities, and raising the shoulder girdle barely off the surface for a moment. This movement, together with extension of the lower extremities, sends the body forward as the legs are extricated. The next developmental step is indicated when it appears as if the extension of the lower extremities is made possible only by the activity in the upper extremities and the shoulder girdle. That is, the development of the upper part of the body seems to have checked the reflex activities of the lower extremities. The ability to raise and support the face up off the surface becomes more marked, until finally the baby is less likely to fall into the hyperflexed position. His resistance is such that he tends rather to fall slightly to one side. As he does so he extends the lower extremities sufficiently that he lands in a supine or prone position.

In the third or falling posture most partunates manifest little if any resistance to the pull of gravity. The chin is flexed on the chest, the trunk is flexed and falls forward in a helpless fashion. Within a few days there appears a slight but momentary resistance to the gravity pull as shown by the infant's falling forward a little and then jerking himself back. This action may be repeated several times before he finally collapses to the jack-knife position. Later it is observed that the chin is not flexed on the chest during the entire falling posture but will be extended slightly so as still to hold his head up even though there is considerable flexion at the pelvis. Resistance is thus increased to such an extent that he does not ordinarily get into the hyperflexed or jack-knife posture of the newborn. He exerts enough pressure on his upper extremities to check the falling posture and maintain considerable equilibratory control in a forward leaning position. Development is further indicated by a gradual decrease in the degree of pelvic flexion and an increase in the time the infant is able to maintain this forward-leaning posture. There often occurs a brief period, just before the baby is able to maintain an erect sitting posture, when he seemingly exaggerates his resistance to the forward pull of gravity. His excessive resistance is expressed by extension of his spine and a tendency to fall backward. Sometimes it takes considerable effort to push him forward.

It is scarcely necessary to point out that, when in the leaning posture, the infant does not gain a degree of resistance one day and maintain a certain angle of flexion throughout the period; then the next day a greater resistance; and so on—each day showing a little gain over the day before. Instead he maintains a greater degree of resistance for a moment, then drops down to a lower level. On subsequent occasions he will show a little more resistance and maintain it a little longer. Even so there will be days when his reactions are poorer than they were perhaps days or weeks before. Nevertheless, the progressive trend toward improvement is unmistakable.

In the sitting posture the passivity of the newborn is shown in the lack of control over the position of the head and the way it sags from an extended to a flexed position as soon as the body is brought to a right-angle position with reference to the surface. Development in this postural aspect is indicated by an increasing manifestation of control of the head on the shoulders and a decrease in dyssynergia. It becomes possible for the baby to hold his head fairly steady in this upright position long before he can maintain the trunk in an erect sitting position. But gradually the increase in control moves caudad until the infant is enabled to sit in an upright position without the support of the upper extremities. It is interesting that, when he first begins to sit without the support of the upper extremities, he will usually hold them on his thighs or knees as if in a supporting position, or in readiness to use them for support if necessary. Actually, however, the hands are merely resting on his legs and he can make use of his arms in reaching if he chooses. Stress or strain will, of course, make him return to a less mature posture. When the baby is just acquiring the ability to maintain the sitting posture without support, the spine is likely to be curved; but as he gains complete equilibratory control of sitting the spine straightens. He then is able to sustain the erect sitting posture against considerable difficulty or interference.

It is usually easier for an infant to maintain an upright sitting position when seated on a flat surface than when his feet are resting on a lower surface. The lower extremities, flexed and abducted at the knees, serve to broaden his base when he is sitting on a flat surface so as to aid him in maintaining equilibratory control.

In the first or rising position the utter helplessness of the newborn infant is shown by the way his head drops back toward the interscapular spine, the hyperextension of the spine, and the inactivity of the lower extremities, which are ordinarily flexed at the knees and hips and abducted. With development, however, the infant is able to hold his head in the plane of his body as he is raised from a supine position. A little later he actually flexes the neck, bringing the head forward as if to aid in the rising movement. This flexion of the neck is the opposite from the head posture in the newborn rising actions. About this same time he begins to raise the lower extremities during the rising position. His total actions indicate that he is taking an active part not only in resisting but in moving against gravity. Subsequently it is observed that many infants when in the supine position are able to lift the head and possibly the shoulders off the surface without any assistance from the experimenter. They cannot, however, at this stage of development assume a sitting position without some help.

It can be said that the development of a sitting posture has attained maturity only when the child is able to get into a sitting position unaided. The most ordinary method of accomplishing this consists of rolling over from a supine to a prone position, pushing against the surface with the upper extremities, drawing one knee up under the abdomen, and finally flexing and abducting the opposite lower extremity, which brings him to an erect sitting position with the ischii resting on the floor. The movements involved

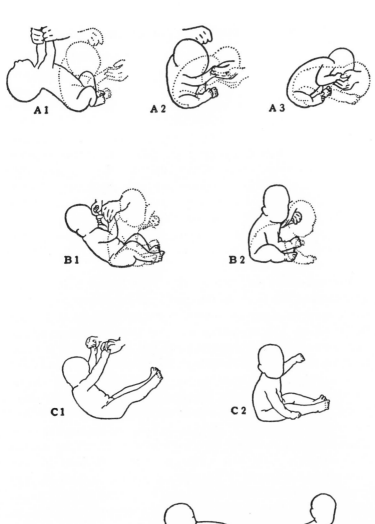

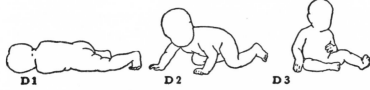

FIG. 10. DEVELOPMENT OF A SITTING POSTURE

A1, 2, and 3 illustrate the passivity of the newborn when raised from a supine to a sitting position. B1 shows infant beginning to take active part in the rising position; B2, dotted line illustrates extension of upper extremities in order to prevent falling forward. C1 indicates a postural reversal from A1; C2 shows maintenance of erect sitting posture. D1 illustrates rolling prone preparatory to the independent assumption of a sitting posture; D3 shows the infant able to maintain erect sitting position without support on upper extremities.

in the independent assumption of a sitting posture are indicated by line drawings D1, D2, and D3 in Figure 10. A few infants, even at this early stage of development, are able to push sufficiently on their upper extremities when they are in a supine position to gain the sitting posture.

About the second half of the second year most infants have eliminated rotation into a prone position as the initial aspect of assuming a sitting posture. At this final stage they are most likely to turn slightly to the side and push with the upper extremity sufficiently to bring the body from a supine to a sitting posture. In this description we have considered the assumption of a sitting position from a reclining one, and not the development of sitting down from an erect posture, which is an entirely different pattern and will be discussed later.

Although there was considerable correspondence in the development of the twins in this performance, Jimmy was on the whole accelerated beyond Johnny in the development of this particular ability. This superiority was recognized even from the time they were newborn infants and continued until the skill of sitting erect unaided was fully developed. Dropping the head backwards in a helpless manner when in the rising posture was a characteristic reaction of Johnny for approximately thirty days longer than it was of Jimmy. Both babies when seventy days old showed the first appearance of a tendency to hold the head in the body-plane as they were raised from the supine to the sitting posture. That is, although the first indication of recovery from the newborn posture appeared in Johnny and Jimmy on the same day, it actually required thirty days longer for Johnny to make a complete recovery than it did Jimmy. The contention of superior development on the part of Jimmy at that time is thus given additional support. His advancement beyond Johnny is better indicated by his resistance to the pull of gravity as revealed by his posture in the third or falling position. He began supporting himself on his upper extremities, so as to avoid falling on his face, fully six weeks younger than Johnny. He also began sitting upright without the use of his upper extremities for support, and began to get from a supine to a sitting position, approximately thirty days before Johnny. Jimmy began sitting alone without the support of his upper extremities when he was 191 days old, or a little more than six months. Johnny was a little more than seven months old, when he acquired comparable proficiency in this ability. The methods used in getting into a sitting position consisted of rotating prone as the initial movement; then pushing with the upper extremities as one lower extremity was flexed and abducted.

It is beyond the prerogative of this investigation to attribute this retardation in the development of sitting on the part of Johnny to the daily use or exercise which he was at the time receiving. It is the experimenter's opinion that Johnny's failure to attain independent sitting as young as Jimmy is merely additional evidence of his inferior development during the early months. The daily exercise which he had received was insufficient to compensate for his poorer start. The exercise which Johnny received was largely of a passive nature. The experimenter merely took him by the hands and pulled him from a supine to an upright sitting position.

Some interesting features of the growth process are made apparent in the records of these babies for the development of a sitting posture. In the first place there are several instances when the emergence of a new aspect of the pattern announced itself, so to speak, and appeared on one occasion perhaps several weeks before it emerged as a characteristic part of the pattern. For example, both infants sat alone for a brief moment without support of their upper extremities when they were 169 days old, but this skill did not definitely emerge as part of the behavior-course until some weeks later. Likewise occasional extension of the neck in the third position is recorded for Jimmy and Johnny when they were fifty-six days old, but this extension of the neck while they were falling forward did not become permanent until they were 115 and 122 days old respectively. There was a period from about the 100th day until the 200th day when, every time they were raised from the supine position by traction on the upper extremities, the lower extremities would flex at the pelvis so as to be raised above the surface. At this time a resistance to the pull of gravity was rapidly developing. But once the infant had better control over this aspect of the situation he appeared not to put forth so much effort in coöperative use of the lower extremities when he was being raised from the supine to the sitting posture. In other words, as the child gained control over the action the movements involved became more specifically limited to the actual needs of the performance. With slight help from the experimenter, beginning when they were 238 days old, both infants raised themselves from a supine to a sitting position and scarcely moved their lower extremities in doing so. Furthermore, there was a reduction in the flexion of the neck at this stage from that which had occurred earlier when the infants were just beginning to gain control over the rising position. The shift from the hyperextension to the hyperflexion at the neck is illustrative of the tendency to overdo a given pattern when it is in its early stages of development. But the predominating action-pattern finally becomes fixed between the two extremes.

The Assumption of an Erect Posture

An analysis of the progressive phases in the development of erect locomotion, once the infant is placed in or has assumed the erect standing position, was given earlier in the chapter. We would now like to consider the steps involved in development in the infant's own assumption of an erect standing posture. The writer has elsewhere pointed out that the newborn baby will not infrequently show such a degree of muscle tone in the lower extremities that when one attempts to raise him from a supine position he will tend to rise on his feet. This reaction is a fleeting reflex response of the newborn and is not easily elicited in infants a couple of months old or more. A few months later, however, when the infant is raised from a supine to a sitting position he may press both feet against the surface, extend the lower extremities, and thus pull himself to a standing position. At this point the whole body seems to move at once, with the legs rigidly extended and the feet on the surface acting as a more or less fixed point. Within a short time, however, the infant when slightly helped by traction on his upper extremities will place first one foot and then the other carefully on the surface and push his body upward. The trunk and head at this stage are moved upward by the gradual extension of the legs from the position of the feet, whereas in the former position the body moved radially through a segment of an arc with the position of the feet as the center.

The next outstanding phase in assuming the erect posture appears after the infant has begun to balance himself for a little while alone. Soon the baby also learns to raise himself to an upright posture from a squatting position without holding on to anything. Most infants, if not all, are able to stand up from a squatting position a few days or weeks before they can get from a sitting to an erect posture. As a matter of fact a baby can rise from a squatting position almost as soon as he is able to stand.

The characteristic method employed by infants, when they begin to develop the ability to rise to their feet from a supine position, consists first of rolling into a prone position, then placing both palms on the floor, and finally flexing the legs at the knee and pelvis so that the soles of both feet rest on the floor. In this way the baby assumes a quadrupedal or "all fours" position. From this position in one sweeping movement he elevates the trunk so as to gain the erect standing posture. Later it is observed that the child in the quadrupedal position draws the pelvic girdle backwards before raising the trunk upward. At a subsequent stage in the development of this performance the infant does not turn over from his back into a complete prone position, but merely rolls over on his side and pushes up with one upper extremity into a sitting position. From this sitting position he gets into the quadrupedal posture in order to gain the erect one. Older children and adults usually eliminate this quadrupedal posture as a preliminary to standing up. In the sitting position they ordinarily flex the lower extremities beneath the body, using one upper extremity for support as they do so, and then rise to their feet by extending the legs. A rapid recapitulation of those progressive phases easily demonstrates the costly and roundabout method used by the baby who rolls completely prone preparatory to rising. Later, although he has eliminated rolling entirely over, he has not integrated the movements involved in getting from the sitting to the standing posture, so he continues to get in the quadrupedal position before standing erect. The rising of the older child is so well integrated that it appears almost as one movement. Just when the quadrupedal position is eliminated in the rising movement the writer has not ascertained. Certainly it occurs in most children during the second year.

It will be recalled that at birth Johnny was an unusually flaccid baby. It is not surprising, therefore, that tonic resistance in the lower extremities was not elicited from him at any examination period during the early months. Jimmy was in advance of Johnny

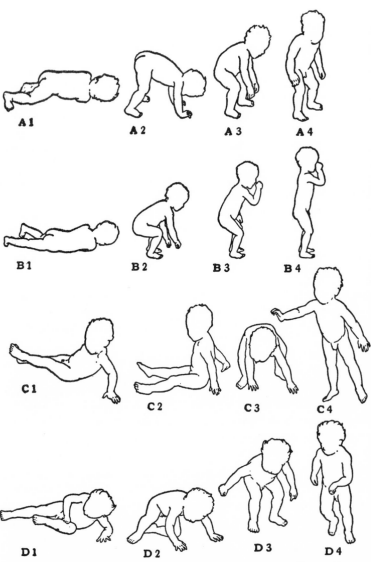

Fig. 11. Development Phases in the Assumption of an Erect Posture

A1, rolls from supine to prone position; A2, both hands and feet securely placed on floor in quadrupedal posture before raising the trunk as in A3 and A4. B1, continues to roll in prone position preparatory to rising but has begun to reduce the quadrupedal posture as an isolated movement; still uses quadrupedal posture, but it merges with rising movement as illustrated by B2. C1, has eliminated movement of rolling into prone position; preparatory to rising from sitting position, reverts to quadrupedal posture. D1, 2, 3, 4, assumption of erect posture has now become so well integrated as to appear practically one movement. The sitting posture is eliminated, and the waste activity in the performance has been reduced to a minimum.

in postural adjustments of this nature. On the 140th day he showed the tendency to place his feet securely against the surface, and by traction of the experimenter on his hand he raised his entire body, columnar fashion, from the reclining to the upright posture. Johnny showed a similar reaction on his 176th day. Placing the feet beneath them and pushing into a vertical position occurred at intervals in the behavior of both infants for a period of about seventy days when they were between six and nine months. They began rising to a standing posture from a squatting position when they were a little more than eleven months old.

Babies and young children squat differently from older children and adults. In the squatting posture of infants the most striking features are the position of the entire soles of the feet on the floor and the hyperflexion of the lower extremities at the knees and pelvis so that the buttocks are only a few inches above the floor surface. It appears to be easier for children to squat than it is for adults. The method of the adult is to support himself on the metatarsal arches, thereby raising the heels above the floor. Flexion of the lower extremities at the two major foci is noticeably less than it is in the squatting pattern of the child. The progressive phases involved in this change of pattern have not been determined by the writer. But certainly practically all babies are able to rise from a squatting posture before they can from a supine or a sitting position. Johnny and Jimmy first demonstrated their ability to rise from a supine to a standing position when they were twelve months old. Johnny began eliminating the rotation into a prone position and exercised the more mature method of rising about three months younger than did Jimmy. Johnny was twenty months old when this aspect of his method of rising was first observed. This latter method of rising was first observed in Jimmy when he was nearly twenty-three months old. Therefore, it appears that Jimmy's behavior indicated superior development during the early months, but in the later months Johnny not only equaled but advanced beyond Jimmy in the assumption of an erect posture.

Rolling Over

As a developmental performance, rolling over is more than the mere act of getting from a supine to a prone position, or vice versa. We have already seen that the development of rolling over has direct bearing upon the growth of many other functions and that it becomes a part of the patterns of creeping, rising to a sitting position, and assumption of an erect posture.

The first evidence of definite rolling over is shown in the infant by hyperextension of the spine and pressure of one foot against the surface. These movements will tend to pull the shoulder girdle into a lateral position. Presently the baby not only pushes with the lower extremity in such a way as to draw the shoulder girdle laterally, but actively throws the corresponding upper extremity over toward the opposite shoulder. Such movements continue to develop until the baby is able to get into a prone position, but when he has done so the upper extremity on the side which was next to the surface as he rolled will be pinioned beneath his chest. There is a brief period in the development of most babies when this pinioned arm cannot be extricated without help. This period is, however, short and except by daily observations would escape notice. Later as the baby rotates the shoulder girdle further he is able to give himself sufficient support with the opposite upper extremity to free the one which would have been pinioned under his chest.

We have previously remarked that *extension* is physiologically an expensive movement. This early tendency of the infant to engage in hyperextension of the spine preparatory to rolling over bears testimony to the principle of exaggeration and energy waste involved during the initial phases of the development of a behavior-course. This hyperextension of the spine does not characterize the pattern of rolling over as observed in the older infant. The spinal extension method of rolling over is characteristic of the baby during the middle of the first year. Later the initial movement is in the opposite direction. The activity is then initiated not by extension of the spine but by flexion of the head toward the chest, slight ventral flexion of the spine, and flexion of the lower extremities at the pelvis so that they are raised above the surface, while the pelvis and shoulder girdle appear to rotate simultaneously. Subsequently even the flexion becomes limited to the minimum. Either the pelvic girdle or the shoulder girdle may initiate the rotary movement in the trunk.

There was great similarity in Johnny and Jimmy in their development of this activity. Extension of the spine and pushing with the lower extremities sufficiently to get them into a lateral position was noted in both when they were 108 days old. By the time they were 130 days old they were able to get both the shoulder and pelvic girdles into the prone position, though they were not ordinarily able to free the pinioned upper extremity by rolling over. However, at this time they showed a tendency to flex the thigh and extend the leg immediately after pushing against the surface with the foot. When they were 140 days old both rolled over easily and extricated the pinioned arm. Extension of the spine as the initial movement in rolling over continued for some months, although it became much less marked, and about the time the twins were one year old it was observed that flexion of the spine, especially in the cervical region, was beginning to develop. By the time they were twenty-one months old spinal flexion was characteristic of their respective methods of rolling over. There was no outstanding difference in the babies either in the way in which they assumed the prone position or in the ages at which definite changes in pattern were first observed.

Johnny's practice in this performance began as soon as it was observed that he was extending the spine and pushing with one lower extremity. The method of stimulation consisted of attracting his attention to an object and then moving the object on the surface of the bed from a position at one side of his face to one above his head. As a matter of fact, stimulation was scarcely necessary. When an infant first begins to roll over, he does it repeatedly, sometimes almost to the exclusion of other activities. In any event, it was obvious that such stimulation as we were able to give in this investigation in no way modified the development of this performance in Johnny. So the behavior-pattern of rolling over appears to be one which, in the early stages at least, is not noticeably modifiable by mere repetition of performance.

Reaching-prehensile Reactions

Reaching and prehensile activities are considered as constituting one pattern and are used here in contradistinction to the grasping reflex discussed earlier. This pattern of behavior involves an extension of the arm toward the object as well as the prehensile or grasping use of the hand. It stands out the more sharply from the grasping reflex because, even from its inception, the visual and tactile sensory mechanisms are involved. During the first months of life, if an object is held within the visual field, approximately six or eight inches from the infant's face, there is no evidence of an inclination to touch the object. Definite fixation and convergence of the eyes as the object is moved nearer or farther away from the infant indicates that visual perception is developing, although there is at this time no suggestion of a connection between visual perception of the object and an impulse to seize it. While the baby gives evidence of visual perception, and although he will grasp the object if it is placed in his hand, the two activities have not become integrated so that he will extend his arm in order to grasp the object.

Within a short while, however, the baby not only perceives the object but responds to the visual percept with a great deal of general body activity. This activity is in contrast to the previous state when, if the baby were engaged in random activity, visual perception of and attention to the object seemed to curtail the general body activity. In the later phase something new introduced into the visual field stimulates rather than decreases such activity. This general activity is diffuse and gives no suggestion that there is yet any development of an approaching reaction of the upper extremities. A little later, however, it is seen that the baby makes fewer, or less intensive, generalized movements; he gazes intently at the object, and as he looks at it distinct movements are observed in the digits and wrist as if preparatory to prehension. That is, while the arms are still relaxed and abducted, slow extensor movements are observable in the digits. These are partial movements indicative of the beginning of the reaching-prehension action as an integrated function. Eventually the movements become organized into one of greater extension and abduction of the upper extremities, which, however, terminates in an ataxic approach of the upper extremities toward the object. As the upper extremity begins to approach the object, the digits show a greater degree of extension which continues during the entire approaching reaction. This first approach of the upper extremities is extremely ataxic. It is often bilateral, and the hands are more likely to meet below, beyond, above, or behind the object than they are to come in direct contact with it. If the character of these movements is considered, it will be seen that, having overcome the reflex tendency to flex its digits upon palmar stimulation, the infant now shows a tendency toward excessive extension of the digits and a circuitous movement of the upper extremities in making his approach to an object. This overextension and circuitous approach not only indicate his poor control over the performance but illustrate the general growth tendency to overemphasize or overdo any new aspect of a pattern when it begins to develop. Further development of this function is indicated by the gradual decrease

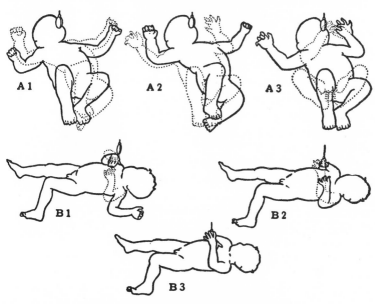

FIG. 12. REACHING-PREHENSILE BEHAVIOR

A1, 2, and 3 indicate total body movements involved in the early stages of the reaching-prehensile behavior-pattern. B1, 2, 3: a well-developed reaching-prehensile act is restricted to movements necessary for the performance.

in ataxia, an increasing tendency toward a unilateral rather than a bilateral approach; the development of a direct rather than a circuitous approach to the object; a lessening in degree of the extension of the digits; and a delay in the extension of the digits until the hand has come nearer to the object.

The older child or adult in going through this performance not only approaches the object definitely and directly but does not extend the digits until they are practically upon the object and then extends them only enough to encircle or take hold of it. In other words, the adult wastes no energy in this performance.

It is said that from a biological point of view extension is a more costly function than flexion, and it is easily seen that the development of reaching and prehension from infancy to maturity is one of reducing the extensor movements to the minimum and eliminating all excess activity. In the development of this function, as in the growth of other behavior-patterns which have been under discussion in this chapter, there may be observed the general principles of increasing specificity of performance, a decrease in excess movements, and a temporary tendency for a new aspect of the pattern to go farther than is necessary for a most efficient, most economical, and well-coördinated act.

A discussion of the development of reaching-prehension would be incomplete without consideration of the proximo-distal tendency in growth. The general opinion of those who have studied the development of prehension is that prehension is at first palmar and then digital. To this point of view the writer has taken exception. We have already observed that the grasping reflex is decidedly digital in the newborn infant; we have seen that the inception of the reaching-prehension activity is ordinarily an extensor movement of the digits. This movement in the initial stage does not at first involve the proximal segments of the arm, and for that reason the approach of the hand toward the object is not observed. For that reason also, casual observation may not discern a primary digital movement as the inception of the reaching-prehensile action. When the entire arm participates in the act so that the hand is brought close enough to touch the object, the prehension is then palmar. But this is not, in the writer's opinion, the *beginning* of the reaching-prehension behavior-course. The pattern is well along in its development by that time, and in its final stages it takes the form of digital prehension in seizing many types of objects.

It is impossible to consider fully matured prehension as palmar or digital without taking into account the nature of the object which is being grasped. It seems to the writer that, once prehension is developed, palmar or digital grasping is determined by the size and shape of an object and also by the circumstances under which it is being grasped. A stationary small object, such as a pellet, is likely to be grasped between the thumb and the index finger. An equally small moving object, such as a fly, will be grasped in the palm of the hand. The type of the grasp used, once the function is fully developed, is a matter of individual discrimination and not therefore developmentally diagnostic.

In the present investigation our method of studying the reaching-prehensile activity was, during the early months, to place the baby in a supine position and then to hold a watch suspended from a string just above the thorax of the infant. The object was in this way easily within his visual field and easily within arm's reach. Beginning on the 106th day Johnny was thus stimulated to exercise the reaching action at four different periods five days a week at intervals of two hours. Objects were, on the other hand, withheld from Jimmy during the hours that he was at the clinic. Despite the daily exercise of this function given to Johnny, the development of the pattern was extraordinarily similar in the two babies. By the time they were 108 days old both were making ataxic approaching movements of both upper extremities toward the object, and all digits were being extended early in the approaching act. The approach consisted of extension and abduction of the upper extremities followed by slight flexion and adduction. If they touched the object, they would likely set it swinging. The swing of the object would act as a disturbing factor and cause a reversion to more generalized excited activity. By the time the twins were 323 days old both babies were extending their arms directly toward the object. When they were 534 days old it was observed that extension of the digits was noticeably less, and that it did not begin until the hand was within a few inches of the object. At this time the prehension of the object such as a watch was more digital than palmar.

It will be recalled that Johnny and Jimmy developed considerable skill in rolling from a supine to a prone position when they were around 140 days old. For this reason it was almost impossible to keep them in a dorsal position without enforcing undesirable restriction. It was not easy, therefore, to follow through the study of reaching for a suspended object to its ultimate maturity while the infant was in a recumbent position. Hence, we continued the study of the reaching actions with the infant in a prone or sitting position. Although this complicated the problem so far as the total body adjustment to the situation is concerned, it did not alter the developmental sequence of the actual reaching-prehensile actions as outlined above.

Reaching in Prone Position

Reaching-prehensile behavior-courses begin to develop in an infant about the same time that he is developing skill in supporting his chest well off the surface by resting on both palms. Both upper extremities are obviously needed in maintaining this position. The young infant who still has a tendency toward bilateral extension of the upper extremities is likely to raise both palms off the surface, and in doing so he drops his chest toward the bed, so that his contact on the surface becomes abdominal, though he extends the neck and attempts to hold his face up in order to see the object. The upper extremities are partially flexed and abducted. In this poorly supported position he is unable to make a complete movement toward the object. The thwarting of his reaching-prehension impulse incites an excess of generalized activity in the lower extremities as well as upper extremities. In some instances he may drop the shoulder girdle sufficiently to support himself on both elbows and approach the object with the forearms only. Later, with the lower abdomen and pelvic girdle on the surface he will support himself with one hand and reach toward the object with the other. During a still later phase the infant will, if an object is presented to him when he is in the prone position, get on hands and knees or finally in a sitting position before he attempts to reach. The child of eighteen months or older, who does not find it necessary to go to all this trouble of getting into a sitting position, makes a minimum bodily adjustment to the situation by supporting himself on one forearm as he speedily and directly reaches for the object with the other arm.

In the details of the actual reaching-prehensile pattern, such as was outlined above, Johnny and Jimmy were similar in their development, but in bodily adjustment Jimmy was somewhat accelerated beyond Johnny. From the time they were 154 days old both infants showed the characteristic reaction pattern of dropping the chest and trying to reach with both hands, supporting the chest with first one hand and then the other while trying to reach and take hold of the object with the other. The characteristic ataxia, hyperextension, and abduction of upper extremities in the approaching movement were present. During this period, however, Jimmy showed greater control than Johnny in supporting himself on one hand and reaching with the other. Fewer occurrences of generalized activity were observed in Jimmy than in Johnny. Jimmy also began getting into a sitting position before reaching for the suspended object when he was 231 days old, whereas Johnny did not make this sitting adjustment until he was 283 days old. Nevertheless, in the process of passing from one phase to another both babies show the same characteristic transition reaction of shifting from the prone position to one on both knees and one hand, while reaching with the free hand. At a slightly later stage they would support themselves upon one buttock, one knee, and one palm as they reached with the opposite upper extremity. Jimmy at least manifested a stage of grasping the object while he was in the hand-knee position and then getting into a sitting position before manipulating it. In the final development of this stage the babies would get completely into a sitting position before reaching. This sitting adjustment is itself a transitory stage. But after they began to make the adjustment of getting into a sitting position, further study of the reaching-prehensile reactions was continued with the baby in the sitting position only. This is unfortunate, since we did not therefore determine at what age the assumption of a sitting posture as a preparatory movement to reaching-prehension was eliminated. When we look back to the records of the babies' development in the assumption of a sitting posture we find that the very week in which they began to get into a sitting position without any assistance is identical with the week they began to take the sitting adjustment before reaching and grasping a suspended object.

This fact brings up the question of the influence the development of one trait has upon another. Shirley (56) has touched upon this problem in her report of a study of the first two years of life, but the field is still new and is one that warrants more intensive investigation. In general the visual perception of an object stimulates an immediate movement in the upper extremities, but at this stage of development rapid growth of a newly acquired skill (in this instance the assumption of a sitting posture) was sufficient to delay the arm movement until a complicated bodily adjustment had been made. Apparently after the ability to raise the trunk from a recumbent position becomes a well-developed and easily performed act, it is then eliminated as part of the bodily adjustment to the reaching-prehensile reaction when the baby is in a prone position.

Reaching-Prehension in a Sitting Position

When placed in a sitting position, an infant will attempt to reach for an object even if he cannot maintain an upright sitting posture. There is then a period when a conflict appears between these two developing processes. He needs the upper extremities in order to support himself in a forward-leaning sitting posture. If he raises the upper extremity in order to approach the object he falls forward, or over on his side. Later, although he does not need his upper extremities in maintaining an upright sitting posture, his reaching-prehensile activities are still ataxic, so that efforts to reach the suspended object are likely to disturb his equilibratory control. As a result, when he starts to approach the object he begins to lose his balance, and then the approaching movements are interfered with, since his arms, suddenly becoming indispensable to the maintenance of balance, are extended and abducted to aid in "catching himself" or regaining equilibratory control. The infant at length has no difficulty in maintaining perfect equilibrium and extending his arm directly in front of him in order to grasp the object. In this way, integration of the two developing processes is attained.

In the actual reaching-prehension behavior-course the development of Johnny and Jimmy was parallel. In maintaining a sitting position Jimmy was unquestionably more advanced. When only 231 days old Jimmy maintained an erect sitting posture as he reached for an object suspended in front of him, although his reaching or approaching act was still more or less circuitous and the digits were prematurely overextended. At this time Johnny was still supporting himself with one hand as he extended the other toward the object. Even when 232 days old he was likely to lose his balance and need the use of his upper extremities to regain equilibrium, although he could maintain a perfectly erect sitting position for some time if the disturbing factors of interest in an object were not introduced. When 245 days old Johnny was also able to maintain an erect sitting position and reach for a suspended object. But Jimmy attained this ability at least two weeks younger than did Johnny.

We believe that we have brought out some of the most salient aspects of the developing patterns in the reaching-prehensile behavior-course, but we do not claim to have analyzed this pattern in its finest detail. For example, we have not included approaching reactions of the head or feet or attempts of the infant to take the object with the mouth, especially when he needs the hands for support. Nor have we considered the development of thumb-index finger prehension of small objects, nor the differences between prehension of fixed and of suspended objects, or of moving and stationary ones. These are all developmentally significant and are essential to a complete understanding of growth in this function. However, in the development of the behavior-pattern as it was manifest in the particular situations we have studied, we are quite safe in concluding that the daily stimulation given Johnny to exercise this particular skill did not accelerate or materially alter the form of sequential phases in the course of development.

Since visual acuity obviously plays a major rôle in the development of reaching-prehensile activities, we endeavored to judge the development of prehension when the stimulus was tactile rather than visual, but the tactile contact was made to some other part of the body than the hand. It is known that tactile stimulation in the palm of the hand (pressure stimulation) will elicit immediate digital flexion, or grasping, on the part of the newborn baby. We therefore placed a light, thin watch on the chest of the infant, at the level of the costal angle, while the infant was in a supine position. In this position he could not see the watch.

For some weeks after an infant has begun to bring his upper extremities toward an object in the visual field he is, so far as can be judged from his overt behavior, indifferent to an object such as a small watch placed upon his chest. Later it becomes apparent that he realizes something is on his chest but that he cannot localize the exact position of the object. Sometimes he will lift his head as if to locate the object through the visual sense. Failing in this method, his hands are likely to touch the abdomen somewhere in the region of the umbilicus, and move cephalad on the abdomen, one on each side until his hands touch the object. Then he will shove it toward the mouth or pick up the object and lift it to the mouth. As the hands move on the abdomen all digits are extended preparatory to prehension. In the later stage of development of this pattern the hands do not roam over the abdomen. Instead both hands go directly to the object on the chest. Finally only one hand is used in reaching and prehending the object, and the digits do not start extending until they practically touch the object. Thus all the excessive and unnecessary movements are gradually eliminated.

In the development of this activity Johnny was considerably accelerated beyond Jimmy. Daily stimulation of this behavior began when he was 106 days old, and he showed no definite evidence of awareness of the presence of the object on his chest until he was 176 days old. But by the time he was 231 days of age his hands no longer roved over the abdomen. Instead both hands approached the object directly and seized it—the digits being extended during the approach. Jimmy on the other hand did not register an awareness or interest in the presence of the watch until he was 187 days old, and when he was 276 days old he still engaged in moving the hand over the abdomen before definitely grasping the watch. He made a direct contact with the object by the time he was 337 days old. While Johnny showed superiority in his reactions to this situation, the experimenter feels that caution should be observed in attributing this superiority to the daily exercise or stimulation in the activity. The only aspect of the pattern which could have been modified was the localization of the point of stimulation. It is u doubtedly suggestive that the daily stimulation hastened Johnny's localization of the object, but the experimenter believes that these results merely raise the question, so that it is still subject to proof and calls for further investigation, with other variables—particularly interest in the object and general attitude in the situation—as nearly equal as is experimentally possible.

Rotation

The method used by the experimenters in studying the reactions of infants to being rotated were rather crude and subjective, but the same method was used for all the infants whom we were studying. Since we have, even in this crude method, determined unquestionable developmental sequences in the behavior-patterns of babies when placed in this particular situation, its inclusion in this report is warranted. An infant was held at the axillæ by the experimenter. Thus holding the baby at arm's length in front of her the experimenter made several whirls so as to rotate the baby in an orbit. A stop-watch record was kept of the number of seconds the experimenter spent in whirling, and count was made by the recorder of the number of turns that were made on each occasion. In this way it was possible to calculate roughly the rate of rotation. While the rate and the frequency of turns varied somewhat, this variability was not great and was equal for all the children.

Newborn infants when rotated in this fashion manifested extreme muscular weaknesses. Unable to resist the force of the movement, both the face and the eyes move in a lateral direction with the rotation. Usually they maintain this position during the turning time. The upper extremities are ordinarily flexed and adducted. It is not common for the newborn baby to show a great deal of evidence of perturbation during the performance. Gradually, however, it is observed that the infant begins to hold his face forward. Sometimes he will overdo it and turn his face *against* the direction of rotation. The eyes in their resistance to the force of the movement begin to shift back and forth, bilaterally, from left to right slowly and grossly; the upper extremities begin to extend and abduct. At this period the infant will cry or show other signs of being disturbed by the rotary movement. With development the infant is able to maintain his face in a forward position. Not only does the nystagmus grow more rapid but finer movements are involved. Often there develops an axial rotation at the neck. The period of perturbation may subside, so that older babies often show signs of enjoyment during the movement.

So far as somatic actions are concerned, Johnny and Jimmy closely paralleled each other in their developmental behavior in this situation. The modal rate of rotation was in both cases 1.3 cycles per second. The following ages on which their reactions were recorded will make a comparison of their development possible:

Turns the Face in the Direction of Rotation
Jimmy: Birth to 56 days
Johnny: Birth to 84 days

Turns Eyes with Rotation
Jimmy: Birth to 63 days
Johnny: Birth to 84 days

Upper Extremities Flexed and Adducted
Jimmy: Birth to 70 days
Johnny: Birth to 78 days

These reactions are the identifying features of the newborn reaction pattern. In recovery from these newborn features it is apparent that in every case Jimmy was a little in advance of Johnny. They constitute, it seems, additional evidence of Johnny's poorer development at birth.

Face Forward
Jimmy: 70 to 701 days
(Though there are seven instances when he is recorded as turning the face against the direction of rotation.)
Johnny: 78 to 701 days
(Two instances of turning face against direction of rotation.)

Nystagmus: Gross
Jimmy: 63 to 427 days
Johnny: 78 to 456 days

Fine and Rapid Nystagmus
Jimmy: 427 to 701 days
Johnny: 413 to 701 days

Out of thirty-three examination periods Johnny is reported to have cried only once as against Jimmy's six times. Neither cried very often. Beginning when they were between six and seven months old both infants began to show signs, such as smiling and laughter, which indicated enjoyment of the situation. After they were able to stand they were placed on the floor immediately following rotation. Ordinarily they would stagger and fall, and their disturbed equilibratory control was further indicated in their effort to rise to their feet again. They seemingly experienced, as a result of the turning, a visual sensation which was at one stage of their development a matter of curiosity to them. For example, on one specific occasion at the age of twenty-three months when Johnny was placed upon the floor and did not immediately fall, he apparently experienced the illusion of having the furniture rotate around him, for he extended his right hand extremely cautiously to touch a near-by piece of furniture. He extended it in just the fashion one would if a revolving object were being touched. When he touched the furniture the illusion was apparently interrupted for he then turned to the experimenter with an expression of great surprise.

The experimenter had an occasion to witness Jimmy experiencing the phi-phenomenon some weeks later. Jimmy had developed a specific excited vocalization when he observed moving objects such as elevated trains. He was standing in the seat of the car looking out the window one day as we drove rapidly along the highway. The writer observed him looking wide-eyed for a moment at the grass along the road-shoulder. Then he began to dance up and down, voicing the familiar squeal which he so frequently gave at the sight of rapidly moving objects.

Reactions to Cutaneous Irritation

No reaction pattern more neatly illustrates the process of growth from a general to a specific state than the changing reactions of the growing infant to a peripheral irritation such as a pin-prick. For the purpose of studying these developmental reactions we have followed the practise of stimulating the infant with a blunted pin-point in four different bodily areas. We arbitrarily selected the following areas as stimulation points: (1) the medial aspect of the leg, (2) the volar surface of the forearm, (3) the ventral surface of the trunk, just below the nipple line, and (4) one cheek, just below the zygomatic prominence. These areas include the four major anatomical divisions, viz., head, trunk, upper extremities, and lower extremities.

Many partunates and infants just a few hours old manifest no overt response to cutaneous irritation of the type just described. So far as can be determined by observation, many newborn babies are insensible to peripheral irritation of this sort. This failure to respond overtly does not apply to all babies who are just born, but it does to a great many, and certainly none manifests an acute sensibility to cutaneous irritation. By the time they are a week or ten days old, however, they generally show decided irritability to such stimulation. Their reaction at this stage may be merely a reflex "withdrawal" of the body member stimulated, but it is more likely to consist as well of crying accompanied with some diffuse body activity. During the weeks immediately following, this diffuse body activity becomes more marked, indicating a more intense sensory experience. Although the infant is undoubtedly sensitive to the irritation, it is obvious that he not only is unable to localize the area stimulated but he is quite helpless to do anything about it. He can neither escape nor defend himself from the stimulus even if he senses pain. But by the end of the first two or three months of post-natal growth a change has occurred resulting in a gradual diminution of the diffuse body activity. During the following period of a few weeks the most conspicuous action-pattern in response to this type of stimulation is simply crying. Apparently there have by this time occurred inhibitions of the general body activity, although the voluntary specific reactions have not as yet become manifest. The baby will at this period merely lie and cry. He makes no attempt to draw his arm or leg away from the stimulus, he makes no attempt to push away the irritating object, and even the diffuse reactions are noticeably reduced.

Soon, however, the baby begins to show signs not only of irritability but also, in a broad sense, of locating the general region of the body being stimulated. At the initial stage of development in this aspect of the behavior-course it appears to be related to the development of visual acuity. One of the first evidences of localization on the part of the infant is that his gaze follows the position of the hand which is stimulating him. Later he will not only watch the hand as it stimulates him, but he will turn and follow it with his eyes as if to see where it goes and whence it came. But at the beginning of this localizing ability the baby still makes no movement to escape the stimulus or to combat it.

In a short time, his development has progressed so that his hands will approach the part of the body being stimulated, though in the beginning it is unlikely that he will actually touch the stimulus or the stimulated area. Shortly thereafter he may be able to carry the movement further and actually touch the stimulated area, but his reaction is usually delayed so that his hand reaches the part just after the stimulus is removed. In the beginning he merely touches the part and does not rub it or in any way attempt to alleviate the pain. These indications of partial localization merge with or overlap with the development of voluntary withdrawal of the stimulated member. This type of withdrawal is distinct from the early reflex response in that the reflex response is ordinarily nothing more than flexion of the stimulated member at the major flexion foci, whereas the voluntary response may be flexion, extension, abduction, or adduction—in fact any movement that succeeds in getting the body member away from the source of irritation. Furthermore it is apparent to the observer that vision plays an increasingly active part in this reaction.

As the voluntary aspect of the reaction begins to develop, the infant again resorts to a total body response, or a tendency to overdo the withdrawal or escape aspect of his behavior. If he is lying on his back, he is likely to roll over away from the side stimulated. If he is sitting up—which he is most likely able to do at this stage of development—he will bend over as if to start creeping away from the source of irritation. Finally the baby eliminates much of this excess activity, such as attempting to creep away. He then sits up and deliberately knocks away the stimulus. As this ability is developing he is also profiting by experience, and presently he puts up a defensive arm as soon as he sees the stimulus approaching. As a matter of fact, he makes the association between the pin and the irritation much younger. Even before defensive reactions have begun to develop he may voice disapproval at the sight of the familiar pin. Later he not only voices disapproval but at the sight of the pin he raises his arms in front of his face in a protecting manner. It is conceivable and highly probable that the older child will be not only defensive but offensive when he sees the pin. He will not only shield and protect himself from stimulation but will attempt to retaliate and inflict pain on the experimenter. The writer has not, however, observed this reaction in any of the infants under two years of age who have come under her observation.

In these activities, as in others which have been discussed in this chapter, development is extremely gradual and there is in every aspect the characteristic overlapping of one phase with another. The reflex withdrawal response and crying accompanied by general body activity constitute the predominating pattern during the first two or three months. There is a succeeding period of another three or four months when the prevailing reaction is mere crying. It has been observed that the initial escape and defense patterns are only partial responses: the hands move in the direction of the stimulus but do not make definite contact with it. The localization becomes more and more specific until the baby is able not only to push away the source of irritation but in a measure to protect himself against its repetition.

We shall not in this report go into the question of variations in reactions when different parts of the body are stimulated, since these variations are not great. It is sufficient for our purposes here to mention that even from the earliest the cheek is the most sensitive region. The region supplied by the trigeminal nerves is more advanced in sensori-motor development than the other areas stimulated. Not only is a more intense reaction elicited, but new phases of the patterns are likely to be educed somewhat sooner when the trigeminal region is irritated than when any other area is stimulated.

Johnny and Jimmy were tested for their reactions to peripheral irritation in these four areas at their regular examination periods. Neither of them received any systematic stimulation of this type between examination periods, and their experiences in these particular situations were essentially equivalent. Although there was a great deal of correspondence in the somatic aspect of their reactions, it was no greater than in other traits discussed earlier in this chapter, in which Johnny had received frequent stimulation. Since the behavior-patterns were on the whole quite constant irrespective of the part of the body stimulated, we shall for the purpose of convenience take the average of the four different records made for each child on each examination day. The newborn action-pattern is characterized by the reflex withdrawal reaction, crying, and diffuse bodily activity. If we consider each phase to extend from the time it was first observed until it was last recorded as the predominating reaction, we shall find that this newborn pattern was likely to be the characteristic response of Jimmy from birth to the 140th day and of Johnny from birth to the 150th day. From the 81st day to the 292d day crying was found to be the predominating reaction in Jimmy, and the same type of reaction was elicited from Johnny during the period from his 76th to his 266th day. The period during which escape patterns represented the most characteristic reactions extended in Johnny from the 202d day until the 701st day and in Jimmy from the 223d day until the 670th day. The period during which defense reactions were recorded covered from the 338th day to the 780th for Johnny and from the 378th to the 780th for Jimmy. Johnny began to assert protective or defense reactions at sight of the pin when he was 328 days old, and Jimmy showed similar behavior on the 408th day. Johnny unquestionably localized the point of irritation on the 343d day and Jimmy on the 344th, though discrimination in this respect had been developing in both infants during the previous four months.

It is apparent that the overlapping of one phase with another was most extensive. Although there is a great deal of overlapping in these phases, they are not entirely coincident. Moreover, these dates do indicate that Jimmy was discarding the typical newborn reaction a little younger than Johnny. It may be recalled that Jimmy showed a tendency to discard newborn phases of behavior-patterns a little younger than Johnny in practically all the behavior traits so far discussed. On the other hand, it is noted that Johnny later began to manifest escape and defense reactions a little younger than Jimmy. These differences in later developmental patterns are perhaps more apparent than real, since Jimmy was less adjusted to the experimental situation during the first twenty-two months and sometimes cried so much that the test could not be completed.

There are twenty-five occasions during the 780 days when Jimmy is recorded as having cried so much as to preclude the test situation, and there are only seven such occasions when Johnny cried to that extent. All of these occasions when Johnny cried occurred before he was 200 days old. A more striking contrast shows that there are seventy-three occasions when even the pin-pricking did not stimulate Johnny to cry. In contrast there are only twenty-three times when the stimulation failed to bring out crying in Jimmy. In the last six months or so of the experimental period the situation became often a matter of play for Johnny. Taking the pin from the experimenter he would gently prick himself, laughing as he did so. This playful reaction has not been observed in Jimmy or any of the other babies under observation.

Summary

In considering behavioral growth it must be kept in mind that at any one chronological period different behavior patterns are phylogenetically and ontogenetically at different stages of maturation in a given individual. Therefore in order to understand the principles of development it is desirable to study the growth of a behavior-pattern rather than the growth of an individual infant. Study of each course of behavior should be initiated at its inception and followed through to its consummation or decline. Since human subjects are generally not available for study of growth in behavior-patterns until the time of birth, it should be recognized that at that time some action-patterns are fully developed and others have not even begun to develop. Therefore it is infeasible to begin study of all behavior-patterns from the point of inception.

Since it is impossible to analyze all behavior-patterns from functional anlages, it is expedient that the maturity of each pattern be determined in so far as possible at the time study of that particular pattern is initiated. In estimating the maturity of a behavior-pattern both phylogenetic and ontogenetic development must be taken into account. Although development is continuous, there are four convenient points of reference in the development of any behavior-course. These are as follows: (1) the inception, or the first appearance or suggestive appearance of a phase of the pattern; (2) the incubation or rapidly growing period, (3) maturity, or the period of most extensive and precise functioning, and (4) decline, or period of evanescence or diminution of the overt manifestation of the pattern. In estimating the maturity of reaction-patterns in newborn human infants it is well to make the following inquiries of each mechanism:

(1) Is this action-pattern fully developed and does it continue to function during the life of the individual in essentially this same fashion?

(2) Or, is this merely a rudiment of a pattern which functioned more precisely and more purposefully earlier in phylogeny?

(3) Furthermore, is it of cortical or infracortical control at the time of its inception?

(4) Is the overt somatic pattern, at the time it is first observable, representative of its period of inception, incubation, full maturity, or decline?

(5) If the action-pattern as observed is tending toward a decline, is it succeeded by a kindred behavior-pattern controlled at a higher structural level?

In the present investigation we attempted to make a cursory inventory of the most prominent somatic behavior-patterns of the newborn infant. From these we selected a limited number of behavior-patterns which obviously undergo remarkable change during the course of development. Behavior-patterns which are fully developed and continue to function during ontogeny were not included in this study, since they do not during post-natal development reveal outstanding growth changes. Having selected a few behavior-patterns, we thereupon endeavored to analyze meticulously and step by step the phases and processes involved in the development of each of these action-patterns.

In the meticulous analysis of each behavior-course we have been concerned with the earliest manifestation of new aspects or new phases of the pattern; with its period of rapid development, or more specifically the rhythm of its development; and with the influence development of one action-pattern may exercise upon the growth of another.

In order to analyze the developmental processes involved in the growth of these behavior-patterns we have examined periodically and systemically the behavior of approximately sixty-eight infants over a period of two years in such a way as to elicit the following reactions: the Moro reflex, the suspension-grasp reflex, inverted suspension, crawling and creeping movements, erect locomotion, the assumption of a sitting posture, the assumption of an erect posture, reaching-prehensile reactions, reactions to rotation, and reactions to cutaneous irritation.

When the stage of maturation level of these behavior-patterns is fully reckoned, it is possible to see that there are certain fundamental growth principles which cohere irrespective of the type or form of the pattern. In the first place no action-pattern appears fully grown or functioning with perfection and precision from the moment of inception. There occur periods of rapid development in each behavior-course, but the rapid periods of development of one behavior-pattern often check or alter the development of another. Not only is no behavior-pattern fully developed at the time of inception, but there is also a definite overlapping of one phase with another in the course of development. There are no sharp lines of demarcation in growth; there is no sudden change from one phase to another. There is not only an overlapping of phases in the growth of a behavior-pattern but there is both a temporal and functional overlapping of one behavior-pattern with another.

Although the inception of a pattern or a particular aspect of a pattern is inchoate, there is in the early stages a tendency for it to become overemphasized or exaggerated. This excessive manifestation of a pattern is itself temporary, so that soon there follows an exaggerated development in an opposite direction. Ultimately the behavior-pattern becomes crystallized somewhere between the two extreme forms of behavior.

We were also concerned with the modifiability of behavior-patterns and the factors, especially extrinsic, which are of great import in modifying behavioral growth—altering either the speed of growth or the nature or sequence of growth phases. It is proverbial that practice makes perfect, and an indisputable truism that one learns by doing. On the other hand, there is unlimited evidence that mere exercise of any activity will not result in improvement in the performance. That is, some activities are more susceptible to modification through use or exercise of the act than others.

In order to study the effect of exercise of performance upon the development of activities which had attained different degrees of maturation at the time the special exercise was introduced, and upon activities which were controlled at different structural levels, we followed the daily development of twin boys in the growth of the behavior-pattern mentioned above. The development of these two babies, who were, during the first twenty-two months of life, subjected to decidedly different régimes, was compared to that of the larger group of infants whose daily experiences were not experimentally controlled. The development of the twin who was from early infancy subjected to systematic exercise of these specific activities was also compared to that of his co-twin whose activities were deliberately restricted.

The comparative development of these infants in relation to each other and to the larger group indicates that in general the somatic aspect of the behavior-patterns discussed in this chapter was not materially influenced by exercise of the performance during post-natal development.

However, even from the earliest, more extensive experience appeared to develop a more acquiescent attitude. In some instances the attitude determined the persistence or duration of a particular somatic pattern though it did not alter the essential sequential phases observed in the growth of a behavior-pattern.

Although these behavior-patterns have been referred to as phylogenetic in origin, their developmental sequence has been considered in this chapter merely as it could be observed in the growth of an individual and not as it is passed from generation to generation. The major aspects of these phyletic activities have become determined during phylogeny to such an extent as to be resistant to alteration through external influences during the development of an individual. Minor details, however, are subject to modification through exercise and use of the performance. While use of the activity will not advance appreciably the day a child begins to walk alone and will not alter the general method of progression, exercise may influence the grace with which he steps, his speed, and his mien of progression.

The hypothesis which in the writer's opinion most adequately explains the results which we have obtained with respect to the effect of practice upon these primitive behavior-patterns is as follows: in the human infant rudimentary behavior-patterns function at an infracortical level. Many of these rudimentary activities are replaced by performances similar in function but controlled at higher structural centers. While this structural change is taking place there is a period of reduction in the overt manifestation of activity. This period of time between the infracortical and the cortical activity varies with different behavior-patterns. Furthermore, it seems, the wider the temporal gap between these two levels of an activity the greater are the possibilities of modifying the higher-level action through repetition of the performance.

Chapter IV

ONTOGENETIC BEHAVIOR ACTIVITIES AND THE EFFECT OF EXERCISE UPON THEM

THE preceding chapter discussed the ontogenetic manifestation of behavior-patterns whose origin was rooted in phylogeny. Such action-patterns are, on the whole, indispensable to normal human functioning and stand as landmarks in the development of the human species. In our study of phyletic behavior-patterns we were concerned not so much with their transmission from generation to generation as with their manner of growth and manifestation within a particular individual.

In the present chapter we shall consider the development of performances or activities which are not indispensable to normal human functioning, activities which an individual may or may not acquire during post-natal development. In this way it may be discerned whether the same fundamental principles common in the growth of phylogenetic behavior obtain also in the acquisition of these complex activities. The methods used in studying the progressive steps involved in these attainments were in essence similar to those employed in studying more primitive types of behavior-patterns. The infants were placed in laboratory situations which were as similar from one occasion to the next as the experimental conditions allowed.

The examinations occurred at weekly and biweekly intervals for the purpose of observing (1) the changes in mode of behavior of the same child from week to week; (2) the common factors in the behavior-patterns of all the children studied; and (3) the manner in which one phase of the behavior-course superseded another.

Since these activities are recognized to be under the dominance of higher structural centers, and since they may or may not be acquired by a given individual, it is extremely pertinent to a study of growth that we ascertain the effect of exercise of activities of this order as compared to the influence of use upon the development of more fundamental phyletic behavior-patterns. Therefore in these activities as well as the ones previously discussed Johnny was exposed to daily systematic exercise, while Jimmy's experiences in these particular situations were deliberately limited so as not to exceed that of other infants who have figured in this investigation.

It has been shown in the preceding chapter that the influence of use upon the growth of certain actions during post-natal development was of negligible consequence so far as the sequential somatic phases inherent in the development of primitive types of behavior are concerned.

The method used in stimulating Johnny to greater exercise of these activities was no more of a *conditioning* technique than that employed in stimulating the more primitive types of behavior. Of course, the term *conditioning* has come into such loose usage that it might mean almost anything, but the method employed in stimulating Johnny in these performances in no way resembled the technique made famous by Pavlov in his conditioning experiments with dogs and used by Watson and Jones in their combined and separate conditioning experiments with young infants. On the contrary, we attempted to promote activities which the baby showed the slightest sign of being able to accomplish. As soon as new patterns, or even partial aspects of a pattern, were perceptible, efforts were made to facilitate the growing mode of behavior.

It will be recalled that as soon as it was observed that the baby was trying to raise his trunk off the supporting surface, preparatory to the development of creeping, he was encouraged to do so frequently, and as soon as he began to make definite creeping movements lures were moved before him in order to stimulate his progression. Likewise in stimulating the more complicated activities the baby's attention was directed to a lure so situated that he would have to engage in a particular performance in order to obtain it. Fortunately for the experimenter, babies who are just beginning to creep and discover the world beyond arm's length usually are also avid in their desire to manipulate an observed object, so that the most nondescript object, such as a spoon, a scrap of paper, an old shoe, or a stick of wood, constitute a provoking lure adequate to educe incredible effort on the part of the baby to gain the object. It is possible for the experimenter to capitalize upon this interest in simple objects until the baby becomes interested in the activity *per se*.

In arranging laboratory conditions which would evoke more complex types of behavior the experimenter endeavored to conform to the principles of development observed in the growth of phyletic behavior-patterns. Having observed that growth of primary behavior-patterns is a gradual process, that one phase overlaps with the preceding and succeeding one, we endeavored to arrange laboratory conditions so as to utilize the activities already under the command of the child but to stimulate him to extend his performance beyond that which he had previously accomplished.

The complexity of these later performances in which Johnny was trained precluded a routine schedule in terms of time and frequency of stimulation such as had been adhered to in the stimulation of the simpler activities. The total amount of time daily devoted to systematic exercise, after he began to engage in more complicated performances, would approximate three hours a day. The amount of time given to any particular performance could not be even approximately estimated. It has been the writer's experience that in working with infants and young children any attempt to hold time constant is exceedingly inadvisable and misleading. While the writer is highly appreciative of the value of the time factor in making an experiment appear clean-cut, in dealing with infants insistence upon a rigid time schedule introduces an experimental error which far offsets its advantages. The degree of attention given by the baby to the situation is the most important factor involved in the use of a performance. This factor cannot be evaluated on a time basis. To insist upon holding constant the frequency of repetition and the number of minutes an infant spends at a given activity really clouds the issue. Therefore in this investigation, if Johnny appeared greatly interested in a particular activity on a given day, he would be given greater opportunity to exercise it. On the other hand, he was not allowed to quit an activity just because he complained.

Swimming

Although this chapter purports to discuss the development of behavior-patterns which are of ontogenetic origin, there is one notable exception, viz., the development of swimming. Swimming is undoubtedly of phylogenetic origin, but it is perhaps the oldest phyletic pattern of which there is even a rudiment in the behavior repertoire of the newborn baby. Furthermore, the gap between infracortical and cortical swimming is so great that swimming can no longer be considered indispensable to normal human development. And since cortical swimming is subject to greater improvement through practice than any of the other phylogenetic behavior-patterns, we preferred to discuss the development of swimming behavior in this chapter together with other types of behavior which obviously were influenced through exercise of the performance.

There are four different situations in which the experimenters are studying the aquatic behavior of infants. Although we feel that we have not as yet been able to analyze the sequential phases of development in this trait with the same degree of accuracy and detail as obtained in our analysis of the traits described in the previous chapter, we have to date descriptive notes covering 215 examination periods on thirty-one infants as well as 2,500 feet of cinema film recording the swimming behavior of infants ranging in age from eleven days to twenty-four months. The observations were carried on in such a way as to cover all movements of the extremities, trunk, head, and face. We are therefore convinced that this preliminary analysis is in essence correct, though undoubtedly additional study will reveal details of particular phases in the behavior-course which we are not able to demonstrate at the present time.

Due to the fact that the majority of the experimental infants in this study have not attained their third birthday and due also to the fact that we are not able to pursue the study of infant swimming behavior with the diligence and persistence with which we have followed the growth of erect locomotion, for example, we do not feel justified at this time in carrying our analysis of this trait beyond approximately the first eighteen months.

The four situations in which swimming reactions were studied are: (1) chin support, (2) strap support, (3) submerged in prone position, and (4) submerged in supine position. We shall consider the activities of the babies in detail when they were placed in each one of these positions.

(1) *Chin Support.* In the first position the experimenter grasped

the infant at the chin, thus holding the face above the water surface but allowing the body and extremities free activity in the water. It was found that when supported in this fashion any newborn infant will engage in rhythmical movements of trunk and extremities. These alternate rhythmical movements in the lower extremities consist of two aspects, viz., flexion and extension. While one extremity is in a state of extension the other is in a state of flexion. The movements of the trunk include (1) extension of the spine and (2) rhythmical alternating flexion of the trunk from left to right. These lateral flexions of the trunk are accompanied by flexion of the lower extremity of the same side. That is, when the body is flexed to the right, the right leg is flexed. This association of the ipsi-lateral leg and side of the trunk appears to be representative of the integration which characterizes the swimming movements in all aquatic animals. Swimming is phylogenetically one of the oldest behavior-patterns, and ontogenetically this alternate lateral flexion of the trunk is one of the first movements of the embryo.

In the human infant at the time of birth swimming activity is in a transition stage from the lower-level reflex stage to an activity under higher neuro-structural control. Due to the fact that growth is caudad, the action in the upper extremities has less of a definite rhythmical pattern than have the movements in the lower extremities. That is, the upper part of the body and upper extremities have progressed further in shifting from the reflex to a higher-level activity. It will be recalled that inactivity is characteristic of the phase just prior to cortical control of the performance. For that reason the upper extremities are less active in the newborn phase of the pattern than are the lower extremities. Sometimes, however, the upper extremities engage in circumduction associated with the flexor-extensor movements of the opposite lower extremity. These movements are not likely to be as complete or as rhythmically persistent as is the activity in the lower extremities. The digits are usually extended and abducted. This extension of the digits is a primitive attempt of the infant to widen the paddle as he moves through the water. Since his digits are not webbed, the extension defeats its own purpose. Interestingly enough, however, this aspect of the swimming pattern is long retained. Even after two years of age the children still tend to spread their fingers. In fact any tyro swimmer is likely to spread his digits until instructed to the contrary. Head movements were not possible in the chin-support position, since the experimenter held the baby's head still. An analysis of the head movements will be made in a later discussion of the pattern when the infant was submerged without artificial support.

Supported at the chin the infant can be felt to propel his body through the water for a short distance. The rhythm of these swimming movements easily distinguishes them from spontaneous activity of the newborn baby. By a counting of the 16-mm. cinema film frames from extension to extension of one lower extremity, the rhythmical swimming pattern of the newborn infant is easily established. The time interval from one extension to the next is often surprisingly constant in the behavior of the newborn. During a period of five or six seconds the time interval will run constant even to a sixteenth of a second, and seldom varies more than two or three sixteenths of a second. On the other hand, when the child is older a counting of frames between extension phases of one lower extremity shows the absence of a rhythmical pattern. In the older infant not only is there greater variability in the time interval from extension to extension, but seldom are two consecutive movements similar in form or in time of movement.

While reflex swimming is common to most infants, it is not possible to elicit a typical mode of the pattern any or every time an infant is placed in the water. Sometimes the newborn will remain quite immobile in the water. Usually, however, a slight respiratory stimulation, such as lowering the nose to the water level, will set up the activity. Although reflex swimming is waning at birth, the action-pattern is most easily elicited during the second post-natal month. At first this may seem paradoxical. But if one considers the growth rhythms and the tendency for a fading pattern to flare up with renewed force just before it loses out completely, it is understood that this greater manifestation during the second month is in fact an indication of evanescence.

Development or growth in this action-pattern is shown at first by a decrease in the rhythmical movements and the emergence of a generalized diffuse behavior-mode and not by an expansion of the reflex pattern. These diffuse activities constitute an indication that a higher neuro-structural level is beginning to control the behavior of the baby when he is in water. The reduction in rhythmical activity is first apparent in the upper extremities. The arms, held flexed and abducted, are noticeably inactive. In the course of a few months the infant, becoming more active, begins to show signs of insecurity in the water. He clutches the experimenter's hand which is supporting his chin and the rhythmical swimming movements become replaced by incoördinate struggling movements of trunk and extremities.

But the infant does not arrive at this state of insecurity all at once. Even his realization of insecurity in the water develops little by little. Following the period of comparative inactivity of the upper extremities it is observed that the arms approach or sometimes touch the experimenter's hand for days or weeks before the baby starts definitely clutching. Once the clutching action has made its appearance, the infant will not hold it during the whole time but will revert to the state of flexion and abduction at intervals during a given examination period. Ultimately the clutching act becomes the most persistent mode of behavior as the infant is supported at the chin.

(2) *Strap Support.* The second situation used for studying swimming behavior was designed specifically to determine when the infant would gain sufficient control to hold his head above the water surface. A belt, fastened around the chest of the infant, just above the nipple line, was attached to a ball-bearing roller which moved on a rod above the pool. In this position the face as well as the body of the infant would be submerged if the baby did not of his own power hold his head above the water. Rhythmical reflex swimming movements are more readily elicited in the young infant when the face is submerged in this fashion.

Of course, the babies are allowed to remain submerged for only a brief moment, since their respiratory activities are temporarily interrupted. Apparently, however, the newborn baby is equipped with a respiratory reflex which for the moment comes to his aid, as evidenced by the fact that he tends to hold his mouth closed and gains respiratory control on removal from the water with less coughing than does the infant a few months older. While the newborn baby is swimming with the face submerged, the eyes ordinarily remain open and become somewhat dilated. The appearance of the eyes when dilated in this way has been aptly referred to as "fish eyes." As the infant grows older this dilatation disappears, although the eyes still remain open when the face is submerged.

Likewise in the older baby there is a diminution of definite swimming movements even though the baby is submerged. Sometimes the infant will remain with the spine and extremities extended though immobile, or there may be lateral flexion of the trunk as well as attempts to turn into a supine position. Soon these movements become more expansive, until the reflex swimming has been replaced by incoördinate activity in all parts of the body. Frequently the baby's hands go to his head at the water surface, especially if the crown is just a little above the water. This act gives the impression of an attempt on the part of the infant to wipe the water away. Such actions denote a developing feeling of insecurity when in the water. Gradually the baby compensates or gains control of the situation by acquiring the ability to hold his head above the water. But he does not gain this ability in a day. Instead there is a period when he will raise his head up, drop it in the water again, then raise it again, and so on, until he has finally gained sufficient control to hold it above the water during the entire time he is in this position. His general movements at this time are still of the incoördinate struggling variety mixed with a more purposeful act of reaching with the arms toward the edge of the pool in order to grasp it.

(3) *Submerged Prone.* In the third situation the baby is placed face down in the water without artificial support. In this situation as in the former a rhythmical swimming movement of the newborn is often elicited. In fact the reflex swimming is evoked more easily when the baby is completely submerged than when his face is held above the water. He is unable to raise his face above the water, though often he can propel himself through the water. At no time has the experimenter observed any child under the age of two years, when submerged in water without any artificial support, raise his head above the water surface for breathing and at the same time maintain a horizontal swimming position. Unfortunately the tank used in this investigation is only twenty-eight inches deep, and it has been impossible to follow the development of this aspect of the pattern to its consummation because the children soon learn that they can touch the bottom of the pool. Children of two years are more likely to get into an upright position to walk on the bottom of the pool than they are to engage in swimming activities.

But newborn swimming movements are often better integrated

when the baby is completely submerged. Indeed it is sometimes observed that the head turns to the flexion side as part of the swimming rhythm. An older infant, however, in all probability will not engage in swimming movements but will turn over on his back.

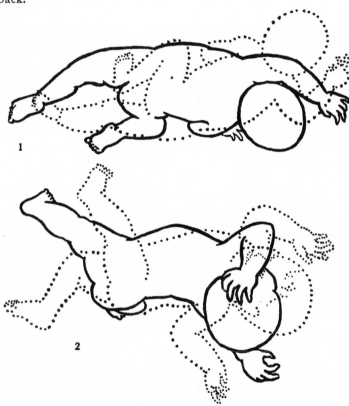

FIG. 14. SWIMMING ACTIVITIES

1. Rhythmical swimming movement of newborn infant. 2. With development, infant shows insecurity when submerged in prone position by rotating into supine position and general struggling movements.

The writer can offer no reason for this mode of behavior in the older infants. Perhaps it is phototropic, or perhaps it is an effort to get the face out of water. It seems more reasonable, to the writer at least, to believe that the rotation in the water is merely a result of a general spinal extension. In threatening situations extensors are brought into utmost function. Extension of the spine would tend to bring the body into a supine position if it had freedom of movement as it would have in water. This interpretation does not, however, explain why the baby should remain on his back, engaging in incoördinate kicking rather than continuing to rotate laterally. The fact remains that the tendency for older infants to turn supine when submerged prone is most pronounced.

Often the child during the early part of the second year will manifest excellent swimming movements. We are not at present prepared to state definitely whether or not these movements are transitory or permanent. It is the writer's opinion, however, that reflex swimming behavior of the newborn bears the same relationship to *voluntary* swimming as the reflex stepping movements bear to *voluntary* walking. Since swimming is an older phyletic pattern than is walking, the gap between the reflex activity and the learned performance is greater. In both of these behavior-patterns there is a shift from a lower to a higher level of structural control. There are two factors of development which should be kept in mind in considering behavior-patterns of this type. In the first place, patterns which are waning at a particular structural level often show an increase in force or action shortly before their regression. In the second place, new phases of the patterns controlled at a higher level often herald their coming. Although these interpretations are admittedly speculative, it seems reasonable that the reflex swimming movements occurring frequently in the infant during the first or second month represent the "dying gasp" of the reflex swimming behavior. The recurrence of swimming movements about the end of the first year is a brief manifestation or heralding of swimming of a higher order. Since at this time swimming is ordinarily not given adequate stimulation, it does not become a permanent behavior-pattern. It requires considerably more conscious effort to attain cortical swimming than it does to acquire voluntary walking.

(4) *Submerged Supine.* Since such a high percentage of the babies older than five or six months showed a tendency to rotate into a supine position when submerged in the prone position, the experimenters wished to determine if the baby would rotate into a prone position when placed in the pool on his back. Although the data have not been tabulated on all the infants under observation in this situation, it is safe to state that, on the whole, newborns and older infants remain in the supine position when

thus placed in the water. There have been a few occasions when an infant has turned into a lateral or prone position, but they have been so few as to be negligible. It is possible that the older child will make the adjustment of turning into a prone position, but the writer is not at the present time prepared to verify the statement, though there have been suggestive actions in a few of the older babies indicating that it is true.

The swimming activity of the newborn in the supine position is much more of a trunk reaction than when in the prone position. This mode of action consists of a sort of alternate lateral flexion at the waist-line which results in a wavelike motion of the pelvic girdle. Circumduction of the upper extremities and flexor-extensor movements of the lower extremities were often associated and rhythmical. The incoördinate movements of the older infants are of the fighting, struggling variety. Frequently the hands go to the face as if to wipe the water away.

The special exercise of Johnny in water was not begun until he was well past the reflex swimming stage. Therefore, this particular study sheds no light upon the problem raised earlier as to whether or not frequent stimulation of the lower-level reflex activities would in any way advance the development of the behavior-pattern when it had attained higher neuro-structural control. Swimming was begun with Johnny in the strap position when he was 231 days old. He was not submerged without artificial support until he was 290 days old. From the beginning Johnny was able to hold his head above the water surface when supported by the strap. At the time training was initiated he apparently was in the inactive stage, as he made only a few slow, incoördinate kicking movements which could not be definitely labeled swimming activity. He never showed the clutching and struggling activity characteristic of most infants at this period. Within a month after training was begun with the strap support around the chest he was able to progress the length of the small seven-foot tank by means of excellent alternate flexor-extensor movements of the lower extremities and some, though less, activity in the left upper extremity. For a while the upper extremities were quite inactive. When he did begin to use his arms there were some weeks when only the left one was active. The right was held in flexion and abduction until he neared the end of the pool when he would reach out with the right hand to grasp the edge.

Daily exercise in swimming was begun with Johnny so late that there was no indication of the respiratory reflex which in newborn infants apparently functions during submergence. During the first two weeks of Johnny's swimming experience there was considerable coughing immediately after submergence as well as considerable swallowing of water during submergence. But by the time he was 276 days old he was observed deliberately to expectorate water if it got in his mouth as he paddled the length of the pool. Furthermore by this time he was showing excellent control of breathing.

No effort was made to teach him strokes. He was merely placed in the water so that his activities could be observed. At times a toy would be placed at one end of the pool in order to stimulate him to swim for it. In order to make the situation increasingly but gradually difficult, the strap was inch by inch lowered in its position around his trunk, so that he would have to depend more and more upon his own abilities in holding his head out of the water. He would usually cry and object the first time the strap was lowered. Either his disturbed attitude or the increased difficulty of the situation would temporarily retard his swimming activity on each occasion that the strap was placed lower around the trunk. However, this period of readjustment to a new factor was ordinarily brief. By the time he was 357 days old the strap was placed at the pelvic girdle, so that in order to keep his face out of water he would have to support practically the entire upper part of the body by his own efforts. Within ten days he had thus learned to hold his head above the water surface as he rapidly swam the length of the small pool.

When he was 419 days old an elastic strap was placed around each groin so that he would have to work even harder to keep his head above the water surface. By this time the child had had sufficient experience swimming with his face under water that he apparently preferred that method to the increased effort demanded in holding his head up with only the slight support of an elastic strap. Consequently he would swim with his face under water just as if the strap were not there. It was evident that he was capable of holding his head up, for occasionally the experimenter would give him additional support at the chin as he started out swimming; then he would continue the rest of the way with his head above the water. That his swimming with face submerged was a matter of preference was further indicated by the fact that when the strap was returned to the chest position he would deliberately submerge his face as he swam the length of the pool.

Johnny was first submerged without any artificial support when he was 280 days old. His actions at that time consisted of an extension of the spine which apparently was an attempt to bring his head above the water surface. This special extension brought him into a vertical position, though still completely submerged. As he was then too short to touch bottom even in a vertical position, he would hold his arms outstretched in readiness to seize the edge of the pool as soon as the alternate flexion and extension (a sort of high stepping movement) brought him within arm's length of the edge. Thereupon the experimenter, in an effort to interrupt Johnny's tendency to get into a vertical position, began holding a hand just beneath the boy's abdomen so as to push him back into the prone posture whenever he started to get into a vertical one. Otherwise support was not given him. Corrected in this way, he was within a month, at the age of 308 days, beginning to swim horizontally without support but with his entire body submerged about six inches from the water surface. There was, however, much overlapping of the tendency to get into a vertical position and the horizontal posture, and it was not until he was 366 days old that swimming in a horizontal position had become a rather permanent characteristic aspect of the pattern. Although in the beginning, as was usually the case when new situations were introduced, he had objected to being submerged without support, he did not turn over on his back as was characteristic of other infants of corresponding chronological age in this situation. By the time Johnny was 308 days old he was thoroughly enjoying the swimming activity when supported in the strap. When 360 days old he was enjoying the performance so much that he would of his own accord release his hold on the edge of the pool in order to swim the length of the pool. This act he would do repeatedly. It was not until he was 411 days, however, that he voluntarily released his grip on the pool edge to swim without the supporting strap.

He continued swimming in a horizontal position until he was 446 days old. Then he discovered that he could touch the bottom of the pool. He so enjoyed walking on tiptoes through the water that it was impossible to keep him in the swimming position in the small tank. For that reason, when he was 484 days old he was taken to an adult swimming pool for practice. At first when in the larger pool there was a reversion to the old tendency of swimming in a vertical position, even though he did not touch the bottom. Practice in this large pool was continued over a period of three months, when the possibility of respiratory infection precluded further pursuit of this type of exercise. During that time, however, he showed marked improvement in his speed and in the distance covered while swimming under water. He never learned to raise his head above the water surface to take a breath. At the time the swimming was terminated he was eighteen months old. From the time he was seventeen months old he had been swimming under water for from twelve to fifteen feet without stopping. It was, however, necessary for the experimenter to raise his face above the water so that he could take a breath. It is unfortunate that we were unable to pursue further the study of swimming behavior in order to ascertain when and how he would acquire the ability to raise his face above water for breathing.

Johnny was not given daily practice in the floating position. However, when 367 days old he was examined for his reactions in this position. He rolled immediately into a prone position and started swimming. It will be recalled that this is just the opposite mode of behavior from that of most infants when placed in this situation. Usually they prefer the supine position when submerged.

Diving Behavior

It was not just in distance and skill that Johnny's swimming behavior exceeded that of other infants of corresponding chronological age. At the age of 393 days Johnny was stood on the edge of the pool as the experimenter gave enough pressure on the back of his head to suggest his bending forward in such a way that he would go into the water head first. The baby objected to this activity at first, as indicated by a stiffened spine, so that it was often impossible to get him to bend forward in order to enter head first. Also at first he cried and complained. However, he soon developed a more acquiescent attitude, so that within a month he did not need even the suggestive pressure at the back of his head in order to get him to bend forward. The experimenter merely said "Down, Johnny." Immediately he would bend over to go into the water in a sort of diving fashion. This deliberate "diving" became more and more frequent, until at the age of 422 days he went into the water head first without waiting for the experimenter to tell him to do so.

One should avoid the impression that, once Johnny began to "dive" deliberately, he did so ever afterwards. Growth does not proceed in that manner. There would be periods when he would regress to the old attitude of resistance. But these regression periods grew steadily less frequent. By the time he was 445 days old his deliberateness and delight in diving in the pool were unmistakable. For a period, however, there appeared to be a conflict between the developing diving reaction and the development of a jumping pattern. The conflict between these two developing behavior-courses resulted in his bending his head forward as if to dive but finally stepping off or landing "flat" on the abdomen. A light touch on the head just as he started to bend over was sufficient to get him flexed enough to go in head first. When he was 480 days old, not only was he enjoying the "diving," but a definite "spring" appeared in his mode of action.

When Johnny was 467 days old he was taken to a lake—a completely new situation to him. In view of his later behavior in an adult swimming pool, it is interesting that he willingly dived off a springboard five feet above the water surface. A command and slight touch on the shoulder were sufficient to get him to dive off the high board. Although it was the first time he had ever experienced outdoor swimming and both the breeze and water were cool, he did not cry or show other signs of antipathy toward the situation.

About the time Johnny was developing most rapidly in his diving behavior it was deemed unwise to have him continue diving in the small pool, so he was taken to the adult pool. There occurred in the new situation a general setback in his manner of performance. At first he refused to dive or jump off the spring board. For the first ten days he complained every time he was placed in the diving situation. Gradually, however, he became more cooperative and began jumping off the springboard, and by the time he was 511 days old a slight touch on the shoulder was sufficient to get him to dive off head first. The spring which was beginning to develop in his mode of action in the small pool did not reappear.

As a matter of fact, although he at times coöperated, he never developed a completely acquiescent attitude in the new situation. Changes in temperature and other factors which were beyond experimental control under the existing circumstances apparently were contributing factors to his resistant attitude. When he was 518 days old he dived off without even the suggestive touch on the shoulder, and he continued to do so daily during the following week. On one occasion when 520 days old he lost his balance as he walked out on the springboard and would have fallen in the water except that he quickly switched the falling uncontrolled act into an excellent dive. During his practice period he never attained this excellent performance again. Unfortunately growth does not proceed in regular fashion, so there followed a period of persistent refusals when he could not be induced to attempt to dive. Even more unfortunately, the study of swimming development was unavoidably terminated before additional development in diving could be ascertained.

Jimmy's swimming behavior more closely corresponded to that of other infants who are placed in water only at periodic intervals. Placed in the water for the first time at the age of 231 days, he would not hold his head above the water surface. When the experimenter gave him support at the chin, both upper and lower extremities were tense and immobile. If his face was lowered so that the nose barely touched the water, vigorous incoördinate movements were educed. When he was 283 days old his feeling of insecurity was definitely manifested by his clutching the experimenter's hand which was giving him support at the chin. Submerged in a prone position he immediately rotated into a supine position. When he was taken from the pool at 308 days he did a great deal of coughing, spitting, and gagging in contrast to Johnny, who had weeks earlier developed considerable breath control. At the age of 337 days Jimmy began to show a characteristic behavior-mode of bringing his hands to the margin of the water around his head or face.

The clinging reactions continued as characteristic of Jimmy's behavior until he was about 413 days old when, in the strap-support position, he began to show alternate flexor-extensor movements of the lower extremities. When he was 597 days old he was able to make considerable progress across the small pool by alternate flexion and extension of the lower extremities in the submerged or supported position. At that time the upper extremities were ordinarily inactive and held close to the body until he approached the side of the pool, when he would reach out to seize it.

In the development of swimming behavior, more particularly in the diving behavior, Johnny showed an unequivocal improvement in performance as well as in the development of a coöperative attitude which can be attributed only to his more extensive experience in the situation.

Ascending Inclines

Climbing up and down inclines is an activity closely related to the development of creeping. Phylogenetically and ontogenetically climbing follows creeping. It would be foolhardy, therefore, to attempt to induce an infant to climb up and down inclines before he is able to creep on a flat surface. While the ability to creep is indispensable in normal human growth, the ability to creep up and down an inclined plane is not. It has been pointed out in Chapter III that daily exercise or repetition of the crawling movements resulted in a *conditioned* response or increased activity in the extremities, but it did not advance the day the baby could raise his abdomen off the underlying surface and proceed in well-coördinated, associated creeping movements. Since creeping *per se* is an activity which is resistant to modification through exercise of the performance, it was desirable to ascertain what effect, if any, repetition of the performance would have upon an activity which was constructed upon the creeping pattern.

Having observed that growth is gradual and that infants work longest and most diligently at activities which are just beyond easy accomplishment, the experimenters endeavored to make creeping more difficult by inducing the baby to creep up and down inclines of varying steepness. Creeping up and down a low incline is a situation more difficult for the baby than is creeping on a flat surface. It is possible, therefore, by carefully grading the slope of the incline to keep the situation just enough beyond the infant's attainments as to make it difficult for him to accomplish, although keeping it within his capabilities. In the present investigation a series of eight columnar stools were constructed so that a 72-in. slide could be fitted into small apertures near the top margin of each stool. The stools measured 18 x 18 in. on the top surface and ranged in height as follows, 14¼, 22¼, 30, 38¼, 46½, 54¼, and 63½ in. When the slide is attached to these stools, varying degrees of steepness are easily procured. Angles indicating the slopes of the inclines are as follows: 11°, 18°, 24°, 32°, 40°, 48°, 61°, and 70°. The slide measured 16 in. in width, with a small ridge 1½ in. high on each side.

The two obvious methods by which the infant's development in ascending inclines may be reckoned are (1) the manner of ascension and (2) the slope of the incline. It is slightly more difficult for an infant to creep up an incline of only 11° than it is for him to creep on a flat surface. Therefore, his behavior on the inclines is at first more or less determined by the degree of maturity of his creeping performance. His first attempt in ascending the lowest incline is to use the creeping method which he favors when progressing on a flat surface. If the low incline presents a difficulty to his progress, there occurs a regression to a more immature creeping movement. The baby who is just beginning to develop associated creeping movements on a flat surface will, when faced with the difficulty of a low-grade incline, revert to isolated movements of upper and lower extremities.

In the beginning the baby is often unable to get himself entirely on the incline. He places both hands on the slide, but apparently does not know what to do with his feet. He definitely has the idea that his feet should go on the slide, as indicated by his raising one foot as if to place it on the slide, then putting it back on the floor, lifting it again or raising the other one, and so on. But he does not succeed in actually placing both feet on the board. Raising his foot constitutes a partial act, but the infant does not carry through to completion. Usually if he succeeds in setting both hands and feet on the incline his method is inadequate and his movements are isolated or staccato. If he starts up with his palms and knees on the surface of the incline his knees may slip back so as to bring his abdomen down on the surface of the slide. Perhaps he will have both of his palms flat on the slide surface, then he will raise one hand, take hold of the slide edge, put the hand back on the slide surface, and then take hold of the other edge, etc. He makes a great many useless, poorly directed movements, although his general direction and purpose are focused on the goal. The staccato feature of his movements is shown for example in the tendency to place one hand securely on the slide surface and get it steadied there before moving another part of his body. In time, however, not only is the excess activity eliminated but the movements become integrated and smooth until it appears as if the associated upper and lower extremities move as one, as he ascends the lowest incline with great facility.

When confronted with an incline of greater steepness, however, the baby will again, in the initial phase, manifest the diffused excess activity. Sometimes he will stand at the foot of the slide and bounce up and down, or he will reach vainly toward the lure which is placed beyond his reach on the slide. He may get both hands and feet upon the slide and then slip back, start up again, only to slide back, and end up with crying. After a few such futile efforts he may give up and direct his attention elsewhere. But in time this slide too is easily scaled. It has been observed that the baby who gets into a palm-toe position will show greater skill in progressing up these inclines than those who adhere to the hand-knee position.

It is unlikely that any child will be able to climb with ease an incline placed at an angle of 61° or 70° the first time he is faced with the situation. Slide-climbing is a type of activity wherein considerable improvement in performance is effected by exercise or practice, and it is possible by gradually increasing the angle of elevation to stimulate an infant of nine or ten months to climb inclines of incredible steepness. The process of growth as well as the comparative effect of practice or exercise upon the development of this function can better be revealed through a critical analysis of the behavior of Johnny and Jimmy in this situation than in discourse about the behavior of babies in general.

Daily practice in slide-climbing was begun with Johnny when he was 239 days old. Reference to his creeping record in Chapter III will show that at that time he was just beginning to develop associated creeping movements. Although he succeeded on this day in covering the entire distance of the slide when it was placed at an angle of 11°, it apparently was due to the stimulating effect of a new situation, since his subsequent performances for several weeks showed less proficiency. His method of ascension was inferior to his manner of progression on a flat surface. He tried the hand-knee position; slipped down so that his abdomen was on the surface; then rose up on his toes, etc. His movements were

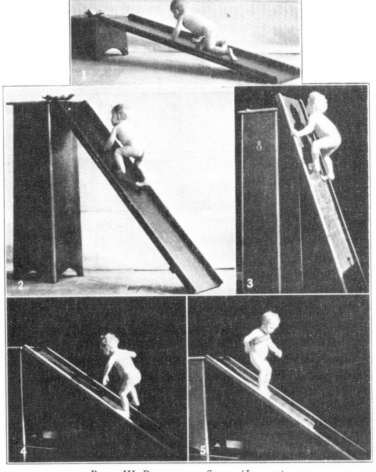

PLATE III. BEHAVIOR ON SLIDES (JOHNNY)

1. Johnny begins ascending a slide placed at an angle of 11° when eight and one-half months old. 2. At ten months he ascends a slide placed at an angle of 48°. 3. At twenty-one months he scales a 70° slope. 4 and 5. Johnny at thirteen months walks up and down an incline of 32°.

isolated and poorly controlled. It was only persistence which enabled him to cover the entire distance. Even so, this climb was better than his performances which followed during the ensuing weeks. Although he succeeded in getting both his hands and feet on the slide, his action-pattern consisted of supporting himself on hands and toes, raising first one foot and then the other, falling down on his abdomen, then rising again. He repeated all these excess movements many times, though he did not actually make much progress.

It was two weeks later before Johnny for the second time crept up the entire length of the slide, although at that time he used associated, fairly well-coördinated movements in doing so. His general method of ascension consisted of placing both palms and feet on the slide surface. The pressure on the feet was toward the ball of the foot, with the heels slightly raised. This method was superior to that of Jimmy, who was still ascending in the hand-knee position. By the time Johnny was 300 days old he had gained excellent control over this performance. After he was 316 days old he tended to creep up the lowest incline on the hands and knees rather than his toes, although his movements in either case were well-integrated associated acts. Once he had gained control of the performance, the hand-knee position was no handicap to his progression up the lowest inclines. In terms of physiological energy it was at this highly developed stage of the performance less costly. A method of action which in one stage of development may be inefficient may, at another stage, be not only the most efficient but the most economical. When Johnny was 347 days old both practice and study of his reactions on the lowest slide were discontinued, since he had in the meantime gained proficiency in climbing slides of considerably greater steepness. In the early performances of the twins in this situation Jimmy showed slight superiority over Johnny, for when they were 261 days old he successfully climbed the low-grade incline, which Johnny failed to do. It is not so much the fact of his accomplishment as it is the method of performance which indicated Jimmy's superiority at the time. Cautious associated movements of upper and lower extremities were a part of Jimmy's reactions as he progressed the entire distance up the incline.

But during the course of development Jimmy, who was creeping up the incline better than Johnny when they were 261 days old, showed a gradual regression rather than expansion of the behavior-course. He succeeded in climbing the slide when he was 261 and 276 days old, although his movements on the latter date were noticeably more slow and cautious. When 294 days old he crept up only one third of the distance of the slide, and when 308 days old he scarcely got entirely on the slide. From the time he was 337 days old until he was 672 days old utmost effort on the part of the experimenters failed to get him to creep up on the low slide any distance whatever. Obviously he had adequate motor mechanisms for this performance. Equally obviously, from his manner of behavior, he was interested in and often coveted the lures set for him, but there was a progressive inhibition of his motor performance due apparently to his general attitude toward the laboratory conditions.

Johnny had been receiving daily practice for five days a week over a period of twenty-eight days before he successfully climbed the entire distance on an incline of 18°, though it was just as easy and he learned as quickly to climb the incline of 24° as that of 18°. For that reason his performances on these two slopes will be considered at the same time. The first occasion on which definitely integrated associated movements occurred was when he was 276 days old, or about five weeks from the time of inception of his special exercise period. His method consisted of placing both of his palms on the surface of the slide and gripping the surface with his toes as he proceeded up in well-coördinated movements. Occasions of reversion to the hesitating isolated movements occurred until he was past 315 days.

Jimmy never succeeded in climbing inclines of 24° or steeper during the period of restricted activity. When he was 283 days old, although he had had only four experiences in the slide situation, he climbed the entire distance on the slide of 18°. Grasping one ridge of the slide with his right hand he climbed up in the hand-knee position, using well-integrated associated movements as he did so. He was slow and cautious. This ascent and the previous achievement on the lowest incline are the only two occasions when Jimmy successfully climbed the entire distance on any of the inclines during the months when his motor activities were limited. In general, sitting on the floor at the bottom of the slide, he would either rest his hands on the slide or hold on to both ridges and cry. He would seldom get both hands and feet on the slide at once. Occasionally he would succeed in making two or three creeping movements which would bring him to a distance of about one foot on the slide, whereupon he would sit on the slide until removed by the experimenter. Except for the fact that he did climb up the 18° incline on one occasion, his actions were essentially the same on all slides. As the months went by during his period of restricted activity, Jimmy showed a regression in his somatic performances on all inclines rather than an expansion or development.

Although Johnny made no differential reactions to inclines of 18° and 24°, when the slope was increased to 32° the steepness became a greater barrier. Johnny had been getting practice in slide-climbing over a period of fifty-one days before he successfully scaled this incline. But he succeeded in climbing up the incline of 40° just as quickly as he did the one of 32°. During the early period of climbing these steeper inclines it was observed that he made less use of his hands than his toes in actually making the ascent. He gripped the surface tightly with his toes. His hands, whether on the surface of the slide or grasping the ridge, were used mainly to steady himself rather than to pull his body upward. The progressive movement was initiated by placing one foot higher and pushing himself up. The use of his feet as propellers continued for several months.

When presented with a higher incline he showed a greater tendency to lose his grip and slip back. Often after the first unsuccessful trial or two he would revert to immature diffused activity, such as holding on the slide and bouncing up and down on the floor. When he was first presented to the slide of 48° he made a few efforts to climb. Failing, he immediately began to bounce up and down on the floor in front of the slide. Within a week he had succeeded in climbing this new height. His efforts were considerably labored, isolated movements for some time, and it was fully three months before well-integrated movements became his established mode of ascent.

In the meantime he had also mastered an incline of 61°. On the first occasion when he was faced with the slide placed at this angle, he failed to get both hands and feet off the floor and on the slide. He slipped back to the floor each time he made an effort. However, after he had been placed about one-third of the distance up on the slide he was able to climb the remaining distance. Frequently the only assistance necessary to get him started was enough support to his feet to stop his sliding back as he made his first movements. If he got started he was likely to continue. A little assistance given at the right moment will greatly facilitate the child's acquisition of a particular performance. Although he climbed up the slide of 61° when he was 358 days old without any assistance, there were occasions when the experimenter would have to give him the slightest help just as he started up the slide. By the time he was 374 days old there was a noticeably greater tendency for him to use his upper extremities more in pulling himself upward than his feet for pushing himself upward. It was not until he was 486 days old that an easy, rapid, well-integrated ascent had become his established behavior-pattern on the incline. In other words, it took him four months to develop an easy command of this performance.

That is, it required considerable time and practice for him to develop an integrated ascent on the 61° incline. This is interesting in view of the fact that in less than a month from the time he was first presented with the incline of 70° he had attained an easy, well-integrated movement in ascending. He was, however, 633 days old when he first met this situation. Although there was a temporary regression to the hesitating, isolated movements as compared with his performance at that time on a slightly lower slide, he nevertheless succeeded in going up the entire distance on the first occasion. By the time he was 652 days old he was scaling this incline of great steepness with incredible facility.

Among the outstanding factors observed in Johnny's learning to ascend inclines of increasing steepness was the fact that a mishap in a situation he was just beginning to learn would be more expensive from a learning standpoint than the same mishap would have been if it occurred in the situation over which he had gained control. For example, if he slipped back on a slide which he had already more or less mastered, he would start up again with renewed vigor. But if he slipped on a new slide, he would probably engage in generalized or excess activity, and it was more difficult to get him to renew his efforts.

An excellent illustration of a newly developing pattern interfering with a previous achievement was indicated in his slide-climbing activity when he was just acquiring an ability to assume an erect posture. For example, he would tend to assume a standing position even when he was on an incline. After he had begun to walk up the low inclines there was a period when he would also attempt to walk up inclines of greater steepness, so steep in fact that to walk up them was physically impossible. But ultimately these fallacies of judgment disappeared, so that he easily distinguished the elevation and obviously knew which slide he should walk up and which he could climb.

No child less than twenty-four months of age under the observation of the experimenters has succeeded in climbing up the steep inclines of 61° and 70°. A few infants have climbed up the incline of 48°. It is therefore evident that repeated practice in this activity did promote the performance of Johnny, while the lack of experience curtailed Jimmy's development in this activity. The modification effected through repetition was indicated both in the method used by Johnny and in the steepness of the inclines he ascended.

Descending Inclines

Descending inclines of varying declivity presents to the creeping baby quite a different problem from that of ascension. On the lower declines, those of 11° or 18°, the infant is able to make use of the creeping pattern as he descends in a creeping fashion. Descending even the lowest incline is in the beginning a more difficult performance for the baby than is ascension. Since slide-descension is a problem to the baby, his performance in this activity exposes the points of greatest weakness in his general locomotor development. In descending slopes the advanced development of the upper part of the body over the pelvic girdle and lower extremities is clearly demonstrated. Ordinarily the baby sets out to creep down the incline head foremost. In so doing he apparently needs to use all the powers of his body to guard against falling headlong; so he extends the upper extremities and presses them against the surface of the slide to avoid tumbling forward. He obviously has a great deal more control in the shoulder girdle than in the pelvic girdle. Therefore he flexes the lower extremities markedly beneath the pelvic girdle and more or less drags them downward as he moves each hand cautiously and deliberately to a lower place on the slide. Gradually the dragging of the pelvic girdle becomes less pronounced and he is observed to move the flexed knees slightly forward. This movement of the knees denotes the inception of associated movements involved in creeping down the incline. It is only a partial movement at first, though it gradually expands until the baby is able to cover the distance on hands and knees with the pelvic girdle well supported above the slide surface.

The baby may continue to use the creeping posture in descending the lowest slides. But when the slope is increased to an angle of 24° or more, if the baby starts down head foremost he quickly realizes that he must exert even more resistance in order to prevent tumbling forward. His resistance becomes so exaggerated that it is likely to place him in a sitting position on the slide. Taking even greater precaution against falling as he gets into the sitting position, he often seizes one ridge of the slide with both hands. This puts him in an excellent situation for the pull of gravity to turn him around. That is, the whole body rotates, as he holds on to the slide, in such a way as to bring him into a prone position with the feet downward. There is a period following this phase of the pattern when the infant will then resume the creeping posture on the slide but start creeping upward. In a short time, however, the infant ceases to start up the slide again and continues sliding downward in a prone position, feet downward. Usually he manages to grasp both ridges of the slide but allows it to pass through his hands as he slides down. There is a very distinct milestone in development when the baby learns to progress backwards toward an object. There is another milestone in development when the infant has learned to release his grip sufficiently on the edge of the slide to allow himself to move easily downward. His first reaction is to grip the edge so tightly that he merely clings to the slide. When he first begins to release the grasp on the slide edge he tends to overdo that aspect of the pattern, with the result that he slides down much too rapidly for comfort. Finally, however, he holds the edges just enough to check the speed of his descent.

Development is also shown in this performance by the distance on the slide at which the baby rotates his body in order to slide down in a prone position. In the early phase of this aspect of the behavior-course he does not make the rotation until he has started down the slide head first. But as development proceeds he anticipates his needs and turns from a sitting position to a prone position while he is still on the stool before starting down the slide. This method of sliding down in a prone position remains the chosen one of practically all infants in descending inclines of considerable steepness. Why the baby should select from all the possible modes the simplest method of descending an incline is an intriguing question, but not one upon which we have adequate data for comment here. However, the baby ordinarily continues to use the associated-creeping method in descending low-grade declines.

Johnny's development in this performance was somewhat atypical in so far as method was concerned. Daily practice in this performance was initiated on the lowest declines when he was 239 days old. Six days later he succeeded in going down the entire distance, though his control over his actions was so poor that he lost his balance, fell down, and struck his face on the slide surface several times. In the beginning he flexed both lower extremities markedly under the pelvic girdle, merely dragging the lower part of his body along as he moved his upper extremities downward on the slide surface. His lower extremities were flexed to such an extent that he was almost in a sitting position. The experimenters encouraged him to descend in a prone position with the *head* downward. It was not until he was 316 days old, however, that his characteristic method of descent consisted of well-integrated associated movements.

About this time too he was learning on a steeper incline to "let go" so that he would slide down in a prone position. Having learned to enjoy sliding down these steeper declines, there was a period when he could not discriminate with respect to the degree of declivity. So even on the low slides of 11° and 18° he would at first stretch out on the slide in a prone position with the arms extended above the head and wait a moment, obviously expecting gravity to pull him down. Since he did not slide by the force of gravity he would give a pull on the slide edge, then hesitate for a moment with his body still extended and relaxed on the surface as if believing the pull was sufficient to give him a downward start. Finding it difficult to pull himself down in this fashion, he would then flex and adduct the lower extremities in order to proceed downward in well-coördinated creeping movements. By the time he was 354 days old he had apparently learned to judge the steepness of the incline sufficiently to adapt his method to the slope of the slide. On the low decline he would start out in associated creeping movements.

When first placed on the steeper declines, Johnny attempted to go down in creeping movements. It was not easy to accomplish in this way. After a few trials on the 40° incline, at the age of 291 days, he began to grip the ridge of the slide, thus rotating his body in a prone position so that his feet were downward. This is the method naturally assumed by infants in descending inclines. But the experimenters interfered with his descending in this fashion and encouraged him to descend in a prone position with his head downward. By the time he was 308 days old he had learned to "let go" sufficiently to slide down head foremost, although the experimenter at the beginning had to check his speed in order to avoid a casualty at the end of the slide. Within a week, however, he had learned to check his speed himself. With his arms extended above his head but downward on the slide, and with the digits extended, he would press with his fingers against the slide surface just enough to check the speed but not enough to stop the sliding performance.

Although he had been encouraged to descend the slides in a prone position with his head downward, when confronted with a declivity of 61° he merely made a few attempts to go down in a prone position head first, after which he deliberately turned his body on the stool, seized the ridges of the slide with both hands, and slid down easily in a prone position but with his feet downward. This continued to be his preferred and characteristic method of descent on the steeper slopes. It is also the characteristic method of other babies who have not had special training in this performance.

Jimmy's behavior when placed in this situation is in sharp contrast to that of Johnny. On the lowest slide, when he was 261 days old he crept about one third of the distance and then assumed a sitting position. When he was 276 days old he crept the entire distance down this low incline. Although he was slow and cautious, he maintained the palm-knee position and his progression consisted of associated movements of both upper and lower extremities. From that time on his characteristic mode of behavior when placed at the top of the lowest slide as well as the higher ones was to sit on the stool and cry. Never once during his period of isolation did he descend any of the steeper inclines, although he was given opportunity and urged to do so at biweekly intervals.

Both in going up and in going down these slides Johnny's experience through daily practice facilitated his development in these activities and Jimmy's lack of experience reduced his performance to something a little below that of other untrained infants of corresponding chronological age who had not been given special stimulation in this activity.

Walking Up and Down Inclines

Since an infant who is beginning to assume an erect posture and engage in erect locomotion will tend to rise often into a standing position if placed on the slides for creeping, further study of the behavior in going up and down the inclines of low grade was continued with the infant in the erect position. There are two factors which are paramount in determining the mode of behavior in this situation. The first is the degree of maturation the baby has attained in the development of walking, and the second is the slope of the incline. Inclines of even low grade will, when the infant is first confronted with them, evoke a more immature ambulatory pattern than that which is at the time characteristic of the baby as he walks on a flat surface.

The first time an infant starts to walk up an incline he flexes the lower extremities at the knees and the pelvis and extends and abducts the upper extremities, even though he is able to walk on a flat surface with a well-integrated heel-toe stepping movement. He is also likely to revert to a wide base, even though he characteristically steps one foot in front of the other when walking on the floor. Even if his locomotion under ordinary conditions is a well-coördinated, consecutive, smooth stepping movement, when he first starts up an incline his movements become isolated, cautious, and hesitating.

The incline presents an unfamiliar situation to the baby, and for that reason many more of his extensor muscles are brought into action. The great toes are extended and adducted, and the other toes tend to grip the surface of the slide as he edges his feet along inch by inch. In the beginning the baby will make only a few steps before he reverts to the creeping posture. Of course, the speed with which he overcomes these immature behavior-modes is determined by the maturational state of his walking patterns. The older infant who is walking well the first time he meets the acclivous situation has only his attitude to reëducate. Therefore, as soon as an acquiescent attitude is achieved a well-developed walking pattern on the slide is at his command. But the younger infant who is just acquiring the ability to walk alone must develop the somatic activities involved, together with a cooperative attitude. These two developing factors may at times counteract each other. For example, an eager, acquiescing attitude may spur the child on to more daring steps, and his daring may take him beyond the possibilities of his motor performance; consequently he will lose balance and fall.

However, as the baby becomes familiar with the situation and as his control over the acts of walking develops, it is observed that in ascending the low inclines flexion in the lower extremities decreases, the upper extremities are held down by the sides, and the infant walks up the incline with a smooth, integrated gait. But an increase in the acclivity will again bring out a reversion to the less mature pattern. If the acclivity is sufficiently steep, the child retains the isolated movements, the extended and abducted position of the upper extremities, and the flexion of the lower extremities at the hips and the knees. This flexion of the lower extremities brings the body forward so as to aid in the maintenance of balance. In fact, adults make essentially these same adjustments when walking up steep slopes. In many ways it appeared as if the young child experienced less difficulty in walking up the steeper inclines than an adult would. It is possible that the difference is really due to a difference in bodily ratios, but so far as the data of this investigation are concerned this is merely an impression.

One interesting feature on the part of young children when walking up steeper slopes was a noticeable proclivity to assume a creeping posture as they neared the top of the slide. The actual relation of the child to the slope remains constant whether he is near the top or the bottom. The fact that the babies tend to fall over into a creeping posture near the top of an incline on which they have already walked two thirds of the distance, together with the fact that in descending they are likely to break into uncontrolled running steps near the floor, suggests that visual perception is exercising an important influence in determining the child's behavior.

It is more difficult for the infant to walk down than to walk up an incline. The initial behavior-mode in descending consists of the same aspects of flexion of the lower extremities, extension and abduction of the upper extremities, gripping with the toes against the surface of the slide, and isolated or poorly integrated movements. When descending a decline of unfamiliar steepness the baby will start out with tiny, slow, isolated steps˗ for a short distance, then lose control and run down the balance of the way. The running is an indication of inadequate rather than superior control over the performance. When going down the steeper inclines these modes of activity remain as characteristic of the infant's behavior-pattern. As a matter of fact they are common in the behavior repertoire of the adult when confronted with similar situations. But the infant soon masters a smooth, easy gait when descending the low declines, so that ultimately his later running up and down an incline of 11° becomes indicative of advanced development rather than inadequate control.

There were slopes of five different degrees on which Johnny had repeated experience in walking up and down. His activity on each slide will be discussed in order from the lowest to the steepest. The degrees of slope were as follows: 18°, 24°, 32°, 38°, 40°. Daily practice in walking up and down an incline of 11° was begun when Johnny was only 336 days old. He had been walking alone only a short while. Therefore he was still walking with a wide base, using his upper extremities as a balancing accessory, and his progression was extremely dyssynergic. When he was placed on the incline these aspects of the behavior-course became more accentuated. Even when using all the equipment at his command he was able to make only two or three consecutive steps before falling. Improvement was soon apparent, however. Although his movements were dyssynergic, within three days he succeeded in walking up the length of the 72-in. slide without falling once. By the time he was 366 days old his behavior in walking up this low-grade slide consisted of modes of locomotion as well controlled as were observed when he was walking on the floor. When 347 days old he had walked alone up the incline of 18°, though with considerably less efficiency than showed in walking up the incline of 11°. This poorer control was indicated by his tendency to take short steps and pause between steps and by an impulse to stoop over and creep, though he did not actually do so.

His mode of action in coming down these low slides consisted of tiny steps, so tiny indeed that he scarcely lifted the foot off the slide as he moved it forward. During the last half of the slide he would lose control and break into running steps or fall forward. His lower extremities were flexed at the knee and pelvis; the upper extremities were extended and abducted. There was a marked tendency for the toes to grip the surface of the slide. In ascending acclivities of 24° and 32° there was a tendency for him to fall over into a creeping position as he neared the top. By the time Johnny was 414 days old he was able to go up and down the incline of 24° with considerable proficiency. Though he still used his upper extremities for balancing, he did not lose balance frequently. During the early phases, if he did lose his balance assistance was necessary to enable him to regain a standing posture on the slide. When he was 427 days old, if he lost his balance he regained it himself and continued on his way upward or downward.

When he was 396 days old he walked up the slide placed at an angle of 32°. It is noted that, at the age of 414 days, if he started to lose balance when descending this incline he would not allow himself to fall off but would get into a squatting or sitting position, in that way checking the fall. For a long period he continued to make tiny steps when descending an incline of this steepness. As a matter of fact at times his feet movements could scarcely be called steps since they consisted essentially of extending and flexing the toes so as to move the foot forward. The distance was less than an inch at a time. He began making quite well-controlled walking steps in descending an incline of 32° when he was 463 days old.

When Johnny was 722 days old he successfully walked up an incline placed at the incredible angle of 40°. It is possible that he would have accomplished this younger had the situation been presented to him earlier. For several days he had been walking about two thirds of the distance up but as he neared the top he would bend over slightly and grasp one edge of the slide in order to aid himself in balancing. In ascending this steep grade it was impossible for his steps to be plantigrade. The pressure of the foot against the surface was at the metatarsal arch. His heels did not touch the slide, but he had sufficient gripping power in his toes to make the ascent. He was much more proficient in descending than in ascending this steep incline. This is interesting, since earlier he walked up the other slopes with greater ease than he did down them. His manner of action in walking down this 40° slope was essentially the same as that used in descending the incline of 32°, except that all of the compensatory balancing reactions were more marked. There was greater flexion in the lower extremities, greater use of the upper extremities in balancing, more isolated movement, and a greater tendency to lose control and revert to running steps as he neared the bottom. Even so, his performance excelled that of the older children or adults whom the experimenter has had the occasion to observe in this situation.

During the period of Jimmy's service as a control the divergence of his behavior from that of Johnny in this situation was beyond comparison. In walking up or down these slides Jimmy made no progress. He would stand at the end of the slide reaching vainly for the lure which was held just beyond him. Sometimes he would stoop to get into a sitting position. On only one occasion, when he was 473 days old, did he walk the entire distance up the 11° incline. Never once during his first twenty-two months of life did he walk up or down the slide when it was placed at an angle of 18° or greater, though he was given an opportunity to do so at biweekly, and finally monthly, intervals. Obviously Jimmy's failure to walk up and down these low inclines cannot be attributed to an undeveloped somatic mechanism. His uncoöperative attitude to the total situation figured largely in determining Jimmy's somatic pattern of behavior.

There is surely no doubt that in performances of this sort repetition of the activity influenced not only the development of a more coöperative attitude on the part of Johnny but a definite expansion in the somatic aspect of the activity during the practice period. Jimmy's lack of experience obviously influenced the development of an uncoöperative attitude, and his attitude in turn inhibited his somatic performance. It is impossible, therefore, to ascertain how much his limitation of experience directly influenced his motor performance.

Development in Getting Off Stools

It was noted in connection with the development of a sitting posture that infants are able to sit erect on a flat surface before they can maintain an erect sitting posture with the knees flexed over an edge so that the feet rest on a lower plane. It was also observed that an infant can sit in the latter position and maintain a fair degree of equilibrium before he can maintain comparable balance when seated with the lower extremities hanging from the knees over the edge of the surface on which he is sitting. The first phase of the behavior-course in the infant reveals a lack of control over the act of sitting and a tendency to topple forward, usually head first. As he begins to gain greater resistance against gravity he is likely to fall backward. Finally he is able to maintain an erect sitting position, though he will use the upper extremities, extended and abducted, to aid in the maintenance of balance.

For a while, though he is able to maintain the sitting position with his feet hanging over the edge, it is necessary for him to give his utmost attention to the task. If his attention is drawn to an object out of reach or if for any reason he becomes excited, he is likely to topple forward again in the immature fashion. Soon, however, he learns to maintain balance and at the same time focus his attention upon the object out of reach. He will reach forward toward the object, but discovering that it is beyond the length of his arm he will again straighten up into a sitting position. He learns to judge how far he can bend his trunk forward without losing control and falling over. Presently it is observed that the infant does not continue to reach vainly for the object beyond arm's length. He perceives that it is beyond arm's reach, though he has not yet learned to bridge the gap between him and the line. We endeavored to study the progressive development of the child in meeting this difficulty. Stools of various heights ranging from 7½ in. to 63¼ in. and measuring 18 x 18 in. on the top surface constitute part of the laboratory equipment. The child is seated upon these stools of varying height and his attention is directed to a lure or object on the floor in front of the stool. When he first begins to realize the difficulty of the situation, the object excites a great deal of diffuse activity, though he is able to maintain a sitting posture. The first inchoate movement toward the development of a definite pattern is indicated when his upper extremities, which are no longer indispensable as a balancing accessory, are held down by his sides. He holds them down toward the surface of the stool as if preparatory to the next phase of development in this activity, which involves his grasping the edge of the stool.

He now begins to show a glimmer of understanding that if he is to bridge the gap between him and the lure he must get himself off the stool. Placing his hands on the edge of the stool is an inchoate act in that direction. This partially developed movement is often accompanied by some rather useless, excess movements such as drawing the lower extremities up on top of the stool, putting them down again, and in other ways indicating a lack of cognition and mastery of the total situation. At this stage, although the baby perceives that in order to achieve the object he must get off the stool, he has not the vaguest notion as to how it can be accomplished.

But gradually these excess movements are eliminated, and the baby turning his trunk slightly to one side takes hold of one edge of the stool with both of his hands. After he grasps the edge of the stool he begins to pitch his body forward a little. Of course in so doing he loses control and tumbles helplessly to the floor. This failure to retain his grasp on the edge of the stool until he has carefully let himself to the floor represents a fusion of the tendency to rotate his body preparatory to getting off the stool and the evanescent penchant thrusting his body directly forward toward the object. One phase overlaps with the other both in time and in pattern. Consequently, there is a time when either response may be elicited. Presently it is observed that he is gaining greater use of the grasp on the edge of the stool, as is indicated by the fact that both hands retain a grasp of the same corner as his body swings around sufficiently for his feet to reach the floor, thereby avoiding a fall.

A successive phase of development is indicated when the baby learns to rotate his body from a sitting to a prone position while he is on the stool, thus flexing his body over the edge of the stool about the level of the waist-line. In this position he can then grasp opposite edges of the stool with each hand, in order to slide them along the edge of the stool, thereby lowering his body until his feet touch the floor. When he has attained this phase of development he has an adequate mechanism for getting off the lower stools. While it is an adequate technique for getting off the lower stools, it is not the most economical. As will be seen by his later method, it is possible to get off the stool without going into the complex movement of rotating into a prone position. There is less waste motion when he holds on to one side of the stool and slides his buttocks forward on the stool surface until his feet are near the floor; then a slight extension of the spine, just as the buttocks get to the edge of the stool, is sufficient to get him off into a standing position on the floor.

There is a period when the baby can get off the stools if he is placed in a sitting position with his feet suspended over the edge, but if he is placed in a standing position on the stool new difficulties are introduced. At one period he will step off the stool into space, apparently having no appreciation of height. This period is followed by a time when he engages in considerable purposeless activity. He steps first on one foot and then the other on top of the stool but does not move forward or step off. This action is another illustration of disorganized activity when an understanding of the total situation is inadequate. Subsequently he begins to squat on the stool and grasp the stool edge while he is in the squatting position. He has great difficulty learning to move one foot from beneath him in order to get into a sitting from a standing position on the stool. As he squats on the stool he may, from fatigue, drop lower and lower until finally the buttocks rest on the stool. In this way he seats himself too far back on the stool to have the lower extremities dangling over the edge.

Being seated far back on the stool introduces a new difficulty, for it necessitates the infant's learning to edge himself forward on the stool surface until his lower extremities will hang suspended from the knees over the edge of the stool. With further development he avoids this difficulty. From the standing position he bends over enough to grasp the stool edge, then he flexes and abducts one lower extremity preparatory to getting himself in a sitting position. This method allows him to get seated in the middle of the stool so that his legs are suspended from the edge. Later when getting off a low stool from a standing position he will not go to the trouble of assuming a sitting position as the initial move. He will instead merely stoop on the stool, grasp one edge and drop both lower extremities off the opposite side. In this way all excess movements are eliminated so that he makes the performance in the most economical fashion.

Although a baby has acquired the technique of getting off low stools, when placed on stools higher than his body length he is confronted with new difficulties and engages in a new type of excess activity. He will turn immediately into a prone position so that his lower extremities are suspended over one edge of the stool. When he cannot touch the floor with his feet he draws himself again to a hand-knee position and turns sufficiently to try another edge of the stool. Still he cannot reach the floor, and he continues to try different sides of the stool. On some occasions he lets himself down a little lower, so low indeed that he cannot again get up on top of the stool, though he is still grasping the opposite edge with his hands. He holds this obviously uncomfortable position as long as he can until, utterly fatigued, he drops helplessly to the floor.

In the next phase of development in this activity the baby not only rotates into the prone position over the edge of the stool, but gradually slides his hands forward, grasping the opposite edges of the stool until they are near the front edge. With first one hand and then the other he takes hold of the edge of the stool which he is facing in order to lower his body as far as possible. Finally he deliberately releases his grasp so that he will fall to the floor. This is the characteristic method used by young children in climbing off pedestals such as were used in this study. There is considerable individual variation in the height of a stool from which a child will undertake to climb down.

While the writer has spoken of a sequence in the phases of development in this behavior-course, it must not be inferred that once the infant has acquired a new method he ceases to use the previous one, or that once he has overcome a particular difficulty he is never stalled by it again. There is the same characteristic overlapping of one phase with another in the development of these activities as has been noted in the development of other more primitive behavior-patterns.

In the comparative study of the twins in this situation, striking differences are revealed in the performances of Johnny and Jimmy between the ages of eight and twenty-two months—differences which can be explained adequately only in terms of the effect of daily repetition of the activity which composed part of Johnny's schedule. Jimmy began, three weeks younger than did Johnny, to develop equilibratory control when he was seated with his feet hanging over an edge. But soon Johnny began to excel both Jimmy and other babies of corresponding chronological age in the activity of getting himself off pedestals. By the time he was 261 days old he could maintain balance sitting on top of a stool with his lower extremities dangling. But if a new element such as interest in an object were introduced, it would generally disturb his equilibratory control so that he would topple over. Within a week, however, he was able to maintain a sitting posture even if the presence of an object stimulated a great deal of excited and excess activity. If at that time he started to reach for the object, he would bend his body so far forward that he fell helplessly to the floor. At this age he had not acquired any understanding of differences in height, as was indicated by his reaching for the object until he fell head foremost, no matter what height stool he was placed upon. The fact that he had no appreciation of differences in height at this age was further demonstrated when he was placed on the stools in a standing position. If the object were held beyond his reach he would walk off the stool into space. There was no flexing of the lower extremities at the knee as he stepped off to indicate that he expected to step down on a lower plane. Furthermore, he would step off into space regardless of the height of the stool.

Johnny began to receive daily exercise in turning off these stools when he was 269 days old. Since the experimenters had observed that the chosen method of older infants was to rotate in a prone position on the stool in order to get off, Johnny was directed during practice to take hold of the edge of the stool and turn his body to one side before throwing himself forward. When he was 347 days old he began deliberately turning his body to one side as he grasped one edge of the stool with both hands, but it was practically a month before he was able to turn his body sufficiently to get his buttocks entirely off the stool. When he was 373 days old he was, when placed in a sitting position, able to get entirely off the stools without assistance from the experimenter. Therefore the situation was made more difficult for him by having him stand on the stool instead of sitting with his feet hanging off before he was directed to get off the stool entirely. Since he had by that time begun to develop sufficient cognition of height levels to prevent his blindly stepping off into space, the standing position on the stool created something of a new problem for him.

When placed in this position he was obviously in a situation

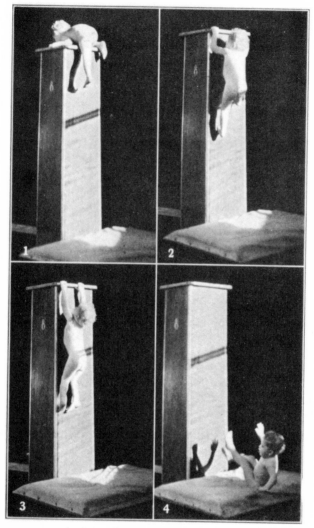

PLATE IV. GETTING OFF STOOLS

1, 2, 3, 4. Johnny gets off a 63¼-inch stool at twenty-one months.

PLATE IV. GETTING OFF STOOLS (*continued*)

5. Jimmy refuses to climb off a lower stool.

beyond his control. His difficulty was indicated by his tendency to squat on the stool, then rise, then squat again. He was unable to get into a sitting position on the stool, although from a sitting position he could readily get off a stool 38¼ in. in height. He succeeded independently in getting into a sitting position on the stool the first time when he was 399 days old. But after he had seated himself he discovered he was so far back on the stool that he could not turn into a prone position. In order to rotate into a prone position, preparatory to dropping his body off the stool, it was necessary to get his legs extended over the edge. Otherwise when he turned he would fall off. The next step, therefore, in his learning was to edge himself forward until his knees could flex over the stool edge. He edged himself from a position toward the back of the stool by shifting his weight from one ischium to the other and pulling with his hands on the stool edge as he did so. It was approximately a week before he learned to edge himself forward so that the lower extremities were dangling off the stool, thereby making it possible for him to rotate into a prone position preparatory to dropping his body down. There followed a period when the shifting of weight from one buttock to the other was reduced until the movement consisted merely of pulling his body forward until the lower extremities were well off the stool. Ultimately he eliminated this difficulty of edging himself forward by flexing and abducting one leg as he changed from the standing to the sitting position on the stool. This movement seated him sufficiently near the front that his legs were over the edge by the time he got himself seated. Later he often eliminated even the phase of sitting preparatory to rotating his body. He then stooped and placed one knee on top of the stool as he dropped the opposite lower extremity over the edge of the stool. The movements at this stage were so integrated as to appear almost as one. If one considers for a moment the steps involved in Johnny's preparatory movements in getting from a standing position on a stool onto the floor, it is easily discerned that the process during the initial phase of each aspect of the pattern is primarily a matter of eliminating excess movements. At that stage the movements were isolated. The final stage of development is primarily a matter of integrating these isolated movements so that the several movements are put together until they constitute almost a single movement.

Johnny had developed an adequate method of getting off stools higher than his body length by the time he was 400 days old. He had learned to shift his grasp on the edge of the stool in order to hold on to one edge with both hands as he lowered his body as near as possible to the floor. He also would then deliberately release his grasp in order to drop himself to the floor. As he dropped himself his face struck the vertical side of the columnar pedestal, but he very quickly learned to kick his left foot against the side of the stool just before he released his grasp. This little kick against the side was sufficient to throw his body out enough that his face would not strike the side of the stool as he fell. To throw himself out from the stool in this way was an adjustment of his own creation which followed after several occasions of striking his face against the side of the stool.

Additional evidences of his growing discrimination with respect to height differences was indicated when at the age of 413 days and subsequently he would readily get off a stool of familiar height but, when placed upon a higher one, would engage in more excess and preparatory movements or even complain and reach to be lifted down. When he was 464 days old he began getting off a stool 63¼ in. high. Differences in the height of the stool did not alter his method of getting down provided the stool was higher than his own body length. On the other hand, differences in height did modify his attitude or willingness to climb down. On one occasion when he dropped off the 63¼-in. stool he bit his tongue. There followed a period of resistance to climbing off the pedestal of this height. This resistance lasted only ten days, and by the time he was 486 days old he was taking such delight in this activity that he would ask to be placed upon the stool.

The emergence of a newly developing activity sometimes interferes with performances previously acquired. In this instance jumping interfered for a while with the act of climbing off a pedestal. Johnny was exercised in standing upon the same 63¼-in. pedestal and jumping into the arms of the experimenter. He came to delight in that performance. Often then when placed on the stool he would hold out his arms, indicating that he preferred to jump rather than climb off, but never once did he jump from this high stool when an adult was not standing beside it to catch him. Furthermore, he was always able to distinguish by the position of the adult which performance was expected of him. On one occasion when he preferred to jump rather than to climb down but the experimenter, insisting on his getting down himself, would not stand near to catch him, he sat on top of the stool for an hour. Whenever the experimenter passed in the room he would extend his arms, thereby indicating his desire to jump. But he did not jump, since the experimenter never stood near enough to receive him. He was contented and gleeful in his high position on the pedestal, so at the end of an hour the experimenter, acknowledging him the victor, assisted him in getting down. The conflict in jumping and climbing off stools was an interference of attitudes toward the two acts rather than an interference of somatic aspects of the two performances.

The behavior of Jimmy during his period of limited activity, between eight and twenty-two months of age, was strikingly different. Although he had between the ages of 245 and 260 days shown a better start than Johnny in the maintenance of balance when seated on the edge of the stool and although he gained the ability to maintain equilibratory control in this position as he reached for an object in front of him younger than did Johnny, his subsequent behavior indicated a definite retardation in this performance. At the age of 308 days, when he was placed on a stool 14¼ in. high, he reached for the object shown him until he lost control and then fell forward on the floor. When placed on a higher stool he reached toward the object vainly but restrained himself from falling forward. He was then evincing some slight discrimination. From the time he was 337 days old until he was 672 days old he did not succeed in getting off even the lowest stool. In general his mode of behavior consisted of reaching futilely toward the object, a great deal of crying, and calling to the experimenter for help. Neither the desire to have the lure or his aversion to the situation was sufficient inducement to stimulate him to get off the lowest pedestals.

It is, therefore, quite safe to conclude that so far as this particular activity is concerned the effect of practice materially advanced the performance of Johnny during the practice period and that the lack of experience curtailed the somatic actions of Jimmy. Since Jimmy would not attempt to get off stools only 7½ in. high, his failure to do so was not a matter of inadequate motor ability. His attitude toward the situation interfered with his performance on both low and high stools, so that it was impossible to determine to what extent the somatic aspect of his performance *per se* might have been impaired by virtue of his lack of experience.

Skating

Growth in equilibratory control is one of the important aspects in the development of independent walking. In this investigation the experimenters essayed to devise schemes of studying the development of a particular function under conditions which would make the activity gradually more difficult for the child to perform. Therefore, when the baby first began to show signs of developing equilibrium in the upright position, we designed situations which would gradually increase his difficulty in maintaining equilibrium. It was for that purpose the baby was placed on roller-skates.

Since we have not attempted to measure development in roller-skating behavior of all the babies who have been under the observation of the experimenters, we must draw primarily upon the intensive study of Johnny for an analysis of the phases of development in this activity. Other infants have on occasions been studied in the roller-skating situation, but their performances have not been followed systematically over a period of time. Since, however, our records of Johnny in this respect consist of descriptive notes made on eighty-nine different days plus 500 feet of motion-picture film covering his development in this performance during a period of fourteen months, we believe that the essential phases in the development of this activity have been revealed. Furthermore this detailed, day-by-day study of a particular individual in the development of a particular performance or skill is extremely illuminating with respect to the fundamental processes of growth. Because of the intensity of the study this detailed report, even on one individual, is warranted.

When 350 days old Johnny, still in a stage of erect locomotion when his walking was quite dyssynergic, had his first experience on roller-skates. At first non-ball-bearing skates were used and he was stood upon a mat 6 mm. in thickness so that his feet should not constantly roll from under him. When on the mat he could for a few moments maintain the erect posture even with the skates on. If he started to move forward his impulse obviously was to lift his feet up as if making a walking step. Without the aid of the fairly thick mat he was unable to maintain an erect posture. He cried, sat down, and pulled at the skates and tried to get them off. Two days later he absolutely refused to stand up on the skates; even on the mat he became limp and dropped in a heap. This attitude, however, was transitory. In order to correct his tendency to make walking steps when on the skates the experimenter pushed his feet along alternately so as to suggest to him the act of rolling his feet on the surface. Within four days he had apparently begun to get the idea, as was indicated by his first attempt to roll his foot rather than lift it. However, this was only an ephemeral, inchoate response indicating the inception of an association, while his most characteristic behavior on the skates continued to be that of lifting up his feet to make steps. Gradually the idea took root, and four days later he made eight consecutive rolling movements with his feet. On this day he also demonstrated his ability to stoop and pick up toys from the floor while he was on skates on the mat.

Since the experimenters endeavored to seriate the difficulties of the situation for the child, he was on the 360th day placed on a thin mat, 1 mm. in thickness, instead of the thicker one. His sliding steps were as good if not better on the thin mat than on the thick one, though he did tend to fall more frequently. Four days later he was placed on the floor. There was a greater tendency for his feet to spread, and he would lose his balance, but once he got started he was able to make more sliding steps than in previous situations. This difference in performance is easily understood, since the mats would impede movement but would aid in the maintenance of balance. When his feet began to spread he was unable to make the accommodation of adducting the lower extremities, thereby narrowing his base.

By the time he was 364 days old he showed no signs of picking up his feet to step. The notion of pushing his feet forward rather than stepping had become established. Accordingly, at this time he was placed upon ball-bearing skates. The differences in his activity on ball-bearing and ordinary skates at this time were not noticeably great, so from that time on practice was continued on the ball-bearing skates only. Although he rolled his feet on the floor, the movements of the lower extremities were isolated and slow. The upper part of the body appeared not to be actively involved in the movement of progression. Of course the body moved forward, but it gave the impression of moving forward because the feet carried it and not because it was actively engaged in the associated complementary movements which constitute a part of the well-developed skating performance. An objective measure of the isolated character of his movements is revealed in a count of the 16-mm. cinema frames from one stride to a successive one. Such a count shows that it took him on the average one second to move one foot forward and that there was a pause of ⅝ second before the other foot started moving. At the age of 375 days a slight sway of the shoulders and trunk was observed to accompany the rolling motion of the feet forward. He used the upper extremities a great deal in extension and abduction as a balancing accessory. He was by this time well adjusted to the situation. His movements were slow and cautious, but his development in equilibratory control was evidenced by the fact that he fell only infrequently, even when covering a distance of fifteen or twenty feet. As a matter of fact, he became so acquiescent in the situation that for a period of twenty days or more there was no appreciable evidence of progress in his performance.

In order to stimulate him to put forth more effort the experimenters placed him in a situation where he would have to skate up and down a slight acclivity in the hall. The slope of this incline was 3.6°. In going up this slope he would push a foot forward, but before he could get sufficient control to push the next one forward the first one had slipped back. Soon, however, he began to make the adjustment of rotating his right foot externally in order to prevent slipping back. This tendency was carried over to his method of skating when on a flat surface until he began to use his right foot as a pusher in order to make progress. This method and his increasing acquiescent attitude improved his speed of progress both on the flat surface and the gradual incline. Four days later practice was begun on a steeper cement incline. As usual he complained and experienced greater difficulty, and his mode of behavior was of an immature type. The slope of this steeper incline was 4.5°. But practice on the steeper incline soon appeared to be improving his skating performance.

When he was 441 days old there was not only a greater increase in speed but a noticeable reduction in the tendency to use his right foot as a pusher. He began to move the right and left foot alternately. There was more evidence of a sway in the upper part of the body concurrent with alternate pushing with his feet. It was observed when he was 469 days old that his initial move was not a movement of the lower extremity forward, but that movement of the lower extremity was preceded slightly by a movement of the shoulder girdle. In other words, the upper part of his body was beginning to play not only an accompanying but a leading part in his skating movements. By the time he was 548 days old this movement had developed into a sweeping stroke with one foot, then a short coast before the opposite foot pushed forward in rhythmical sequence. This type of movement became more and more manifest, so that by the time he was 694 days old his mode of action consisted primarily of the broad rhythmical body sway which is characteristic of a proficient skater. Count of the cinema frames at this time shows that there was no pause between glides but that the left foot started moving before the right had stopped. In other words the act had become integrated.

Since Johnny was showing such extraordinary control on the four-wheel ball-bearing rollers he was placed upon two-wheel ball-bearing rollers when he was 599 days old. The gap between this situation and the ball-bearing four-wheels was so great that it practically constituted a new situation for him. There recurred many immature aspects of the behavior-patterns when he was first placed on these skates. He experienced great difficulty in maintaining balance, and his lower extremities would become abducted. As they did so he was unable to adduct them in order to reduce his base to prevent falling. There did not recur the tendency to lift his feet for stepping. The connection of skates and rolling his feet had become sufficiently established to withstand the new factors in the situation. Even the first day, he managed to take two slides on the two-wheel rollers, though most of his energies were devoted to the maintenance of an erect posture.

In less than a month he was able to traverse eight or ten feet across a cement floor on the two-wheel roller-skates. He would complain and object to these skates, but there was no indication whatever that his objection to them was transferred to the four-wheel rollers. In fact he appeared to enjoy the four-wheels all the more. When he was 639 days old he was showing a slight body sway when moving on the two-wheeler rollers, although it was a transitory pattern which appeared at infrequent intervals. He never succeeded in getting a graceful skating rhythm on these two-wheel rollers during the period of this investigation.

At the time daily experience of the skating activity was terminated he was making rapid progress not only in skating *per se* but in the assumption of an erect posture when he was on skates. Although he did not in the beginning know how to adduct his lower extremities when his feet began to spread, he could, within only a week after his first experience on skates, stoop to pick up toys from the floor and then regain the erect posture. He could not, however, get into an erect posture from a sitting position when he had his skates on until he was 426 days old, more than two months after his first experience on skates. When he did begin to rise from the sitting position, his method of getting up consisted of rolling into a prone position, getting into the hand-knee position, and then planting his hands securely on the floor. Holding his hands steadily on the floor, he would extend the lower extremities at the knees so that his body for a second was suspended above the floor, his only support being on his hands and the toes of his skates. Then he would flex both lower extremities at the pelvis and flex the foot on the leg slightly, thus bringing his feet in juxtaposition to his hands on the floor. When his feet were securely placed on the floor in this position he raised up the superior part of his body. In the initial phase of this rising act he frequently lost control so as to fall over on his side after he had gotten both hands and feet on the floor. The experimenter would occasionally lend slight assistance by holding the pelvic girdle steady as he raised the trunk upward. By the time he was 428 days old he seldom needed any assistance in rising. Further efficiency in this aspect of the performance was indicated by the speed and control with which he exercised the act rather than any major change in method. When rising on the two-wheel rollers there was a reversion to many of the immature phases first noted in the activity on the four-wheel skates. He would lose control in the pelvic region and topple over in a lateral position. Although he succeeded in getting into an erect position, the first time he had the two-wheel skates on, it was a transitory performance. It was twenty days before he did it successfully **again**, and thirty-five days before it was an established, well-developed behavior-pattern.

Coasting on Skates

Johnny had his first experience in coasting down a gradual slope of 3.6° when he was 413 days old. At first the movement surprised him, but he was able to maintain his balance as he coasted for a short distance. It is strange how infants can perceive a solution in situations which are known to be perfectly new to them. Even on the first day, as he started down he turned in toward the wall soon after he had started coasting. Although his feet had slipped from under him several times, causing him to fall, there is no reason why the experience of falling should suggest the wall as a solution to prevent it. It is, however, possible that his turning into the wall was not a matter of discrimination initiated to avoid a fall but instead an indication of the lack of ability to steer his course straight. A desirable check on this problem would have been to observe his coasting behavior in an open space. If he turned off to one side when there was no wall to break his progress, it might reasonably be presumed that his doing so was due to undeveloped steering abilities and not to an appreciation of the situation. Unfortunately the facilities of the clinic did not offer this possibility, but—in so far as the experimenters' judgment, not supported by definite experimental evidence, can be of value—the infant's turning toward the wall was an act of inadequate steering ability rather than discrimination or the selection of a means to break the coasting movement.

Johnny soon recovered from his surprise or perhaps antipathy toward the coasting situation and even during the second experience was showing some evidence of delight and enjoyment in this activity. When 425 days old he had learned to adduct the lower extremities and rotate the foot inward if his feet started to spread as he was coasting down the grade. Five days later he started coasting down a steeper grade of 4.5°. At first on the steeper grade he would tend to turn into the wall. But by the time he was 450 days old he was not only steering a straight course but could steer around curves even when he was coasting at a rapid rate. Further development in coasting was indicated by an increase in speed and distance over which he could maintain control without falling. When he was 520 days old he was able to coast a distance of 188 feet on a gradual slope of 3.1°. Although he was gathering momentum all the while, he was able to maintain his position without falling. There were days, of course, both before and after this date when he would fall or stop several times during the distance, but this was the first occasion that he had been able to coast the entire distance without stopping. The stops and falls grew steadily less frequent.

Development was also indicated not only in the fact that his frequency of falling was reduced but in his method of falling when coasting. At first his feet got ahead of him so he thumped to the floor in a sitting position, having lost all control over the activity. Later when he started to fall his upper extremities would became greatly extended and abducted, the spine would extend but he would still fall heavily on the buttocks. Gradually, however, he learned to squat as he started to fall. He would bend his trunk forward to compensate for the fact that his feet were getting ahead of him, then he would flex the lower extremities so that by the time his feet were in front of him his buttocks were not so far above the floor. In making this response the upper extremities were not extended and abducted above the head but were held down by his sides, and a flexion at the wrist placed his hands in a position to strike the surface and thus to break the force of the fall.

When Johnny was 600 days old he was playing at the top of the steep cement decline when the force of gravity started him coasting down backward. He appeared surprised at the sensation, but after turning around and seeing the experimenter's approval he deliberately turned again to give it another try. From that day on practice was given at each period in coasting backward as well as forward. From the beginning he would attempt to steer, although he was not very successful in doing so. Within five days, however, he was trying to steer not only by adjusting his feet but by turning his face slightly to one side so that he could watch the wall in order to guide his course. He continued to gain in steering abilities and in the distance he would coast backward before turning around. Coasting down the steeper incline backward when he was 730 days old, he spontaneously stooped over to place his hands on his feet. In this way he could see between his legs in order to steer more efficiently. When 773 days old his proclivities for trying new techniques were further evidenced by his lightly touching his fingers on the floor as he coasted down backward, still steering himself as he looked between his legs. Friction of his fingers on the floor checked his speed. It probably irritated his fingers, and he apparently did not favor the method, since as soon as he tumbled once he resumed his position of coasting backward with his hands on his feet as he coasted. He never tried holding his fingers on the floor as he coasted again. One cannot avoid noting the difference in the way a deliberate experimental act on the part of the child is eliminated in contrast to the way excess activities associated with developmental stages of a behavior-pattern are gradually reduced to the minimum.

In giving this account of Johnny's learning the performance of skating the writer has mentioned specifically the dates when particular modes of behavior were first observed and has not attempted to convey the complete picture of the overlapping of successive patterns. This analysis does reveal, however, the outstanding phases in the development of this performance.

Jimmy was not exposed to this situation during his period of restricted activity. Nevertheless, the skating performance of Johnny is so outstandingly beyond that of any other child of corresponding chronological age that it would be impossible to deny the influence of daily exercise or repetition of performance upon the development of a specific skill of this type.

Jumping

Jumping is one of the most interesting activities in the behavior repertoire of the young child. In most children it does not begin to develop until the latter part of the second or the first part of the third year. The situations used in this investigation for the purpose of studying the development of the jumping activity consisted of: (1) having the children jump off low stools onto the floor and (2) having them jump from high pedestals into the receiving arms of an adult. It will be necessary to analyze their actions in these two situations in order to reveal both the phases of development and the many factors which enter into this behavior-course.

The fully developed act of jumping embodies initially (1) flexion of the lower extremities at the three major flexion foci, (2) a momentary resting of the weight on the metatarsal arches preparatory to the extension and springing aspects of the act, and (3) a slight flexion of the spine which brings the body forward. The flexion of the lower extremities is followed by (4) an immediate extension at the pelvis, the knees, and the ankle, and (5) extension of the spine. The extensor movement is synchronous with (6) a thrust of the body forward, backward, or laterally. Usually the arms are extended and abducted during the spring forward. Infants of seven or eight months, before they can stand alone, will when held erect flex and extend their lower extremities in rapid succession while their feet are held in position. This activity has been referred to as "jumping" in an earlier Chapter, but it must be distinguished from the later type of behavior which develops in the child of two years or older. This latter activity involves not only the flexor-extensor movement but a change in the locus of the body-position.

The mode of action in the jumping behavior is contingent upon (1) the maturational status of the child at the time he is first confronted with the situation and (2) the distance demanded in the jumping situation. In the present investigation we did not begin to study jumping activity until the infant was able to stand erect. By that time many and complex elements have already entered into the behavior-course which determine the character or form of the initial act. For example, the baby at this stage is beginning to have appreciation of differences in height, and he is also learning or has learned to extend his arms to an adult to be lifted. The initial act of an infant at this stage of maturation when placed on a high pedestal and urged by an adult to jump into receiving arms consists of extending his arm toward the adult as if indicating that he wishes to be taken. His height discrimination prevents his stepping off into space. The outstretched arms of the adult activate an impulse on the part of the child to be taken, and he responds to the outstretched arms of the adult in a familiar way. If the adult does not take him, he stoops in order to shorten the distance between him and the adult. The stooping becomes more and more exaggerated until it results in his squatting in order to bring himself nearer to the outstretched arms. He reaches his utmost to touch the adult. Unable to do so, he may throw his body forward head foremost or he may resume the standing position.

In a later stage of development when the idea of jumping is making an appearance, he is less inclined to stoop or squat imme-

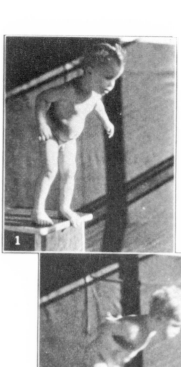

1, 2, 3. Johnny has developed a spring as he jumps from a high stool. 4. Jimmy refuses to jump from the high stool.

PLATE V. JUMPING BEHAVIOR

diately. Instead he stands on the stool shifting his weight from one foot to the other as he reaches toward the experimenter. His reaching is now more of a symbol indicating an impulse to jump than it is a definite effort to bridge the gap between him and the adult. He has obviously become aware that the gap must be bridged in order to meet the situation adequately, but he does not yet have command of a technique for bridging it. Being unable to complete the act while standing, he regresses to the squatting phase and reaching toward the experimenter. But this time his reaching involves a good deal more than merely raising up his arms to be lifted. There is also a muscular tension, or straining, deliberately to throw his body forward. His cognition of height and distance inhibit his actually throwing himself forward, and hence he resumes the standing position. By and by the impulse to throw his body forward becomes more dominant, but it is not as yet integrated with the flexion of the lower extremities. Hence he raises one foot and steps off the pedestal, throwing his body forward as he does so. The next phase in the development of the jumping pattern consists in a flexion of the lower extremities as if to jump, but as he tends to overdo this aspect of the performance he gets into a squatting position. Squatting which occurred earlier was, so far as the child was concerned, but an aspect of the effort to bridge the gap between him and the adult. This later squatting represents an exaggeration of the flexion phase which is an initial movement in the jumping activity. Unable to jump from the squatting position, he again stands on the stool and steps off. He has now developed two necessary aspects of the pattern: flexion and extension as well as thrusting the body forward. But the exaggerated and isolated character of the movements prevents their working together to complete the act of jumping. The two aspects are still isolated movements and are not knitted together as a coordinated act. The final stage of development in jumping involves the integration of these two aspects. It consists of preparatory flexion of the lower extremities followed by immediate extension synchronous with thrusting the body forward. The movements are so well integrated that they appear practically as one.

In jumping off a high pedestal into awaiting arms an infant's appreciation of difference in height is well demonstrated by the fact that he will often jump from a pedestal of a particular height but will consistently refuse to jump from one slightly higher. In any event, when a child who has attained a fairly well-developed jumping technique is placed on an unfamiliar height for jumping there appears at first a regression to the less mature patterns such as squatting and reaching toward the receiving arms of the adult. Soon, however, adjusting to the new height, he is as capable in jumping from that as from lower levels. His discrimination of differences in distance is also indicated by the fact he will jump if the adult is standing only a few feet away. If the adult steps back to widen the gap, the infant will refuse to jump off the pedestal.

Most infants between the ages of two and three years acquire the ability to spring from a slightly elevated place onto a lower one. In many respects an analysis of this behavior-pattern discloses the same phases of development as those mentioned in the situation where the infant jumps from a higher pedestal into the arms of an adult. However, there are certain aspects of the performance which are evoked only in this second situation. We began study of this activity by placing the child on a pedestal only 7½ in. high. As he developed the ability to jump from such low elevations we endeavored to increase the difficulty gradually by increasing the height of the stool from which he should jump. A mat of 4¼ in. thickness was placed at the base of the stool for him to land on. A genetic analysis of the development of this behavior-course manifests the following phases:

    (a) a type of excess or diffuse activity when the child stands upon the stool shifting his weight from one foot to the other but is unable to thrust his body off the stool in any fashion;

    (b) a period when the infant extends one lower extremity over the edge of the pedestal but without flexing the lower extremity throws his body forward;

    (c) a subsequent phase when he apparently realizes he must flex the lower extremities in order to jump off but overdoes it and gets into the squatting position;

    (d) a fusion of (b) and (c) when the child begins by flexion of the lower extremities but, as he does so, steps one foot over the edge of the stool;

    (e) flexion and extension of the lower extremities as well as a thrusting of the body forward, but with the two aspects of the reaction poorly coördinated, so that he is likely to land on his knees or the upper part of his body rather than his feet;

(f) rapid flexion and extension of the lower extremities, and an extension and abduction of the upper extremities synchronous with throwing his body forward, but landing flat-footed or on the soles of his feet;

(g) finally a well-integrated flexion and extension of the lower extremities, and extension and abduction of the upper extremities as he springs forward, so that he lands on the metatarsal arch.

While these are the essential steps in the development of a jumping reaction, one phase always overlaps with another. A change in the situation, such as increasing the height of the jump, will evoke the less mature aspects of the performance. Often when a new height is introduced the child will refuse to jump alone, but if the experimenter merely holds his finger, in no way actually aiding in the somatic aspect of the performance, he will jump readily and easily.

Daily practice of Johnny in the jumping performance began when he was 395 days old. He was seated upon a pedestal 63¼ in. high with the lower extremities flexed at the knees and suspended over the edge. At this age he would throw his body forward in order to thrust himself into the outstretched arms of the experimenter. One of the most interesting aspects of his behavior was the facial expression. His eyes became dilated; there was a marked contraction of the platysma muscle and decided tension of all facial and trunk muscles. The facial expressions indicated a feeling of insecurity on his part as he threw his body forward. It is interesting that his urge to throw himself forward was sufficiently strong for him to do so notwithstanding. Within a few days, however, he had acquired an acquiescent attitude and these facial tensions were no longer evident. In the course of time his expression became one of superb delight preparatory to and during his jumping off the high pedestal.

When he was placed on the stool in a standing position at the age of 396 days while the experimenter held extended arms toward him, he would squat on the stool and strain to throw his body forward. Three days later when his straining efforts were still ineffectual, he stood up on the stool and stepped from one foot to the other, in this way indicating his desire to carry his body forward in order to bridge the gap between him and the experimenter. When 413 days old there was a conflict in the impulse to flex the lower extremities and thrust his body forward. This conflict resulted in his throwing himself forward head first from the squatting position. With rapid flexion and extension of the lower extremities as preparatory movements he successfully threw himself forward from the standing position on the high pedestal when he was 435 days old. Even so it was not then a permanent mode of behavior. Ordinarily at this stage of his development his performance did not involve the flexion and extension of the lower extremities. Usually he extended the left foot over the edge of the stool, then thrust his body forward without flexing the lower extremities in preparation. By the time he was 494 days old he was flexing the knees only slightly, and both feet were leaving the pedestal at the same time as he thrust his body forward. But his action did not at this time even include the "spring" which is a necessary part of a mature jumping pattern. When 581 days old the flexion of the lower extremities was followed by an extension of the spine just as he thrust his body forward, and the springing aspect was obviously beginning to develop. By the time he was 656 days old the springing jump from the high pedestal was fully developed.

Johnny's behavior in this respect is in sharp contrast to that of Jimmy and to the behavior of other babies of corresponding chronological age who have been under the observation of the experimenter in this situation. Jimmy was first stood upon a stool for jumping into the arms of an adult when he was 473 days old. Although he was quite happy before being placed upon the pedestal he began crying and clinging tenaciously to the experimenter. This or kindred behavior such as squatting and clutching the edge of the stool was his characteristic manner of behaving in this situation during the entire period that his motor activities were restricted. Never once did he make the slightest move to throw himself off the stool.

Daily practice in jumping from a low stool onto the floor was initiated when Johnny was 427 days old. In order to convey to him the idea of jumping off the stool rather than climbing off, an activity in which he had previously been exercised, the experimenter placed him on the stool, then holding him at the axillæ pressed sufficiently on the shoulders to get him to flex the lower extremities, and then lifted him off the stool onto the floor. It was not until he was 433 days old that he showed any signs of comprehending just what was expected of him. On that day he spontaneously flexed his lower extremities and got into a squatting position, but he did not throw his body forward. At 476 days he flexed one lower extremity and stepped off the 7½-in. stool onto the floor. Within another two days his initial move was to flex both lower extremities, but he overdid it and flexed them to such an extent that he got into a squatting position. He would hold the squatting position for a moment, then rise and step off. This was his mode of behavior on either the stool of 7½ or that of 14¼ in. in height.

When 484 days old his performance consisted not only of flexion and extension of the lower extremities but also throwing his body forward. But he did this only if he held one hand of the experimenter. Four days later he was jumping off by himself, but the tendency to hyperflex the lower extremities in the initial aspect of the act was so great that he was landing practically in a prone position rather than on his feet, even though the elevation of the stool was not great. When 499 days old he jumped spontaneously off the stool of 14¼ in. in height. Although both feet left the stool surface at the same time and there was some flexion in the lower extremities, the flexion was not followed by the extensor movement which constitutes the "spring" in jumping. He landed on the soles of his feet rather than the metatarsal arch. The springing movement was beginning to appear in his jumping action when he was 541 days old. At the age of 597 days there was a suggestion of his landing on the ball of the foot. This was an incomplete, transitory aspect of the behavior-course, however, and did not reappear until seventeen days later. It was not an established aspect of the pattern until he was 743 days old. There was an overlapping of approximately five months in the tendency to hyperflex the lower extremities preparatory to jumping and the springing aspect. Regression to the earlier squatting phase was determined in a large measure by the height of the stool from which the child was expected to jump. Even after he had a fully developed jumping technique from an elevation of 14¼ in. he would regress to a less mature manner of action when placed on pedestals of twice that height.

Observation of Jimmy in this jumping situation began when he was 473 days old and his behavior was in essence the same irrespective of the height of the stool. He made no attempt to jump off the stool but cried intensely and reached toward the experimenter. Never once during the time of limited activity did he jump off even the lowest stool onto the floor. The behavior of Jimmy corresponded more closely to that of other clinic babies than did the mode of jumping attained by Johnny.

In the development of jumping, experience and practice brought about not only a more coöperative attitude and an improvement in performance, but it apparently advanced the day this particular type of activity made its first appearance in the behavior of Johnny. He acquired this ability not only considerably younger than Jimmy but younger than any of the other babies who have figured in this investigation.

Manipulation of Graded Stools

As the behavior of the infant grows more complex it becomes increasingly difficult to find adequate terms for expressing the different aspects and phases of the pattern in a particular situation. We have used the term "manipulation of graded stools" to designate a complex act. The elements entering into this experimental situation were multitudinous, and no term is descriptive of the factors involved in the sense that "jumping" or "erect locomotion" designate these particular behavior-patterns.

The laboratory equipment included a series of eight columnar stools ranging in height from 7½ in. to 63¼ in. Except for the differences in height and weight the stools were quite alike. The weight and height of these stools respectively were as follows:

Number	Height	Weight
1	7½″	10 lbs., 4 oz.
2	14¼″	18 lbs., 8 oz.
3	22¼″	26 lbs., 4 oz.
4	30″	36 lbs.
5	38¼″	38 lbs.
6	46½″	44 lbs.
7	54¼″	52 lbs.
8	63¼″	60 lbs., 10 oz.

For the purpose of convenience of expression we shall refer to these stools by numbers, from 1 to 8.

Suggestions came from the baby for most of the experimental situations in this study in which improvement of performance was attained. This situation is no exception to that rule. The time comes when a child appears to take delight in what seems to be the random activity of pushing pieces of furniture about the room. This activity observed in many of the run-about children suggested the possibility of an experimental situation which would offer an incentive not only for his pushing furniture but for his selection and discrimination both as to the pieces of furniture he would push and the destination of his pushing activity. For that purpose the child's attention was attracted to lures which were set beyond his reach. In order to attain the object he had not only to adjust the position of his own body but to manipulate the situation to meet his ends.

About the same time the child begins to push furniture around spontaneously he also acquires the ability to climb up on low chairs, stools, etc. Unfortunately the writer has not made an analysis of the developmental processes involved in climbing up on pieces of furniture. But it was the combination of these two abilities which made this particular experimental situation possible. The present situation is concerned with the purposive arrangement of the equipment to meet an end and not with the climbing ability which was necessarily involved.

The situations involved in the study of behavior development of this type were essentially two:

(1) A lure was placed on a stool too high for the child to reach. In order to get the lure he would have to place beside the higher stool a low one on which to climb.

(2) In the second situation the object was suspended from the ceiling out of reach of the child so that he would need to place a sufficiently high stool beneath the suspended object in order to attain it. Sometimes one stool placed beneath the object was inadequate since he would need to use other smaller stools in order to climb upon the one under the object. The purposive selection and manipulation of these stools constitute the problem in this situation.

Development of behavior in these situations consists of the following phases:

(1) The child's initial mode of action is to stand beneath the object reaching vainly toward it, whether it is suspended or placed on a stool too high for him to reach.

(2) This initial phase is followed by an incipient connection between the lure and the available stool which is in the field of vision, so he runs to the stool and starts pushing it. But by the time he gets to the stool the connection is broken, and he pushes the stool about the room without consideration of the position of the lure.

(3) In the third phase there is a manifestation of an incipient concept of the possible use of the stool in connection with the object. So he runs to the stool and climbs up on it, though it is nowhere near the object. He may push it a short distance before or after climbing on it. If his attention is again drawn to the object he will look toward it and will appear to be puzzled that he cannot obtain it even when reaching or pointing in its direction.

(4) The next step in the development of this behavior-course is indicated when the child has attained a *complete* connection between the lower stool and the higher one on which the object is placed. He then pushes the low stool beside the higher one in order to climb up. If the low stool is sufficiently high for him to reach the object, then all is well. But if he has selected a stool too low for that purpose, then his immediate subsequent behavior is usually placing the low stool on another side of the high stool, climbing up, and again trying to reach the object. Some infants will try all sides of the high stool several times, but most of them give up and direct their attention to extraneous activities after trying two or three sides of the high stool.

It is easier for a child at this stage of development to place a low stool up against a wall or another piece of furniture in order to reach an object than it is for him to place it beneath a suspended object. Also at this stage of his comprehension he shows no signs of height discrimination in the selection of stools. For some reason he is likely to select the smallest or the lowest one. Just why he ordinarily selects the lowest one is a matter of conjecture, although it seems reasonable that he does so because it is lighter and easier to push. After placing it on several different sides of the high stool but still finding his efforts ineffectual, if he is further urged to obtain the object his attention falls upon other stools, slightly higher, in the field of vision. So he starts pushing one of those usually against the low one which he had already placed beside the high stool on which was located the lure. That he has no sense of differences in height or space is definitely

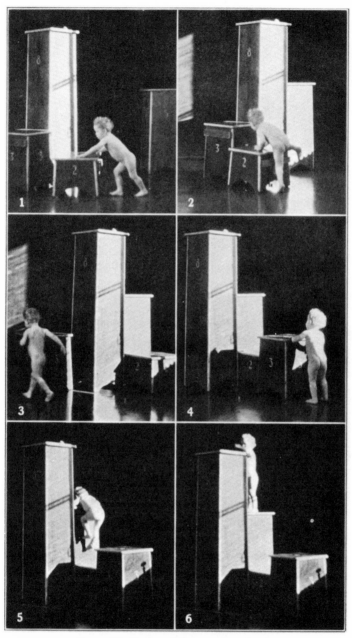

PLATE VI. JOHNNY MANIPULATING STOOLS

Situation 1.—At nineteen months he understands need of more than one stool but not their serial arrangement.

PLATE VI. JOHNNY MANIPULATING STOOLS

Situation 2.—At twenty-six months he manipulated eight stools of different heights in order to obtain an object suspended nine feet above the floor.

indicated by the fact that he not only places the lowest stool in between his second choice and the one containing the object but he climbs from the lowest stool to the outer one only to appear bewildered that he cannot obtain the object from that position.

If, however, he so placed the second stool that he could reach the object, then he seemingly gets the notion that the additional stool solves the problem. This notion of an additional stool leads to a manifestation of a subsequent stage which is an excellent illustration of the tendency to overwork a new aspect of the developing behavior-course.

(5) Having conceived the idea that an additional stool brings about a solution, he will for a time push many more stools than are necessary around the one on which is placed the object. Furthermore, he does not even pretend to make use of all of them in climbing up to get the object, and he shows no appreciation of gradation or sequence in their arrangement.

(6) In the next step of development he begins to show discrimination of differences in height, especially of the lower stools. Such, discrimination is indicated when he deliberately moves a lower stool in order to place a slightly higher one next to the stool on which is the lure. Presently it is observed that he is able not only to discriminate sufficiently to move the lowest stool in order to make space for one slightly higher, but he discriminates in his selection and starts pushing a stool of slightly higher gradation at the beginning so as to place them seriatim. In other words, he does not go to the trouble of actually placing the lowest one, then removing it in order to make way for a higher one. He exercises discrimination before he starts moving the stools. In that way excess activity is eliminated.

(7) The final stage of development occurs when the child not only places the stools in serial order but carefully discriminates and selects only the minimum required for him to climb up and reach the objective.

In outlining these essential steps in development the writer would not like to convey the impression that the child moves from one phase to another as if passing through separate chambers. There is an anastomosis, so to speak, in the developmental manifestations of these behavior-patterns. That principle is just as true of these higher-level, more complicated activities as of the primary, more fundamental behavior patterns. The detailed account of the development of Johnny and Jimmy in these situations will readily reveal this principle of growth.

Training Johnny in the use of furniture to compensate for his inadequate height in attaining objects beyond reach began when he was 539 days old. He had already been observed to push furniture around the room. On this day an object was placed on a stool just beyond his reach and a low stool, adequate for his reaching the object, was placed conspicuously in the field of vision a few feet away. When his attention was first attracted to the object he stood beneath it on his toes in order to reach as far as possible with his arms extended toward the object. When he could not get it he turned to the experimenter and complained. Since help was not given, he directed his attention elsewhere. Then the experimenter placed the low stool directly beside the higher one and called his attention to the lure. At first he stood by the stool and tried to reach. After some delay and complaining, he stepped upon the low stool and got the object. A little later during the same day the first arrangement was again set and his attention was directed to the object. Again he stood beneath the higher stool for a while, trying vainly to reach the object. Then he turned around so that his gaze rested on the low stool a few feet away. He made another futile effort to reach the object, then ran directly to the low stool a few feet away and began pushing it about the laboratory. But the connection between the stool and the object (which had been unquestionably indicated by his going directly toward the stool after gazing at it) was broken by the time he started pushing, so he began pushing the stool aimlessly about the room.

The situation was not presented to him again until he was 550 days old. His initial mode of behavior on that day was to reach vainly for the object as he stood beside the high stool on which it was placed. Unable to reach it, he got the low stool, placed only a few feet away, pushed it beside the one on which the lure was located, climbed up and successfully reached the object.

Five days later when the object was placed on a stool 63¼ in. high, so that it was necessary for him to make use of more than one of the lower stools in order to reach the object, there was no doubt that he had established the association of placing the low stool beside the high one in order to reach his object. But he had no appreciation of differences in height, as was shown by the fact that he placed the lowest stool (#1) between the stool on which the object was located and the second stool. The next day his performance in this situation revealed definite discrimination. He placed the second stool beside the tall one, then the lowest stool beside the second so that he could climb from #1 to #2 in order to reach the object. But this perfection was transitory— beginner's luck. There followed many days when he would still place the lowest stool next to the one on which the object was located, although a higher one was necessary for his reaching. He not only failed to place the stools in order, but also pushed more stools around the tall one than he even attempted to use. By the time he was 582 days old he was fairly consistent in showing discrimination in his selection and placement of two stools in order to obtain an object placed on the tall stool.

Therefore, when he was 581 days old the situation was made more difficult for him by hanging the object from the ceiling so that it was necessary for him to make use of more than two or three stools in order to gain the object. This situation also presented a new problem involving spatial discrimination in order to place the tallest stool in a position on the floor directly under the suspended object. At this time his spatial adjustment was not fully developed and there would still occur times when he would climb up on a stool placed far to one side of the object. Then he would appear bewildered that he could not obtain the object.

Since there is a great deal of overlapping of one phase with another in developmental patterns, the experimenter endeavored to have an overlapping of the problem situations set for the child. For a period he would get practice with the object placed on the stool and also the more difficult situation when it was suspended. At the age of 605 days he showed some understanding of the factor of distance in his problem. With the lure on stool #8 he placed stools #2 and #3 beside it, but #2 was in between #3 and #8. He started to climb up on stool #3 when he paused and looked up at the object and down at stool #2 in between. He immediately got off the outer stool to climb up on the middle one. Although it was so low that he could not reach successfully from it, it nevertheless was the one nearest to the object. Two days later his discrimination had proceeded to such an extent that, before climbing upon stools, he removed a low stool to replace it by one slightly higher. At this stage there was a glimmer of understanding of both height and spatial differences, but the two cognitions were as "isolated" reactions. They were not completely developed, nor were they integrated.

Having conceived the idea that an additional stool would solve this problem, there was a tendency for him to overwork or exaggerate the notion. So during this period when the object had been suspended from the ceiling, his characteristic mode of behavior consisted of pushing all the stools under the object, although there was no indication of order or sequence either in his selection or his placement of the stools. Ordinarily he would select the small stools first. At the age of 601 days there was a slight suggestion of cognition of the serial order of the stools. Six days later his performance indicated a spurt in his discriminative development. The suspended object was nine feet two inches from the floor and the eight stools were available for his use in solving the problem. As usual, they were scattered helter-skelter about the room. He took one look at the object, then definitely selected the highest stool and pushed it toward the object. He quite definitely gauged the distance in placing the stool under the object. Obviously the stool towered several feet above the child's head. But his discrimination of distance was indicated by his pushing the stool a few feet, then pausing, stepping back and taking a look at the object, then pushing it a little farther and so on until it was placed directly under the object. This stool was 63¼ in. high and the only one from which he could reach the object. His next selection was stool #5, which he placed beside stool #8. He then started toward stool #6 and pushed it a little distance, paused and gazed at the arrangement of the two stools already placed. Immediately he deliberately abandoned stool #6 and started pushing stool #3. Stool #3 he first placed beside stool #8; then he paused, looked the situation over, and removed #3 to a place beside #5. He then gleefully ascended the series to gain the object. In this performance all excess stools were eliminated and he indubitably discriminated both height and spatial differences in the selection and placement of the stools in order. Not quite all excess motion was eliminated, but it was, nevertheless, a performance of rare proficiency.

Such excellence of performance had not become established as a characteristic mode of behavior. Parenthetically, these transitory spurts and subsequent regressions constitute one of the most interesting features of growth, but adequate explanation of their appearance must await more intensive study than this investigation affords. After this spurt in Johnny's development, there followed a period of unusually poor performances. It is possible that Johnny's well-developed skill in climbing from one stool to another actually hindered his learning the serial order of these stools, for all too often when he had not exercised utmost judgment in placing the stools they were so placed that he could climb from one to another in order to reach the objective. As a matter of fact, when he was 639 days old he demonstrated his ability to reach across a gap of twelve or fifteen inches (caused by having stool #2 placed between #4 and #5). He was standing on stool #4 when he grasped the edge of stool #5 so that he could swing his body across the gap and climb up on stool #5, which was more propitiously placed with respect to the object.

By the time he was 665 days old he was showing an unquestionable appreciation of serial order of the stools so far as the first five heights were concerned. But he was unable to make such distinction with respect to the higher stools. He still had a tendency to place all the stools available under the object, though he made no use of them in climbing. It was a little more than three months after the first excellent performance in this activity before he equaled it again in selection and discrimination. This second instance occurred when he was 704 days old. When he saw the object nine feet from the floor, he started to push stool #3 beneath the object, but as he pushed it he took another look at the object, then gave the low stool an additional shove so it would not be directly under the suspended object. He then selected stool #8 and placed it directly under the object, with stool #5 beside it. After getting those placed he turned around and got stool #3 and placed it beside stool #5. This record was also followed by a briefer period of inferior performances.

When 714 days old, although he did not make a perfect performance in his initial move, since he placed stool #7 under the object rather than stool #8, his behavior indicated that he was well aware of both the difficulty and the solution. He went so far as to climb up on stool #7, located under the lure, found himself unable to reach the object from there, pointed across the room to the highest stool, and repeated "stool." During the following months there were several instances when his performance showed a high degree of discrimination and proficiency. Not only were his performances gradually approaching perfection, with excess activity being eliminated, but he made superior performances at more frequent intervals. When daily practice in this situation was discontinued at the age of 743 days, Johnny's characteristic mode of behavior in the situation still showed a tendency to use more stools than was necessary for a successful performance, and often he failed to arrange them in serial order. But during the six and one-half months in which his development in these situations had been under daily observation, the fundamental principles of growth were in essence the same as those shown in the development of the early primitive patterns of behavior.

The first evidence of Jimmy's making use of furniture to climb up and reach an object was when he was 665 days old. It was during spontaneous behavior and not under the laboratory conditions that this activity was first observed. During the time Jimmy's activities were restricted under laboratory conditions he never once succeeded in making a complete performance which involved manipulating furniture or stools upon which to climb in order to obtain a desired object out of reach. He had attained such a stage of development that he made a connection between the position of the object and the available stool, but he had not been able to use the stool purposively for climbing. When his attention was first drawn to the object he would stand beneath it reaching up vainly. Then he would start toward the stool, as if to make use of it, but would get no further than pushing it around the room aimlessly. Never once did he place the stool under the object and climb up for it. It is admitted that had Jimmy been free so that his behavior could have been observed more frequently than the examination schedule at this time allowed, a more advanced type of behavior might have been elicited. Certainly under the laboratory schedule his behavior in this particular performance did not approach that of Johnny.

On the other hand, his achievements corresponded more closely to those of other clinic babies of corresponding chronological age in the same situation than did Johnny's. No child under two years of age has under these particular conditions succeeded in combining three or more stools in order to climb up and secure the desired object out of reach. It was not, however, in just the actual performance that Johnny excelled other children of similar age in this situation. More striking even were the differences in persistence and his manner of pausing at intervals to look the situation over before acting. There were occasions during his practice periods when he worked persistently at arranging the stools for thirty to forty minutes without giving his attention to anything else in the interim.

Certainly it stands without question that daily exercise in activities of this type greatly accelerates the performance. How much transfer there would be from these particular situations to kindred ones is another matter, beyond the province of this investigation.

Manipulation of Graded Boxes

In the preceding situation the child had merely to push stools of different heights in juxtaposition, whereas the situation of graded boxes called for his stacking one box on top of another in order to gain the object. As soon as the experimenter observed the child spontaneously picking up small pieces of furniture such as chairs and carrying them about, instead of just pushing them around on the floor, situations were designed for the purpose of stimulating the child to greater effort in stacking furniture, in this instance boxes, one on top of the other. Four boxes of different sizes were constructed of three-ply board. They varied in size and weight as follows:

Number	Size	Weight
1	9½ × 13 × 13	5 lbs., 4 oz.
2	11 × 16 × 16	7 lbs., 4 oz.
3	11½ × 18 × 18	11 lbs.
4	12½ × 23 × 23	13 lbs.

On the three smallest boxes a ridge one-half inch wide projected over two sides. The boxes could be lifted by this ridge.

The experimental situations were so arranged that an object was suspended from the ceiling at such height that it could be reached (1) if the child stood on only one box, (2) if he piled one upon another, (3) provided he piled three boxes upon each other, and (4) only if he climbed upon all four boxes stacked one upon the other. For the purpose of convenience in writing the boxes will be referred to as 1, 2, 3, and 4, from the smallest to the largest. At the beginning of this experiment the boxes were painted blue, yellow, green, and red. Since only fifteen of the larger group of experimental infants had attained an age sufficiently mature to have had experience in this laboratory situation when the present report was made, and since none of these had actually succeeded in purposively placing one box upon another, the writer must depend rather heavily upon the behavior-patterns of Johnny and Jimmy in this situation in deriving the following analysis of the phases and factors entering into the process of development.

When a child's attention is first drawn to the suspended object, his reactions are similar to those observed in manipulation of graded stools. He stands directly under the object and reaches vainly, often engaging in a great deal of excess activity such as bouncing up and down, grunting, and beseeching the adult to help. Sometimes he will go to the extent of pulling the adult by the hand to the suspended object. If that avails him nothing, then the child runs to a box (showing no evidence of discrimination of size) and starts pushing the box about the room. Apparently he has lost interest in the object and enjoys the activity of pushing the box about. If attention is redirected to the object he may climb up on the box although it is not placed under the object. The next step in his development is indicated when he pushes the box underneath the object and then climbs up on it.

This activity is adequate if the object is hung sufficiently low for him to reach from that height. When, however, the object is placed at a height which requires his climbing upon two boxes in order to reach the object, the child's next move ordinarily is to place two or more boxes in juxtaposition. Then he climbs up on them. Unfortunately, he may place them side by side under the object or in some other place in the room. He has merely gained the idea of using more than one box, but he does not know how or where to use them. In the next phase he has apparently learned to place the box under the object. When one box does not enable him to reach the object, he pushes it away and tries another one. Sometimes he will try all four boxes, one at a time, in this fashion. When no one box is adequate, there is often a regression in his behavior to more immature phases of the behavior-course. He is likely to start pushing the box around the room or to stand under the object vainly reaching toward it.

Finally the day arrives when he starts lifting one box. But it is

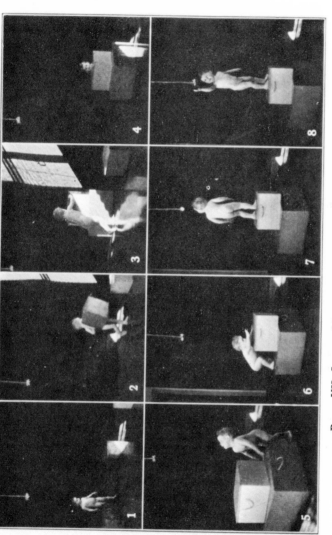

PLATE VII. JOHNNY MANIPULATING BOXES (TWENTY-ONE MONTHS)

1. Looks the situation over. 2 and 3. Selects a smaller box and places it upon the biggest one. 4 and 5. Pushes the two boxes beneath the object. 6, 7, 8. Although the smaller box projects over the edge, he is successful in climbing up to reach the object.

observed that as he lifts the smaller box he is likely to look toward another box or even approach it seemingly with the idea of placing the smaller one on top of the other. Unfortunately, the idea is only ephemeral and inchoate. The connection is quickly broken, and he merely carries the box a little distance about the room. In the next phase of his development, the connection which was only partially indicated is now complete and he successfully places one box upon another. But he has no appreciation of serial order in placing the boxes. Apparently, since he has gained in one aspect of his development another is for the moment interrupted, for he shows less discrimination in correctly locating the two boxes under the object than he previously had shown in placing one. He pushes them somewhere in the neighborhood of the object, then starts to climb up.

The child's climbing technique is poorly adapted for climbing upon unsteady pieces of furniture. In this respect he is different from the simian. The simian is able to touch lightly with his hands the unsteady box as he pushes against the floor with the lower extremities and bounds up on the top box. But the climbing technique of the young child consists primarily of grasping tightly on the edge of the top stool or box and pulling himself up with the upper extremities rather than pushing up with the lower. Obviously if he pulls upon an empty box placed upon another one, he will pull the box off. Therefore, the next step in his development involves his learning to hold gently upon the top box as he uses his lower extremities to do most of the actual work in climbing. It is not that he reverts to the simian technique, but rather that he holds on to the top box just enough to steady himself as he cautiously steps on the ledge of the lower box.

In this connection he must also master the problem involved in balancing one box upon another. There is a period when the child has no appreciation whatever of that problem. He will place them so that one may be resting as much as a third over the edge of the lower box on which it is placed. He still has no sense of size differences and will try to balance a big box on a smaller one. The next phase in development is indicated when the child learns to select his boxes so that the larger one is always under a smaller one. Furthermore, he must learn to place one on top of the other in such a manner that one box does not project over the edge of a lower one. When the child has these connections adequately established so that all excess movements are eliminated in his selection and placement of the boxes, further development is indicated by the number of boxes he can successfully stack and use in this fashion.

Whenever an additional box is required in order to meet the desired height, there is ordinarily a regression to a less mature phase of the behavior-pattern. It is not only under stress or strain that regressions to less mature modes of action are evident. Regression is a natural part of development. A child does not once "perceive" the possibility of placing one box upon another in order to gain his objective, then ever afterward immediately and directly make that type of performance when confronted with the situation. Nor is his behavior purely trial and error. He does not move about helter-skelter until he *chances* upon the correct solution. From the beginning the first moves, though incomplete and accompanied by diffuse activity, are nevertheless directional. An ephemeral and inchoate movement, shrouded with excess and diffuse behavior, indicates the emergence of a growing pattern of action. For example, the child at first makes only a partial connection between the two boxes and the object. Furthermore, after he has successfully placed one box upon another and successfully achieved his objective, there may be days before he repeats the act of stacking two boxes. An appearance of a successful response by no means indicates that the child will henceforth make an equally successful response. Little by little, waste activity is eliminated, and little by little new aspects of the pattern are expanded and integrated.

Practice in this situation began with Johnny when he was 595 days old. He had already been observed to carry small chairs and other portable pieces of furniture around the room, but he had never been observed to combine two pieces in order to reach an object. Furthermore, he had had previous experience in getting an object suspended from the ceiling by climbing on chairs or stools. Therefore, the initial phase of the pattern indicated by standing beneath the object and reaching futilely was, from the beginning, eliminated. When first confronted with this situation, his inceptive movement consisted of pushing the boxes side by side, stepping from one to the other. Since boxes were the new element in the situation, he was more interested in them than in the object suspended from the ceiling. Johnny's first attempt to lift one of the boxes was during spontaneous play when he tried to put the smallest box in the largest one. At that time the boxes had no conspicuous handles—only the half-inch projection of the lid over the side of the box. Johnny's method, therefore, of trying to lift the box was to place both palms against opposite sides. It was necessary for him to get into a squatting position in order to span the width of the box. Having placed both hands on the sides, he would try to rise to a standing position. This was impossible, and the result was that the box slipped out of his hands. The experimenter then pointed out the lid projection by which the box could be grasped.

In less than a week he had acquired the idea of placing one box upon another, but he did not always place them directly under the object. He had considerable difficulty in climbing upon the boxes because of the instability of the top box. His tendency in climbing was to seize the edge of the top box and pull himself up. Once he fell over backward with the box on top of him, and for several days afterward there was a reversion to the earlier pattern of pushing the boxes side by side and climbing up on the higher one. Because of the unsteadiness of the boxes and the possibility of his building up an inhibiting attitude toward the situation, it was necessary in the earlier stages for the experimenter to give more assistance in the way of holding the box steady while Johnny climbed up than was given in other experimental situations.

When 613 days old, Johnny was able to place a small box upon a larger one and climb up unassisted for the object. He was always extremely cautious in climbing up on these boxes. At this time he showed no evidence of actual discrimination in balancing the boxes one on the other. Although he most frequently began by placing the smallest box upon the largest, he actually exercised no size discrimination in his selection of the boxes. His selection of the smallest was apparently due to the fact that it was easier to carry. When the object was hung so that he could reach from the top of the two boxes, the arrangement of box 1 upon box 4 was an excellent compensation for his difficulty in climbing as it allowed ample space for him to step upon the biggest box before climbing upon the smallest one. The size relationship between these two boxes did not appear, however, to be apprehended, nor were they selected in order to make the climbing easier. The absence of appreciation of size relations was indicated by his often placing box 1 upon box 2 or 3 and climbing up. If he had understood the advantage of the wide ledge he would have used 1 on 4 consistently. When 618 days old there was a transitory aspect of using a third box beside the two piled under the object. He did not attempt to lift it up on the two, but used it as a stepping-stone in climbing on top of the stacked boxes.

By the time he was 631 days old, he had command of the situation when only two boxes were required for his reaching the object. Although he usually placed the smaller box on the bigger one, it was not an indication of size discrimination but rather was due to the fact that he could not at his age lift the two largest boxes. When he was 632 days old he not only successfully balanced box 3 on top of box 2 but also succeeded in climbing up on them after he had so placed them. There were still occasions when he did not place the boxes immediately under the object before climbing up, although he was beginning to show signs of watching the position of the suspended object as he pushed the boxes toward it.

The object was hung sufficiently high when he was 646 days old to require three boxes in order for him to reach the lure. He successfully pushed the two boxes under the object, but it was not until he was 652 days old that he deliberately tried to place the third box on top of the other two. His lack of discrimination with respect to size was further evidenced. Having established the pattern of placing box 1 upon 4 or 3, he now attempted to place box 2 on top of 1. In his effort to place box 2 on top, however, he would usually knock box 1 off. Then having placed 2 on 4, he would again pick up 1 and place it on 2. Since 1 weighed less than 2, it was possible for him to raise it high enough to place it on top of box 2 without knocking the second one off.

When he was 676 days old he showed specific discrimination in placing the boxes under the object. Although he spent twenty minutes in getting the boxes correctly placed, he would not start climbing up until they were directly under the object. More than a month earlier he had indicated an awareness of this difficulty when he had the boxes placed to one side of the object. Discrimination in that respect had continued to develop, and this concentrated attention for twenty minutes on just placing the boxes under the object is illustrative of the tendency to overemphasize an aspect of development once the learner is beginning to feel a

PLATE VIII. JOHNNY MANIPULATING BOXES (TWENTY-SIX MONTHS)

1, 2, 3, 4, 5. Successfully piles three boxes in order to obtain suspended object out of reach. 6. Discovers three boxes inadequate.

PLATE VIII. JOHNNY MANIPULATING BOXES (TWENTY-SIX MONTHS) (*continued*)

7 and 8. Removes the boxes which he has piled beneath the object. 9, 10, 11, 12. Starts to rebuild them but is physically unable to get the fourth box placed on top of the other three.

degree of certainty about it. When 693 days old his behavior evidenced awareness of size differences in placing the boxes. He placed box 1 on box 4. Then he picked up box 2 and started toward the pile, paused, put it down, *lifted* box 1 off box 4, and put box 2 in its place. Then he placed box 1 on box 2. During that same week he also, for the first time, began stacking the boxes more carefully. If one box projected over the edge, he would go around and push it from the other direction. Later he did not go to the trouble of running around to the opposite side in order to push the box to the center; he would pull it toward him. Further development in his discrimination of size differences in the boxes was indicated at the age of 704 days when he picked up box 1 and started toward box 4, but pausing before he reached 4, deliberately put 1 down, turned around and looked over all the boxes, then started for box 2, which he placed on 4. He had eliminated the step of getting 1 placed on 4 before realizing his difficulty.

By the time he was 725 days old he not only looked the boxes over and selected them with respect to size but he looked up at the object to judge the height as if deciding before he started stacking them how many boxes would be needed. His unquestionable discrimination in this respect was indicated when occasionally the object was placed lower than usual. He then placed one box on another and got so far as to place his hand on the third box, when he turned, looked at the object, left the third box, and pushed the other two under the object. He seldom stacked the boxes under the object. By piling them in the location of the biggest box, and pushing the entire series under the object, activity was reduced to the minimum.

At the time the daily practice in this experiment was discontinued, Johnny had attained great facility in stacking and carefully balancing three boxes seriatim. He was quite capable of judging when he needed a fourth box in order to reach the object, but his stature was too short for him to lift without some assistance the fourth box on top of the other three. For that reason a stool was added to the pieces of apparatus available in this situation for the purpose of determining when he would make use of the stool to stand on in placing the fourth box on top of the others. Up to the time of the present report, this had not been accomplished.

During his control period Jimmy never succeeded in getting

beyond the stage of pushing the box around the room. His initial mode of behavior when the situation was first presented to him was to run under the suspended object, dance up and down, and reach vainly for it. Then he would start pushing the boxes about the room. When he could not obtain the lure he quickly directed his attention to other activities. His lack of perseverance was in striking contrast to Johnny's persistence. Since Jimmy's attitude was generally less coöperative in the laboratory, an adequate estimate of his discriminative powers could not be obtained in any situation, though in these manipulative situations he was ordinarily more acquiescent than in any of the others.

No child under two years of age has in the experimenters' experience been observed to lift purposively one box upon another and then make use of them in climbing for an object. In this respect Jimmy's reactions were more similar to those of the other children who have figured in this investigation than were Johnny's.

In activities of this type daily exercise and practice undoubtedly improves the performance. The improvement was evident in somatic performances, in cognition, and in developing and maintaining a persistent coöperative attitude.

Summary

A study of developmental processes of behavior-patterns the origin of which is definitely ontogenetic indicates that the fundamental principles of behavorial growth are constant despite the complexity of the activity. Each aspect of a behavior-pattern may manifest a general diffuse phase at its inception. The first directional movement is inchoate and transitory. This partial pattern, however, gradually becomes more and more expansive until it is perhaps exaggerated in form. Presently there appears another aspect of the pattern, the development of which curtails the exaggeration of the former. Finally, the excess activity is eliminated until the essences of both aspects of the action-system become integrated.

Therefore, development in behavior embraces both a process of narrowing down the activity to minimum essentials and a process of knitting together or integrating two or more aspects of a particular behavior-pattern. The process most prominent at a given time is contingent upon the stage of development a particular aspect of the behavior-pattern has attained. During the early stages of development the most obvious process appears to be from the general to the specific, but once an aspect of a pattern has attained a certain degree of determinateness then the process of development becomes essentially one of integration.

Ontogenetic behavior-patterns are subject to far greater modifiability by repetition of the performance than are activities of phylogenetic origin. This difference in variability may be due to introduction of the additive experience nearer the inception of the growing aspect in the behavior-pattern. There is some reason to believe that the time when a new aspect of a behavior-pattern arises, before it has attained definition, constitutes also the period of greatest susceptibility to modification. The developmental status of the behavior-pattern is as important, if not more important, in determining its modifiability than is the chronological maturity of the individual.

Development is extremely gradual, there being ever a wide margin in the overlapping of one phase with another. Not only is there an overlapping of one phase with another, but there is an actual interdependence of the different aspects of a behavior-pattern. The appearance of a new aspect may for a time retard or promote the development of another.

Chapter V

THE DEVELOPMENT OF ASSOCIATIONAL ACTIVITIES

IN this discussion emphasis has been placed upon the development of specific behavior-patterns. The purpose in so doing has been to bring out the sequence and phases of the development of each pattern, especially as they have reference to the fundamental processes of growth. We have insisted that the genetic method is indispensable to an analysis of the *processes* of growth. Mere increments of development will not disclose the process. Since in human subjects behavior has by the time of birth become complex, it is necessary for the purpose of analysis only to study the growth of particular patterns of behavior. We would like, however, to avoid any impression that specific behavior-patterns grow as individual stalks among a field of grain. In emphasizing the development of behavior-patterns we would not like to lose sight of the total individual in whom these behavior-mechanisms are embodied, for the development of one behavior-pattern is interconnected with the development and function of other action-systems. But since behavior-patterns do not attain the same degree of maturity at the same time in a given individual, it is really inaccurate to speak of an individual's maturity in terms of chronological age.

Nevertheless, if a particular chronological period is considered in terms of the greatest increments of development, the first two years of a child's life may roughly, but conveniently, be grouped into four chronological periods, as follows: (1) from birth to the fourth or fifth month, (2) from the fourth or fifth to the eighth or tenth month, (3) from the eighth or tenth to the fifteenth or eighteenth month, and (4) from the fifteenth or eighteenth month to the twenty-fourth month.

During the first four or five months the behavior of the baby is still at an infracortical level. Therefore, the greatest increment of development in behavior at this time consists of a gradual recession of some overt primitive reflexes as behavior-patterns of a higher order begin to emerge.

Growth during the second period is shown largely by an ever increasing control of the individual infant over motor activities in the upper part of the body, that is, in the region of the head and shoulder girdle.

During the third period the greatest increments in behavorial development are observed in the motor activities involving the lower part of the body—in the region of the pelvic girdle and lower extremities.

During the fourth period great strides are evident in the development of an understanding of relationships—associational, conditional, and symbolic—of retention and recall of these relations, of comprehension and use of language, imitative tendencies, et cetera.

These chronological divisions are sketchy, and it must not be inferred from this division that the infant manifests no evidence of understanding relationships or making associations, or of retention and recall of these associations, before he is fifteen or eighteen months old. Nor does his development in motor control cease at that time. All types of development are going on at all these periods, but in most infants the greatest *increments* of growth would closely approximate this age grouping.

It is the development of behavior-patterns of the fourth group which we shall consider in this chapter. The development of these behavior-patterns is interlaced to such an extent that it is impossible to consider the phases in the development of one without taking into account all of the others. Retention and recall presuppose limited associational connections. Without some power of retention and recall of previous experience a comprehension of conditional and symbolic relationships would be precluded. Imitative tendencies as well as retention and recall of experience are indispensable to the development of vocal language usage.

Obviously behavior is becoming rapidly more complex at this stage. The more complex the behavior-pattern the more difficult is it to outline distinct phases in development. Our problem in analyzing the phases of development of behavior of this order is made more difficult because many activities of this type cannot be provoked under laboratory conditions. Often one must depend upon observing them in the spontaneous behavior of the child. Many of the behavior-patterns which are to be discussed in this chapter have been observed in the general behavior of the child and not as actions which occurred under prescribed laboratory conditions.

Development in Retention and Recall

The young infant—that is, the child of not more than five or six months—appears sensitive only to extrinsic stimuli in the immediate environment, practically within the immediate field of vision. "Out of sight out of mind" is an old metaphorical adage, but literally true of the young baby. Therefore, a distinct developmental landmark is indicated when the baby shows unmistakable signs of responding to objects which are not within his view. In order to stimulate the younger baby to engage in motor activities, it is necessary to hold a lure directly in front of him but just beyond his reach. As the baby grows it is possible to increase the distance of the lure and still activate motor actions on the part of the infant. We observed this especially in stimulating the baby to climb up slides. Although the younger baby would follow the slowly moving object up the slide, he often would not climb if the lure was merely placed at the top of the incline and his attention directed to it. Subsequently, the lure placed only at the top constituted an ample stimulus to activate the motor response of climbing.

Gradually the distance of the object can be increased until it is completely out of view. The baby then will definitely respond to an object which he has seen, but which for the moment is hidden. We essayed in the laboratory to get at some measure of the process of development in this type of behavior by having the child hide an object just before he was placed upon a stool or ladder, and, after he had climbed down, directing him to find it. It was possible gradually to increase the difficulty in this situation by increasing the number of objects to be hidden and the number of activities to be done in the interim before they were recovered as well as to increase the distance of the hiding place from the position of the intervening performances.

Lapse of time is only one element, and perhaps a lesser element at that, in determining the child's abilities in retention and recall of the location of hidden objects. More important elements in the process of recall are (1) the degree of attention devoted to the placement of the object, (2) the intensity of the child's desire to recover it, and (3) the extent of distractibility involved in his intermediate performances. By far the most important of these is the degree of attention paid to the placement of the object before he sets about the other activities. Often a child who has hidden an object has been placed by the experimenters on a pedestal so high that he would or could not climb down. He would stand there crying from fifteen to twenty minutes, trying first one side of the stool and then another, looking out the window at passing objects, engaging in any number of distracting activities. The intervening distractions were many. But after being lifted off the pedestal and requested to get the simple object which had been hidden the infant would go directly to it. Since he would immediately bring the object to the experimenter, his motive was to comply with the request of the adult and not to gain possession of the object. Therefore, there is no reason to believe that a potent urge to have the object impressed upon him its location. His retention in that instance can be attributed to the attention devoted to the act of hiding the object before the distractions were introduced.

Phases in the development of this type of behavior are so intricate that they can be only grossly outlined here. However, the sequence of development in cortical activities of this level is of such moment to an understanding of the processes of behavioral growth that even a sketchy analysis is revealing. Steps in the development of retention and recall in this particular situation consist essentially of the following phases:

(1) The child goes through certain intervening motor or other distracting performances after hiding an object. When directed to find the object after completing the motor performance he shows no indication whatever of being aware that a hidden object is being referred to.

(2) After hiding the object and engaging in the distracting activities the child indicates a slight understanding of the fact that an object out of view is being requested. His reactions in this instance usually consist of turning around several times, then

looking toward the experimenter with a questioning expression, but finally directing his attention to other things without making any approach in the direction of the hidden object.

(3) The third phase in this development is indicated when the child moves in the general direction of the hidden object, but does not definitely locate it.

(4) In the fourth phase the child may look in several places before moving directly toward the hidden object. Especially if he has had experience in hiding objects before, he is likely to look in the place where the object was previously hidden. After some delay he recalls the correct position and recovers it.

(5) In the fifth phase the child goes directly and without delay to the correct hiding place of the object requested by the experimenter.

(6) Subsequent development is indicated by the number of objects and places he can retain in memory, the length of the interim, and the number of distractions he can overcome and still retain and recall the location of the hidden object.

It is apparent from the sequential phases as indicated in the development of retention that out of an undifferentiated state there first appears a partial or inchoate movement. It is not at the time carried through to completion. The child merely gets the idea of an object being hidden. Having conceived the idea of looking for something, he exaggerates that aspect of the pattern by looking in too many places. But gradually the excess motion is eliminated until his acts are directly and immediately in line with the hidden lure.

More striking evidence of development in activities of this sort is observable during the spontaneous behavior of the child than can be gained under set laboratory conditions. It is not, however, easy to observe the phases of development involved unless the conditions are held rather constant. Therefore in making this analysis of the phases of development we have drawn upon observations of the general behavior of the infant as well as observations of behavior in laboratory situations.

Practice in locating hidden objects began with Johnny when he was 429 days old. He observed an object being hidden under a mat on which was standing a tall stool. After the object had been hidden he was placed upon the stool and told to get off and find the object. He had previously acquired skill in climbing off these high stools, but ordinarily the object was in full view on the floor. On this occasion when directed to find the object he looked around on the floor near the stool. When he could not find it, he directed his attention to other things. A few moments later he happened to see an adult pick up the object from beneath the mat. That obviously stimulated recall for, immediately dropping what he was doing, he went directly to the corner of the mat and looked under it. Although he had observed the adult pick up the object, he apparently did not realize that the object would no longer be under the mat.

Two days later he secured the object after it was hidden under the mat without the slightest hesitation. Obviously exercise in this activity was not initiated with Johnny as early as he was capable of utilizing it. Practice was continued and expanded to include many objects and greater distractions. One method of distracting him further during the interim consisted of allowing him to start toward the object after he had climbed off the stool but, as soon as he had made a few steps obviously bent on re-covery of the object, interrupting him by placing him on top of another high pedestal from which he would again need to climb down. He complained slightly when thwarted in this way, but it apparently did not interfere with his recalling the location of the object. After several experiences in this situation he would start toward the object, then pause and wait to be lifted up on the second stool before completing the act of looking for the object. His powers of recollection were determined more by the attention he gave to the placement of the object than to the intervening activities or distractions.

In the beginning his recall of the hidden object appeared to be based primarily upon an appreciation of the general direction in which the object was located. Once he got into the vicinity of the hiding place, he made thereupon the direct connection with the actual spot where the object was to be found. This aspect of the developing behavior was evinced in the following manner. After the object had been hidden in a box in a particular place in the room, the experimenter removed the box into another part of the room while Johnny was not observing. At first the child would respond only to the previous location. That is, he would go to the original location of the box. If a box of a different color or size had been placed there, he would look in it for the lure. If he did not locate the object, he would then direct his attention to other activities. Subsequently, having failed to find it in the original position he would look about the room in other places for the box, although he began looking in other places only after he had gone to the original location of the box. A little later in his development he would start toward the original location, but before he actually arrived at the point he would pause and look around the room to see if there had been an exchange of boxes. Obviously he was then beginning to respond not merely to the general direction of location but to the immediate and limited environment in which the object was placed. Finally he would not even make a start toward the original location but would pause and obviously look the room over to see if there had been a change in the position of the boxes before he made a move in any direction. In other words, all lost motion had at last been eliminated, so that his activity consisted of the shortest route toward the objective.

Johnny's development in the ability to recollect the location of hidden objects after he had engaged in irrelevant activities expanded until the time came when he was requested to find an object which had been hidden the night before. Apparently one of the most essential factors in the retention of facts of this type is the realization that the facts will in the future be called for. It was not until he was 586 days old that the first situation was arranged to reveal his recollection after more than twelve hours. The morning following the hiding of the lure he showed no appreciation of its whereabouts, though his reactions indicated that he did realize he was being requested to find something. He would turn around, look about, and repeat his word for the hidden object. When the experimenter moved toward the door of the room in which the object was hidden he apparently recalled the incident of its hiding, for he went directly to the specific hiding place.

By the time he was 598 days old he was showing an occasional tendency to locate the object directly, but these occasions were transitory. There were times following the initial situation when he apparently not only did not recall the location of the object but, from all indications of his behavior, did not recall having placed it there once the object in its hiding place was pointed out to him. Then the time came when a glance from the experimenter, sometimes inadvertent, in the direction of the hiding place was adequate to give him the clue. It was not until he was 668 days old that he was characteristically able to locate the hidden object without the slightest suggestion of its whereabouts from the experimenter. Ultimately as soon as he got off the hospital elevator reference to the hidden object was sufficient to send him scampering down the hall to the right location.

His development in recalling the position of hidden objects was further advanced by the number of objects he was called upon to hide as well as the span of time before he was asked to recover them. By the time he was 715 days old it was possible for him to recall the location of eight unrelated objects, such as spoon, bell, box, pencil, book, screw-driver, dishmop, and key, hidden in eight different places. These he was able to locate correctly on command, although they were not called in the order in which they had been hidden. The fact that he would pause and look around before moving in a particular direction for the named object indicated definite discrimination. Of course, there were days when his performance was better and other days when it was worse, but by the time he was twenty-four months old his ability to recall and locate a number of hidden objects outstripped not only that of other infants under the observation of the experimenter but the experimenter herself, as well as other adults on the clinic staff. Probably any normal adult could easily recall the position of eight simple, unrelated articles hidden in eight different places if he gave sufficient attention to it. But ordinarily he is not called upon to do that specific thing. There was no definite and objective measure of Johnny's retention as compared with that of adults in this situation. The above statement is based not upon the possible performance of adults when reasonable attention was devoted to the task, but upon their casual performances when their attention was really focused upon the child. It was merely casually observed that Johnny recalled the location of the eight objects when the adults in the room did not. To the baby, however, it was a definite task, while to the adult it was a mere incident. The difference does expose the importance of attention in the process of retention and recall. The process of building up memory for specific facts of this type is, in the opinion of the writer, similar to that of an adult who sets about remembering the names of persons whom he meets.

It is interesting that the retentive powers in specific situations of a child under two years of age can through experience be developed to a degree beyond that which is ordinarily expected of an older child or adult. To what extent Johnny may retain his ability in this respect or to what extent, if any, there may be a transfer of his retentive powers from this to other situations is beyond the scope of this particular experiment. But if the writer may hazard a guess, it would be that this type of retention is a specific ability built up for the time being because of the demand made upon him; that it will probably weaken when the demand ceases, but that it could be reëstablished in short order if a similar demand were subsequently made upon him. It is reasonable to believe it could be reëstablished with greater ease because of this previous experience in the situation than would be the case if he had not had this particular experience.

Understanding of Relations

The infant's development in understanding connections between two objects, situations, or activities cannot at this time be analyzed from the rudiments, but illustrative "high spots" are of aid in revealing something of the developmental processes in these higher-level activities. The earliest understanding of relations which is indicated by the behavior of the infant is purely *associational*. Moreover, they are most commonly *spatial* relations.

The younger infant who is just beginning to hold and manipulate objects appears, as judged from his manner of behaving, to make the same association with all objects. But perhaps his behavior at this time is an indication not so much of one association with all objects, as of no particular association with any object. This is an undifferentiated state in so far as associational developments are concerned. Everything, irrespective of size, shape, color, or consistency, is brought to his mouth or banged about in random fashion if it can be handled. Many authorities are of the opinion that one of the first specific associations a baby makes is with the mother's face, the breast, or the bottle. These claims have been based upon the fact that when the baby sees the mother or the bottle he begins to engage in kicking or other excited excess activity. The writer has no experimental evidence to counteract these claims, but since so many other objects—a watch, a piece of paper, or anything held within the visual field—will often excite the same kind of activity in the baby there are grounds for being at least skeptical.

Since there are reactions in the behavior of the baby which positively indicate an *associational* connection, it might be well for us to limit our claims to those situations about which there can be no doubt. Only when the behavior of the baby becomes peculiar to a particular situation can an associational relation be assigned beyond the realm of doubt. The fact that the baby gets excited and kicks when he sees a bottle could scarcely be accepted as indisputable evidence of an associational relationship. But when he opens his mouth in a receptive attitude and also brings his face deliberately toward the bottle, then an associational relationship is indicated.

There is a period of some months in the baby's life when the outstretched arms of an adult toward him evoke not the slightest indication that he expects to be picked up. No matter how frequently adult arms are held toward the baby of two or three months as if to lift him, the baby of that age does not raise his arms in response. At first he pays no attention to the adult's hands; then he begins to look intently at the hands as he holds his own arms flexed and abducted. Both upper extremities and trunk may display excess activity, suggesting that the child wants to do something about the situation but does not know what to do. Later he may reach over to touch the adult's hands as if they were merely objects to be toyed with. Then follows the period when he deliberately extends his arms toward the adult and throws his trunk slightly forward in preparation to being lifted. The motor action is contingent upon his ability to make a meaningful association between the hands of the adult and the expected response. Adult hands then are not held in front of him to be grasped, or to take an object from him. Hands when held in that particular way before him have a very definite and specific meaning for him. His behavior in regard to the adult hand is selective and differentiated. Just how associations become differentiated and specific to the extent of being expressed in the somatic activity is beyond the present knowledge of the writer. It cannot be merely a conditional response due to a close temporal relation between the infant's experience of adult hands and of being lifted. No amount of such *conditioning* would evoke a similar response from the baby only a few weeks old. While temporal spatial coincidence is of primary importance in the infant's development of associational relations, the frequency with which he experiences a particular relationship does not constitute an adequate explanation of the process of development.

Whatever may be the process of associational development, the first evidence of an associational connection is evinced in the behavior of the baby in making an adjustment of his own body to particular environmental conditions. But he develops beyond such limitations and no longer needs to depend entirely upon meeting his problems by adjusting his own body. He indicates the existence of an associational concept by manipulation of environmental factors and active attempts to put the associated elements together. When he sees his shoe he does not just put it in his mouth to be chewed, nor does he merely make the bodily adjustment of raising his foot to have the shoe put on him. Instead he goes to the extent of putting the shoe to his foot. He probably does not have adequate motor and mental equipment for a complete performance, but the fact that he picks up the shoe and takes it to his foot indicates a definite step in associational connections between the two. Likewise, when a baby picks up a comb or brush and takes it to his hair, instead of just chewing on it or banging with it, an associational connection is indicated, but the connection is still lacking in specificity. He has no idea which side of the comb to use, and he certainly could not pull the teeth of the comb through his hair, though the existence of the association is without doubt. He has made a connection between comb and hair, but it has not become restricted to details so that he knows its specific function. The interesting thing about development of connections of this type is that at first the associations are established between *the* shoe and *the* foot only or *the* comb and *the* hair with which he is familiar. Presently the association is no longer limited to a particular shoe but other shoes are connected with the foot. He may be observed attempting to put on himself the shoes of adults. The connection of *the* shoe and *the* foot is an inchoate movement in the development of an association, whereas the following phase is equivalent to the exaggeration or overworking of an act as the association begins to expand. Having gained in broadening his associations, he loses in the specific connection; hence there often follows a brief period of confusion when the child will be observed seriously trying to put a shoe on his head, his hand or some other unrelated part. He will also be observed in serious attempts to put other unrelated articles upon his feet. Gradually, the association becomes more definite until he is able to distinguish shoes in a meaningful way from other objects and to distinguish his shoes from other shoes. Subsequently, when he puts on adult shoes or when he places boxes or cans or hats on his feet it is obviously in play and not an indication of inadequate discrimination.

We have seen that the first evidence of an unequivocal associational relation is indicated when the baby begins to behave specifically to particular situations. When the baby begins to associate two objects sufficiently to put them together, it is observed that his earliest associations of this type concern objects pertaining to himself. He puts a cap to his head, a shoe on his foot, a toothbrush in his mouth. Soon, however, he begins to associate objects or acts which though related in themselves are not definitely connected to him. A comb means not just combing his hair, but combing the hair of some one else; the wash-cloth becomes associated with the basin, and a key is associated with the door.

The steps involved in the building-up of associations and the corresponding change in the child's behavior are well illustrated in the familiar growth observed in the child's gaining urinary control. At first the child takes no responsibility whatever either in urination or inhibiting urination. Many persons consider a child "trained" if he is taken at regular intervals to the toilet so that wet diapers are avoided. As a matter of fact, in that case only the adult in charge has been trained to watch the child's physiological rhythm and to place him on the toilet at the proper hour. At this stage it is quite possible to *condition* the very young baby to a certain postural situation and urination, but even then the baby is not exercising individual control over the function. The child is not really trained until he can assume responsibility so that there is no need of clock-watching on the part of the attending adult. Ordinarily the first sign of development in this situation is that the child makes an association with a particular vessel and perhaps a particular room. Once he has made that association, he will attempt to respond whenever the situation is presented even though he has urinated only a few minutes before. Also at this stage of development he will show some sign of realizing his mistake if he urinates elsewhere. He may go so far as to inhibit until the situation is favorable. Although at this stage of development he responds adequately in the familiar situation, when confronted with an unfamiliar one he becomes excessively inhibited, fails to act favorably toward the situation, and reverts to the uncontrolled phase of the behavior-course which results in urination regardless of extrinsic conditions. Once he begins to realize that there is more than one specific place favorable for this activity, there follows a period when he "overdoes" the idea and deliberately urinates in vessels and situations not previously associated with that activity. Finally, he exercises discrimination and selection as to the places and occasions suitable for the act. At this stage, although the baby voluntarily urinates in a socially disapproved container, his act is prompted by inadequate discrimination. An older child who deliberately urinates in the wrong vessel is not thereby evincing undeveloped discrimination in that particular behavior-course but is probably motivated from some factor in the growth of social-group behavior-patterns.

Often because of the apparent connections between two objects or situations when a child first experiences them, some of his associations appear rather bizarre, and unless the observer is aware of the child's antecedent experiences in which those associations were established, his behavior-patterns appear ridiculous. For example, it appears either absurd or naughty when the child take his finger, puts it in the coffee cream, takes off the thick cream from around the edge and smears it on his face. But if one recalls that he had previously had experience putting his finger in a cold-cream jar and spreading that kind of cream on his face, his performance with the thick coffee cream is indicative of a step in associational development rather than stupidity or naughtiness. It indicates that he is making a specific response to the consistency of the cream rather than its location on a shelf or the type of container. Undoubtedly the behavior of infants and young children would appear much less absurd or random if the observer of his activities were acquainted with and appreciated the previous associations which were influencing his behavior at the time.

It is not possible to set forth rules for the guidance of children of all ages or for the management of a child of a given age in all situations. This does not indicate that the behavior development of infants and children is so individualistic as to preclude the formulation of principles of management. Much of the current confusion concerning the management of children could be obviated if principles of guidance were based upon the process of growth. For example, consider the present differences of opinion as to the desirable amount of parental coercion to be enforced upon the child. There is no agreement as to the amount of coercion that may be damaging to the child's growth or the amount of freedom that may be allowed before it becomes license. There is a fairly general notion that each child is a law unto himself and should be handled individually. If behavior is subject to general principles, then it seems reasonable that the direction of behavior might also be reduced to fundamental principles.

Coercion or restriction of an activity which is just beginning to develop may build into the child an inhibiting attitude which will prevent the action from reaching a desirable stage of development. On the other hand, if the exercise of that particular activity is not checked it may develop excessively at the expense of some newly emerging activity with which it is in competition. For example, to allow the creeping infant, who is just beginning to explore the world beyond his arm's length, freedom in investigating the content of bureau drawers may be a matter of wisdom. Such exploratory behavior is nutriment to his sensory experience, which is advancing most rapidly at that time. To allow the older child freedom in the same activity is not only folly but is actually damaging to his development in discriminating socially approved and disapproved conduct.

There are other types of behavior rapidly developing in the older child. These he should be given a liberal chance to exercise. It would seem that freedom should be allotted to those behavior-patterns or those aspects of a behavior-pattern which are at the threshold of development. In other words, the stage of plasticity of fixity of the behavior-pattern should be the guiding principle for the degree of freedom introduced into the growth situation.

The earliest type of associational relations occurring in the behavior repertoire of the infant are simple connections between things which occur in close temporal or spatial relations. An understanding of *conditional* relations appears later. Then the infant's understanding is no longer limited to simple connections such as that between a bib and his neck. The bib around his neck becomes associated as a conditional relation to eating. Sometimes the conditional relation of bib to eating becomes so established that the child may refuse to eat without the bib. He begins to discover that if and when he pushes a button a light turns on, perhaps some several feet away. The association is not merely between button and light. It is rather that the conditions involved in *pushing* the button bring on the light. Being placed in a high chair means *conditions* during which he has food, and getting pajamas indicates preparatory conditions to sleeping. At this stage of development getting pajamas may sufficiently indicate going to bed as to stimulate his approaching the bed undirected. He does not make the association of pajamas and bed until he has the pajamas. In other words, they have not as yet become a symbol by which he could convey his desire to go to bed.

But out of these primary conditional associations, language and symbolic associations begin to develop. The baby now no longer waits until the adult's hands are in front of him before he reacts favorably to be lifted up. Instead he extends his arms and moves his body forward for the purpose of indicating his desire to be taken up. He no longer merely puts a cap to his head when it is handed to him (pure associational relations); he will bring his hat or coat to the adult for the obvious purpose of conveying the idea of departure, although he has no adequate speech for expressing the wish. The connection is not only between hat and head, nor does it mean simply that when the hat is on he goes out. The hat becomes the symbol for the idea or act of going out. That is, an interpretative association between hat and going out has become established.

Long before Johnny was able to make any recognizable sounds for shoes, at the age of seventeen months, when taken to the adult swimming pool and lead toward the diving board he immediately turned around, walked to the other side of the pool, picked up a towel and the experimenter's shoes, and brought them to the experimenter. The towel and the shoes served as a symbol to express his wish not to dive in the water. These symbols he used adequately in the absence of a vocal language technique. Since the child had inadequate speech equipment, a garment became a symbol for conveying a complete but complex idea.

If language development is considered as growth in symbolic associations, it must be recognized that symbolic associations begin to develop before the child either comprehends or uses words in connection with the specific situation. A child who neither understands the word *cereal* nor makes a sound which he definitely associates with that article will be able to convey his desire to have cereal by holding up the bowl in which it is customarily served to him. The bowl and the gesture become the symbol of the complete idea, though he may engage in grunting or other vocalization in order to attract attention to his gesture. Later, merely a vocal sound which he identifies with cereal is used to say that he would like to have some cereal. Finally, the gesture becomes eliminated and the vocal aspect of the behavior-pattern assumes the major responsibility for conveying the idea.

Language Development

We shall not consider for the time being differentiation in vocalization which terminates in the acquisition of language. It is beyond controversy that crying, babbling and lollalia of the young infant constitute the anlage of vocal speech, but verbalization is only a limited aspect of language development. Since verbal language is a process of symbolic association, the question is legitimately raised as to why the baby does not begin to talk earlier. Is it because he has inadequate speech organs? Or is it because he is incapable of symbolic associations?

It is beyond the scope of this investigation to analyze the steps involved in the development of vocal expression. When the study of language is considered merely from the standpoint of development in associational relationships, significant steps in language development may be summarized in the manner shown below.

(1) *Crying Phase.* For a period immediately following birth the only vocalizations the baby indulges in are pure cry. The cry consists of practically no consonant sounds. There has been considerable discussion among writers on the subject as to the use the baby at the time makes of crying as a means of conveying a state of discomfort or a desire for attention. Some contend that crying is merely a reflex reaction largely of physiological importance in oxygenating the blood. Until more convincing evi-

dence is produced to the contrary, it seems the best we can do is accept the cry of the newborn infant as a reflex activity having no language or associational significance.

(2) *The Babble Phase.* The second phase is that which we have in the absence of a better term called cooing or babbling. It appears ordinarily toward the end of the first month and is distinguished from the crying phase by the fact that the infant is capable of making sounds other than crying which are pleasant to the auditor. These sounds are largely vowels and appear to be more in the nature of vocal gymnastics than to have any meaning or associational value to the infant.

(3) *Lollalia Phase.* During this period the child not only greatly expands the number and combination of sounds he can make, but he begins to acquire variations in pitch and inflexion. His vocalizations take on a conversational tone. They become associated with facial expressions, but they are not, so far as can be determined by the observer, linked in any meaningful way to particular situations. Although the baby may repeat the same sound frequently, none appears to be specifically associated with particular objects.

(4) *Language Comprehension and Use.* Gesture is the primary language instrument of the infant. This is true both for his comprehension and for his use of language. In order to discuss the steps of development in this phase of the behavior-course, comprehension and use of language will have to be considered separately, though they are, of course, developing at the same time and are inherently interrelated.

Development in Language Comprehension

Gestures convey meaningful associations to the child long before he begins to comprehend the spoken word. In the beginning of definite language comprehension it is impossible to estimate the extent to which it is the specific gesture of the adult, the extent to which it is the conditions of the particular situation at the time, or the extent to which it is the accompanying vocal speech of the adult which conveys the idea to the infant. For example, if without gesture an adult tells a child of a certain maturational level to "put the spoon on the table" and he does not understand one word that is spoken, he will apparently pay no attention to the adult. If, however, he is at such a stage of development that he responds to gestures, and if the adult points to the spoon and then to the table, the very circumstances of the situation complete the idea to the child and he complies. It is not the vocal sounds but the conditions of the situation which convey the idea to the child.

Later the child begins to identify the sound "spoon" with a particular object. Once he has made that connection, it is possible to get him to pick up the spoon in response to the vocal word only, although it would still be necessary to use gesture in conveying to him just what he should do with it. If a different spoon were used, it would again be necessary to use gesture in indicating the object to him, though he would comply favorably without gesture to the specific spoon. Gradually, he perceives that more than one object is referred to as "spoon." Expanding development in that respect appears to result in a regression period when he fails frequently to distinguish spoons from other objects and even fails to distinguish the particular spoon with which he first identified the sound. This apparent regression in behavior is not so much a failure to distinguish the spoon as it is an excessive use of the newly acquired idea that other things than the specific object with which he made the original connection can be called "spoon." Little by little he begins to particularize his selection of objects in response to the word "spoon" so as to choose objects of common form, use, or material.

The next outstanding phase in the development of language comprehension is indicated by an understanding of simple commands without gesture on the part of the adult. The first commands which the baby seems to understand without gesture are those which involve his making simple bodily adjustments, such as "lie down," "sit down," and "stand up." Gradually he begins to understand more complicated directions without the aid of gesture. Directions to manipulate certain objects in his immediate environment, or especially in his field of vision, at the time the direction is given soon come within his comprehension. Ultimately he is able to comprehend and follow directions involving the manipulation of objects which are not in his presence at the time the directions are given.

At this stage, although the baby understands simple language directed to him, he does not comprehend the language of adults in his presence. Early in this period he seemingly pays no attention to the conversation of adults. It is necessary to get his attention before speaking to him. A mother touching the face or otherwise endeavoring to get his attention before speaking to him is such a familiar sight as practically to escape notice. But the time arrives when the child unmistakably distinguishes between occasions when he is being addressed and when an adult is being addressed in his presence. His distinction in this respect would not be noted if both adults were obviously present, for in that case he goes about his business, accepting their conversation as not meant for him and apparently paying little heed unless his attention is called for. He distinguishes differences in conversational tone to identify adult discourse as different from language directed to him. Even if the child is never addressed in what is known as "baby-talk" he will, nevertheless, behave differentially to the new conversational situations. Development in this respect has been observed in the laboratory when the child considered himself alone with the experimenter in the laboratory room. Observers were in an adjoining observation room looking through one-way vision mirror glass. Under these circumstances it has been customary for the experimenter to give verbal directions to the child, but occasionally to interpolate explanatory comments addressed to the hidden observers. The observers are instructed not to reply. For many months a child will show no evidence of noticing when these comments to adults were interjected. Later, however, when such comments are made the child will stop suddenly and look around the room to see where the other person is. At this stage, although he distinguishes language directed to adults from language directed to him, he does not comprehend the language directed to adults.

Subsequently he shows a partial comprehension of adult conversation, especially if it refers to him. Illustrations of this phase are common in daily occurrences, when a mother directs a nurse to do certain things to or for the child. The child who was present but apparently engrossed in his play suddenly drops his play in order to run away from or comply with the conditions of the language which he had overheard. Later he begins to understand simple conversation of two adults even though it does not in any way refer to him. The child does not in the beginning grasp the full context of such conversation, but the reality of his partial comprehension of what is said is indicated by the fact that he suddenly stops what he is doing and behaves specifically in reference to the things about which the adults are talking. For example, a child overhearing a commonplace adult remark about a dirty floor may be stimulated to go for a broom.

Final development in language comprehension is indicated when the child understands the general conversation of two or more adults. This phase, of course, is of much later development than the period being covered in this report. Development in language comprehension moves considerably in advance of language usage. Even after the child has begun to show some facility with the spoken word there is considerable time before usage and comprehension are well integrated.

Development of Language Usage

One of the first indications of definite language-molding out of the lollalia stage is the conversational intonations, especially repeated cadences associated with termination of an act. Following this phase there appears a slightly more definite stage wherein the infant begins to repeat essentially the same sound for specific objects and the same combination of sounds in particular situations. These sounds are impure. For that reason it may appear to the listener as if the child is making the same sound for objects of a different variety. But it is evident from the child's behavior, if he is presented with these objects and asked to name them, that the distinction in the sounds he makes is satisfactory to him. The sound the child makes for "cracker" and for "water" may seem to the adult to be the same, but if the two things are presented to the child, it is obvious as he names them that the distinction between the sounds he makes is clear to him. At this stage he is neither capable of sensing or making fine distinctions in speech sounds.

In the beginning of his identification of certain sounds with objects he makes the sounds for specific objects only. Later he begins to generalize and make the same sound for other objects of the same kind. For example, he begins to identify a small cylindrical object with a sound which he makes for "stick." Later he makes the same sound for other objects, different in size and shape. In making this generalization in using a sound for a type of object rather than a specific one with which he is most familiar he apparently becomes confused and makes the sound which was formerly used for "stick" when he sees a pencil, a ruler, a string, a brush, or what not. There may follow then a period of apparent regression when he will not make, even for the familiar stick, the sound which he has formerly used. Subsequently he begins to classify on the basis of use, form, or material a sound for many types of sticks, and does not make the sound for other objects than sticks. Concurrent with this phase of development, in which the child makes specific sounds for specific objects, though the sounds are not pure English words, he is also likely to begin using English words—clear, distinct English words or phrases—in a meaningless situation. It appears as if the child is developing in the control of articulation and in the identification of sounds with objects at the same time, but there is as yet little union or integration in the two developing speech processes.

Language techniques which involve the conveying of ideas more complex than the identification of objects with names are in the initial phase comprised of gesture. The earliest gestures might be said to consist of the withdrawal or defense reactions which the infant makes to disagreeable stimuli. Later the infant begins to point toward objects cherished. With further development, if he cannot make himself understood with pointing, he will take an adult by the hand and lead him to the coveted object. These relatively more mature gestures are accompanied by a great deal of vocalization.

Some infants acquire great skill in conveying fairly complex ideas in the gesture fashion. Ordinarily for the use of the gesture language the object must be within view, but the writer has observed children convey definite ideas about objects out of view although they did not utter one intelligible sound in doing so. To illustrate, when Johnny was nineteen months old, he was observed playing with several objects, among them a pocket comb. After several minutes he came to the writer, who was in an adjoining room. He engaged in an inordinate amount of vocalization and grunting, his eyes dilating with a questioning expression. But the experimenter did not understand. Johnny pointed toward the things he had been playing with. Still the experimenter did not understand. Then he raised his hand to his head and began to make a sort of motion as if combing his hair. Since the experimenter had noticed that a comb was among the objects he had been playing with, his gestures carried the information that the comb was lost. He and the experimenter began looking for the lost comb. Suddenly he turned, looked under a box, and found it. Obviously he suddenly recalled placing it there. He held it up to the experimenter to show that the comb was found. Although his vocal language was meager at this time, he was able to make extensive use of gesture in conveying complex ideas.

There is a distinct milestone in language development when the child begins to substitute a purely vocal symbol for a somatic symbol such as gesture. Further attainment in language development is indicated when the child is able to speak without gesture about objects and situations which are not in his immediate environment. He may be able to talk at a great rate and convey fairly complex ideas although most of his words are slurred and impure. There is a noticeable tendency at about this stage of language usage toward a repetition of syllables. The tendency toward echolalia and the repetition of syllables is representative of the exaggeration phase in manipulation of sounds. A distinct step forward is indicated when the child realizes that he is saying the word incorrectly, that he is putting in too many false syllables. If his awareness is sufficient, he spontaneously makes the correction. For example, there was a long period when both Johnny and Jimmy said "wa-wa" for "water." They were corrected in this, whereupon Johnny began saying "wa-*tear*" and Jimmy "wa-wa-ter." Several weeks later Johnny was heard spontaneously to say when he looked toward the river, "wa-*tear* no wa-wa—wa-*tear*.

Final development in language usage is indicated when the child can conduct intelligible conversation in his native language. Of course, development in this particular behavior-pattern may continue all through life.

It was impossible in the present investigation to arrange laboratory conditions which would stimulate language usage on the part of the child. Furthermore, our endeavors to stimulate Johnny in language comprehension were not systematic or well controlled. Our records consist primarily of observational notes made of some language activities occurring under laboratory conditions and others in free activity. These records are of greater value in revealing the developmental sequence than in showing a comparative development of Johnny and Jimmy under different conditions. As a matter of fact, no effort was made to keep Jimmy from receiving language stimulation, since, although his crib was behind a screen, he was exposed to adult conversation as well as chatter of other children all during the day when he was in the clinic nursery. Therefore, there is no reason to believe that Jimmy received less stimulation in language use and comprehension during his period of restriction than did Johnny. Johnny's experience was no doubt more definite, and systematic effort was made to aid Johnny in making associations of specific sounds with specific objects and types of objects.

When Johnny was 415 days old he unquestionably complied to verbal commands given without gesture, and when 461 days old he was obviously recognizing definite pieces of furniture by name. When commanded to "put your blanket on the chair," he selected the chair from among other pieces of furniture—stool, table, and bench—going past them in order to place his blanket on the chair. Most of the pieces of furniture were stained in essentially the same color. The word *chair* had become particularized to a given piece of furniture. He not only put the blanket on the chair but left it there, thereby revealing his development of the concept *put*. It is interesting to watch the development of verbal concepts. In the initial stages of development, "to put" something on a table signifies merely the act of placing it there but does not carry to the child the meaning of leaving it there as well.

When Johnny was 469 days old the experimenter placed six objects on the floor one by one, and named each as she did so. Johnny was then instructed to pick them up one by one as the experimenter repeated their names. The order in which they were called for varied from the order in which they were first named. These directions were verbal and given without gesture. If he failed and brought the wrong object, the experimenter corrected him, called the object he had brought by its right name, pointed to the one first indicated, and repeated the correct name for it. Even on the second day he was confronted with this situation he was able to select about four objects correctly. He was able to grasp the name of an object if he had had few previous associations with it. If he had established prior associations with the objects used in this situation, then the early association often determined the character of his action at this time. For example, Johnny had already made associations between the word "towel" and the sink. When he was given the towel along with other objects for identification, although he carefully picked up the other objects when directed to do so, every time he was told to bring the towel he would walk over to the sink.

When it was definitely established that the child could select a given number of objects on command, an unfamiliar object, which he had never seen or heard mentioned before, was placed among the familiar ones. It was given no name by the experimenter before the child was requested to select it. After the experimenter had asked him to select two or three of the familiar objects, the unfamiliar one would be called for in order to determine if he could select the unfamiliar object by a process of elimination. This situation was first presented to him when he was 486 days old. By the time he was 529 days old he almost invariably selected the new object by a process of elimination, provided the familiar objects were not too familiar and provided the new object was not too attractive. If the new object was unduly attractive, he would run straightway to it without waiting for the directions of the experimenter. If the familiar objects were so well known that he did not have to consider the situation, then he would not stop to deliberate, and therefore he was more likely to make a mistake. During the latter part of his practice in this activity the idea that he should select the object on command had become so well established that it interfered with his actually picking up the new object even when he was most attracted to it. He would not, however, select the object which had been called for. Instead he would bend over the alluring new object, pointing to it and chattering with great enthusiasm.

After the child unquestionably associated a particular object with its name, for example, "ball" or "bowl," a new object of the same variety but different in color or size would be substituted. This alteration of only one factor would cause him more trouble in making the selection than would an object with which he was completely unfamiliar. Ordinarily the confusion would stimulate him to select an object which he identified by another name. But the cautious way in which he would reach for the other object and the way he would turn to look at the experimenter for approbation as he did so were sufficient evidence that he realized he was making a mistake. For example, suppose the object were a bowl, but the familiar bowl was not present. Since he was familiar with the sound of the word, he would select an object with which he was also familiar rather than choose an unfamiliar object (in this case the bowl of different size and color) in connection with a verbal sound for which he had established definite associations.

It was not until he was 563 days old that he began to make associations and use specific verbal sounds for particular qualities of objects. It was then observed that he made the same sound for "hot" when he touched the radiator as he did for his food when it was smoking, or for steam coming from a sterilizer. Development in Johnny's use of the word "broken" is an excellent illustration of the way language concepts arise. "Boke" is a sound which he began to utter whenever he let an object fall, whether it scattered into fragments or not. Then he apparently learned that "broken" was not applied unless the object was put out of order, so he began to use the work "boke" not when something fell necessarily, but when he could not make use of it. For example, he was playing with a tongue depressor when in an effort to pick it up off the floor he pushed it under a door. Immediately he said "boke," since he could not get it any more. At the same age he was walking on a platform. A frame with black netting extended out beyond the boards of the platform. Johnny started to step on the netting but immediately withdrew and said "boke." It was some months later before he began to associate the word more specifically with things scattered into fragments.

Around the age of fifteen months he began to manifest a tendency to associate a particular word with only a part of an object requested rather than the whole. When he was 596 days of age he used the sound "li li" when he saw merely brightness, when he saw only the button to be pushed for turning on the light, or when he picked up the shade of a lamp. When he was 586 days old he distinguished between language addressed to him and language addressed to an adult, and when he was 700 days old he not only distinguished when he was addressed but he unquestionably understood the context of simple conversation between two adults, especially when the conversation referred to him.

During most of the period when Johnny was under daily observation of the experimenter his language technique consisted of gesture coupled with a great deal of vocalization, some of which approached English sounds. But it was only infrequently that relatively pure English words were evoked. When he was 620 days old the first tendency to limit his action to a verbal reply was indicated. A whistle had been hidden in the box. While he was getting off a stool the experimenter remarked, "Johnny, do you remember where the whistle is?" Instead of running directly to the whistle as he ordinarily did under such circumstances, he merely answered "box." When he was 688 days old it was possible for him to carry out fairly complex commands with reference to specific objects in another room, though none of the objects referred to were in his field of vision at the time the command was given. Children begin to grasp conditional relations in concrete situations long before they understand them in a language situation. It was not until Johnny was 652 days old that he showed evidence of understanding conditional clauses, such as "If you sit down you may do thus and so."

Records on Jimmy during this period are necessarily incomplete, but they are adequate to indicate that, certainly as far as speech is concerned, Jimmy was equal if not superior to Johnny. He tended to use phrases or sentences more easily, although his language did not, during the early period, appear to be as definitely tied up to specific objects and situations. He was more inclined to engage in echolalia, repeating the same sentence or phrase over and over whether or not it was appropriate to the situation. Jimmy could be heard daily behind his crib saying in fairly clear English, "See der ball" or "Dere der ball" innumerable times, though there was no ball in sight. His enunciation was consistently better than Johnny's.

In the earlier stages of language comprehension he did not begin to approach Johnny in understanding directions. When 473 days old he complied with simple commands such as "Sit down." The act of sitting he then definitely associated with a small chair. The first evidence of Jimmy's associating a particular name with an object when only parts of it were observable occurred when he was 611 days old. At the same time he was able to identify objects by names although they were out of sight at the time. This type of behavior had been observed in Johnny nearly two months earlier, but it must be remembered that it might have been noted earlier in the behavior of Jimmy if he had been available to the observers more frequently. When Jimmy was 611 days old he made the same sound for "radio" when he saw the object, though there was no music occurring at the time, when he heard music from the radio but could not see it, and also when he heard some one in the street singing.

From the time Jimmy was 529 days old until he was 626 days old, when confronted with objects to be selected on command, his characteristic mode of behavior was to pick them all up at once, rather than to make a selection one by one. This manner of action is quite typical of that of other children of corresponding development when they do not identify an object with its specific name. If, however, they associate one or two objects with specific names, they will select them correctly, if commanded to do so first, but whenever they are directed to pick up an object they do not know they revert to the less mature mode of action, viz., picking up all objects at once.

When Jimmy was 626 days old, he not only showed some ability in selecting the right objects, but he recognized the unfamiliar name as referring to an unfamiliar object. He selected two objects correctly, but when the experimenter called for the unfamiliar one he hesitated and asked "Where is dat?" Then he went to the unfamiliar object and touched it but did not pick it up. His behavior on this occasion is an illustration of a partial move toward the goal, but the move was not carried through to completion. The experimenter is inclined to believe that Jimmy's superiority in language usage is another indication of his superior endowment and that Johnny's acceleration in comprehension during his practice period was a result of increased experience. Johnny's superiority in language comprehension was not limited to the experimenter or members of the clinic staff or to the laboratory situation. When persons equally unfamiliar to the two children gave them simple directions, there was, at this age, a great disparity in the comprehension of the two children.

On just what basis the child is finally enabled to discriminate objects of a variety or kind and to associate a type of object or a type of activity with a particular word we were not in this investigation able to determine. So far as our data reveal, it appears as if the child, when he first begins to discriminate, does so on the basis of use and position. Form, size, and color discrimination come later, but form discrimination certainly antedates color and size. Children will discriminate objectively both on the basis of color and size long before they will make the distinction in size or color in response to language. Many a mother has heard her child of fifteen or eighteen months complain when she has broken a cracker and handed him the smaller piece. Yet if at the same age he should be confronted with two boxes different only in size and told to look in the big box to find the biggest piece of cracker, he could not discriminate big from little, but would go from one box to the other.

If the child of similar instructional level observed an object being placed in a red drawer, he could later locate it when told to get the object, although the position of the drawer had been changed from the original location it occupied when the object was placed in it and even if it were placed among several others like it in every way except color. However, if the red drawer were placed among several others different only in color and if the child were directed to look in the red one for an object which he had *not* seen placed there, he would be unable to make the selection of the correct drawer. The experimenter has observed no child under two years of age who could discriminate on a color basis in connection with verbal directions only.

In the present investigation we attempted to study the effect of repeated experience in the development of size and color discrimination when only verbal clues were given. The child would have set before him two boxes, two balls, or two bells, alike in every way except size. He would then be instructed to select the little or big one. If the child showed no signs of recognition the experimenter would designate which was the big one and which the little one and then again request him to select one or the other.

Experience in this situation began with Johnny when he was 539 days old. Until he was 592 days old there was no evidence whatever that he made the slightest discrimination in size differences in compliance with language directions. That he definitely understood he was expected to make a selection there was no doubt, for he would reach out his hand to take an object, then look to the experimenter for some indication of approval before actually grasping the object. When none was given he would either select any one of the objects or turn his attention to other activities. From the time he was 592 days old until he was 620 days old there were occasional factors in his behavior which indicated discrimination on the basis of size, but these suggestions of size discrimination were incomplete and transitory. Moreover, there followed a period of approximately a month when he showed practically no signs of discrimination of this sort in connection with language directions. When he was 654 days old, however, he was definitely and unquestionably selecting objects on a size basis in response to a language command, but only when the familiar experimental objects were used. When the practice period of this study was terminated, Johnny still did not discriminate on a size basis in response to verbal directions for objects in general, although he often did so when dealing with the specific objects with which he had been practised. He was obviously capable of perceiving differences in size, and hence it seems justifiable to conclude that the difficulty was one of language comprehension. He had not yet attained a comprehension of adjectival relations.

The laboratory conditions under which we essayed to study the comprehension and discrimination of color differences with reference to language directions were as follows: Doors opening into different compartments were painted red, yellow, blue, green, and white, though they were alike in every way except color. These doors could not be moved, and hence it was impossible to change their relative positions. However, small drawers in bedside cabinets were also painted red, yellow, blue, and green, and these were interchangeable. The experimenter, pointing to the red drawer, would repeat the word "red," likewise to the red door, and so on with the other colors. Then the child would be directed to look in the red drawer to find an object which he had *not* seen placed there.

When Johnny was 457 days old he showed evidence of discriminating on the color basis, but not in reference to language association. On that day he observed an object being placed in a yellow drawer which was arranged in a line beside the red, blue, and green drawers. Then he was engaged in other activities such as climbing off stools. While he was getting off the stool the red and yellow drawers were interchanged. He was then directed to get the object. He discriminately selected the yellow drawer. Discrimination was indicated by his pause to observe all the drawers before making the selection. It was not until he was 541 days old that practice in selecting the colors of the doors and drawers by name was initiated. For a brief period between 548 and 579 days of age he frequently appeared to be discriminating with respect to the red and blue drawers, but since this discrimination was not transferred to the red and blue doors, it is possible that he was reacting on some other clue than color. At 604 days of age and following his behavior consisted more of imitating the experimenter in naming the drawers than in complying with or comprehending the request. He would go from one drawer to the other, touching each with his index finger and chattering. This illustrates the interference of a newly developing function, viz., imitation, with another type of activity. That he was not selectively responding to specific names and specific colors was further indicated by the fact that when he started to open one of the drawers or doors he would look to the experimenter questioningly to determine if he was right in his choice. At a later period, when he was 646 days old, he was apparently selecting both red and blue drawers and red and blue doors on command. A few days later he was discriminating with respect to the yellow door and drawers. But these were only transitory successes, for when he was 662 days old there was a regression to the old habit of running from one door to another and then turning to the experimenter for approval before actually opening one or the other. This period of lack in discrimination continued until he was 704 days old, when there followed a period of two weeks during which he often definitely selected red, blue, and yellow in response to verbal directions. His color discrimination applied, however only to the apparatus with which he was familiar. During the practice period successful reactions were never invariable. When the training period terminated at the age of 743 days, after more than six months of experience in this situation, Johnny was not discriminating generally on a color basis in compliance to language directions. Practice over a period of six months had not materially advanced his attainments in this respect. Since he was able to perceive color differences even fairly early, his failure to respond to verbal directions with respect to color indicates that the difficulty was probably one of language comprehension.

As a matter of fact the child was at this time showing an inability in many situations to differentiate adjectival modifications. For example, if he offered his left hand and the adult requested the *right* hand, there were many months when he showed no signs of realizing that a different hand was being requested. He merely stood holding out his left arm and looking questioningly at the adult. It was not until Johnny was 638 days old that he began to realize that there was a difference between his right and left hands. At that time, when he offered the left hand, if the adult repeated "right hand," he immediately changed and offered the other hand; whereas before he had made no move to change hands in this situation. He was not given special daily exercises in this activity. When his general practice was terminated at the age of 743 days, he still did not distinguish right and left as bilateral aspects of his body. At the same age, however, Jimmy still did not realize that right and left hands were different and would continue to hold the left hand extended even though the adult repeatedly requested the right. This difference in favor of Johnny suggests that his daily exercise in other adjectival terms and his occasional experience in handed discrimination had advanced his development slightly in an appreciation of modifying terms.

Anticipatory Reactions

Another aspect of development in associational activities is indicated by the child's ability to anticipate needs or difficulties. One of the earliest manifestations of anticipatory behavior on the part of the infant is his holding his mouth open to receive approaching food. As soon as behavior begins to assume definite from, it becomes directional. The function of a goal in organizing and determining behavior-courses is more apparent in the infant's behavior after he begins to creep. As soon as the child begins to move about and pursue an objective, it will be observed that he tends to move in a direct line toward it. If the chosen route is blocked, he turns aside only after he has bumped against the blockage. His next move then is to creep around the interfering obstacle. With further development he continues to creep directly toward the goal until he strikes the blockage; then he proceeds to push it aside rather than creep around it. There is a distinct advance in his developmental processes when he perceives and anticipates the blockage and either avoids it or removes it before he bumps up against it. Similar developmental phases are evidenced in the child's manipulation of tools or apparatus in order to obtain an objective. It will be recalled from the situations involving the manipulation of stools and boxes that the first move of the child is to get himself as near the object as possible. Once there and realizing that he cannot reach the object, he starts for a stool or other apparatus to help him out. Later, it will be observed that he does not at first go near the object but goes directly for the necessary apparatus.

When Johnny was 415 days old there appeared distinct signs of anticipatory behavior of an immature type. A ball rolled under a pool in the laboratory. The pool stood ten inches above the floor. Johnny started across the room after the ball. Although the ball was plainly in view at all times, it was evident that he would have to stoop and crawl under the pool a short distance in order to obtain it. As he walked across the room he was observed to stoop three times before reaching the pool. The fact that he stooped, then arose without delay in order to continue the distance walking, is evidence that this was not a mistaken judgment in distance. The fact that the ball was in full view at all times would rule out the possibility of his stooping to reassure himself that the ball was still there. Therefore these repeated but momentary stoops as he approached the ball seem to indicate his anticipating the necessity of stooping once he arrived at the pool. When 596 days old he showed anticipation of obstacles in his way as he pushed stools in a given direction. He started pushing the stool, saw the obstacle, dropped the stool before he came in contact with the obstacle, ran and pushed the obstacle aside, then went directly back to pushing the stool to the desired position. When 611 days old he showed anticipation of the necessity of freeing his hands in order to engage in another activity. He was carrying in each hand a bunch of keys as he skated down the hall. The experimenter had turned the corner about twenty feet ahead of him, when he came rushing toward her. He had just passed an open door to a room containing a blackboard and chalk. As he reached the experimenter he handed over the two bunches of keys, turned and went directly to the blackboard and chalk in another room more than twenty feet away. Here he was anticipating the need of getting his hands free in order to use the chalk. Of course, he had experienced scribbling on the blackboard before, but earlier in his development he would not have bothered to get rid of the keys before starting for the chalk. He would have thrown them on the floor just before he started to pick up the chalk. Twenty days later more advanced development in the anticipation of needs was indicated. Johnny was with the experimenter in the laboratory when he was told to get a spoon. In order to get the spoon he would have to cross the hall, go to the kitchen, and climb up on a chair or stool so as to reach the spoon on a cabinet. When the directions were given in the laboratory he started pushing a stool toward the door, obviously anticipating the need of a stool for climbing once he arrived at the cabinet. Earlier in his development he would have gone first to the cabinet, not realizing the need of the stool until he was in the situation.

One reason why the behavior of children appears to be random and purposeless is that adults do not give them time to carry through their activities to completion. For example, in the particular instance just mentioned, as Johnny moved the stool toward the door he knocked over a box so that the lid came open. He then stopped pushing the stool and spent a good deal of time and effort getting the box right side up and the lid closed. An observer inexperienced in the ways of children would have been convinced that he had lost all sight of the spoon as an objective. In this instance the spoon was not referred to again by the experimenter, neither was his activity with the box interfered with. But as soon as he had succeeded in getting the lid closed he went back to the stool, pushed it across the hall to the kitchen, climbed up, and secured the spoon.

We have had to call largely upon the details of specific instances in pointing out the significant steps in development during the last half of the second year. There are several reasons for this, one being that behavior of this order is very complex, and the more complex it is the more difficult it is to classify and analyze. The stream of behavior has not only swollen, it has also struck rapids. As the experimenter watches each child pass through this period she feels swept away by the rapids and is convinced that a most intense, daily study is essential if the phases in development of these complicated behavior-patterns are to be determined. In this chapter we do not claim to have worked

out the details of developmental processes in associational activities. But these illustrations serve to throw in relief the inception
and more important steps of development in some of the most
common associational activities of the young child.

They also show that the cardinal principles of growth are
in essence the same in the development of cortical activities
as in the development of the more primitive behavior-patterns.
While the same fundamental principles of growth apply in the
development of all behavior activities, the same principles do not
apply through all the phases of development of a specific behavior-
pattern. At one stage of development of a particular action-system
the process involved may consist essentially of elimination of
excess activity and a gradual increase in specificity of response.
During another phase of development in the same behavior-
pattern, the process of growth may be a matter of knitting together or integrating two or more types of growth which have
been moving along somewhat independently prior to that time.
Generalizations on the process of development must, therefore,
take into account the maturational level of specific patterns as
well as the chronological age of the individual subject. Repeated
experience of an activity at one phase in its development may
greatly modify its growth processes, whereas repeated experience
of the activity at an earlier or later phase may have strikingly
little effect upon the growth of the particular behavior-pattern or
upon kindred action-systems.

Chapter VI

MODIFICATION OF BEHAVIOR-PATTERNS AT DIFFERENT STAGES OF DEVELOPMENT DURING INFANCY

IT has been asserted that the extent of influence a particular modifying factor may have upon the development of a behavior-pattern is contingent upon the degree of fixity attained by the pattern at the time the modifying agent is introduced into the growth course. Since within any one individual there are behavior-patterns in all stages of maturation, it is possible to ascertain the effect of a factor such as exercise upon development when the behavior-courses are in different phases of maturation. The factor of exercise might have one type of influence upon walking and another type of influence upon skating, although the exercise of the function was in both instances held constant with respect to frequency and duration of exercise as well as the chronological age of the subject.

One reason the factor of exercise would have different developmental effects upon the two behavior-patterns is due to different states of plasticity present in the two patterns at the inception of the exercise. We have observed that those behavior-patterns which were in a comparatively undifferentiated state at the inception of the factor of exercise were the ones most subject to modification in this way. We desired also to know the influence of increased exercise upon the growth of a particular behavior-pattern provided its inception occurred at different periods in the lifetime of the child in whom the behavior-pattern was being manifested. We have asserted that there are critical periods of susceptibility when the optimum modification of a behavior-course could be deliberately induced through exercise. A fundamental problem in development is to determine when these critical periods occur. It appears that the period of maximum susceptibility to modification closely parallels the period of most rapid development.

Enough evidence has already been accumulated to indicate that these critical periods occur at no one particular chronological age of the subject. It cannot be said that the period of infancy is the period of most rapid development and therefore the period of greatest modifiability. Infancy is the period of most rapid development in certain respects. The critical periods must be determined for each behavior-course, and these critical periods in ontogeny would differ for each behavior-pattern. At any one chronological period in the life of the child a particular external influence may have marked effect upon the development of one type of activity and no noticeable effect whatever upon the development of another. Moreover, a particular external influence may have a marked effect upon the development of a behavior-pattern at one time in ontogeny, whereas at a different period the same external factor would be quite ineffectual in altering that particular pattern. This difference in modifiability of the same behavior-pattern is due to the fact that at the later period it had become specific and resistant to external influences of that type.

We essayed to study the relative effect of exercise of activities in this connection by subjecting Johnny and Jimmy to a repetition of the same activities but at different chronological periods. Since the repetition of the performances was introduced at different chronological periods for each child, the behavior-patterns *per se* were in different states of development when the experimental factor, viz., repetition, was given a chance to influence the growth of the pattern. When the twins were twenty-two months old, restriction of Jimmy's activities was discontinued. He was then subjected to a two and a half months' training in essentially the same situations in which Johnny had been exercised earlier. Jimmy was given specific practice only in those activities in which his performances had been noticeably behind those of Johnny.

Since he had during the preceding months built up a resistant attitude toward the laboratory and the experimental situations, the first two weeks of his training were devoted primarily to getting him in a more acquiescent or coöperative attitude. He was taken daily into the laboratory. Although incentives were placed in position to stimulate activity, he was not given directions, or in any way urged to engage in the activity. For example, an object would be placed on a stool so that he could see it. A slide would be attached to the stool so that if he wished to procure the object he could do so, though it would involve his climbing up the slide. After the first two weeks of his training period not only were the situations arranged to induce the activity but the experimenter directed and urged him to put forth his utmost effort in order to get the object.

While every effort was made to keep the laboratory conditions during Jimmy's practice period comparable to those which prevailed when Johnny, at a much younger age, was getting similar daily exercise, this effort was not carried to the extent of making the situations seem artificial. For example, it was possible for the experimenter to make greater use of language in calling attention to lures when working with Jimmy at the age of twenty-two months than when working with Johnny in a similar situation at the age of twelve months. Not to have utilized Jimmy's greater comprehension of language in the practice situation would have made the practice conditions for him so artificial that the comparison would have been even less justifiable.

It is not correct to say that the practice conditions for Jimmy were identical with those used in exercising Johnny in a similar activity at a younger age. Our purpose was to bring the performances of both children in certain selected activities up to the maximum. Since we were interested in the effect exercise in slide-climbing had upon the child's development in that activity, it was necessary that he should be induced to use the activity as much as possible. Consistency in methods of stimulation was a secondary consideration. It would be unreasonable to expect that the same method of provoking the activity would be equally effective in dealing with infants of disparate developmental states. Methods of stimulating activities had to be adjusted to suit the interest of each child. The infant who is just beginning to take a great deal of interest in the world about him will work at great length merely to obtain a nondescript object held before him, and it is possible to make use of his interest in objects to stimulate specific motor activities. But the child of twenty-two or twenty-four months has become inured to these simple seductions. Not only has he become uninterested in simple objects, but he has also developed many more ways of escaping undesirable situations. He has learned to say "no," to run away from the situation and engage in other activities. He has also learned, when placed in disagreeable situations, to become as limp as a wet cloth so that "all the king's horses and all the king's men" could not make him stand up again if he did not want to. For the older child it is necessary to use more appealing lures, such as food, in order to stimulate his motor activities.

Furthermore the child of eighteen months or more has acquired many more complex behavior-patterns which influence all of his activities. He is often more likely to respond in imitation of another person's performance than to verbal directions. In stimulating Jimmy the experimenter used whatever means were most effective in evoking the desired activity. Sometimes when lures failed the experimenter would go through the performance in order to get him to respond by imitation. He was not, however, allowed either before or during his practice period to see Johnny's performances in most of the experimental activities. Skating and tricycling were exceptions. These he had observed not only in Johnny but in other and older children as well.

Activity on Slides

On the first day of Jimmy's practice period the experimenter placed the slide at an angle of 11° but said nothing to him about going up or down the slide. It will be recalled that he had crept part of the way up that slide when he was 261 days old. He had also walked up once when he was 473 days old, but subsequently he had consistently refused either to creep or to walk up or down this low incline. An illustration of the child's tendency to revert to a less mature mode of behavior when confronted with an unfamiliar or difficult situation is indicated by Jimmy's action. On the first day of his practice period, when he saw the slide he voluntarily stooped to creep up on hands and knees. It is noted that he stooped to *creep* up this low incline, although he walked efficiently on a flat surface. He covered a distance of about three feet; then, dropping his abdomen on the surface of the slide, he grasped the edges and pushed himself backward. Having failed to complete the act of creeping up the slide, he tried another method a little later, starting to walk up. He made about four steps on the slide, became tense, and called "mamma."

Since no one answered his call he again stooped, got into a prone position, and pushed himself off as before.

Jimmy's behavior at this time appeared to be trial and error. He was not, however, failing because of inadequately developed motor equipment for the performance. The motor aspect of his behavior in this situation was matured. The mechanisms of creeping and walking were developed at the time. Ascending a mild slope of 11° did not call for more complicated somatic coördinations than he had already acquired in walking on a flat surface. He failed either to creep or walk up the incline not because of an undeveloped motor mechanism but because of an unfavorable attitude toward the situation. Therefore in so far as we focused upon the motor aspect of his behavior we were not observing development *per se*. His subsequent behavior in this situation revealed growth of a more coöperative attitude.

On the second day he slowly and cautiously crept up the entire distance of the low incline on his hands and knees. He smiled with the satisfaction of achievement. Then he turned into a prone position and pushed himself down the slide with his feet toward the lower end of the incline. Jimmy never during his practice period showed an impulse to creep down the slide head first. At the inception of his daily exercise in this activity he had advanced far beyond the stage where an infant has difficulty in approaching an object backwards. He therefore hurdled the primary phases in the descension of slopes.

Four days later he crept up the slide placed at an angle of 18°, and by the time he was 679 days old, that is within a week, although he was beginning to lose some of his extreme tenseness in this situation, he was still quite cautious in his movements. He crept up the slide placed at an angle of 24° within ten days, though it was not at that time a complete performance. He had not yet attained sufficient command of the situation to climb the entire distance to reach the object. He would get far enough up to see the top of the stool, but he did not know how to release his grasp on the edge of the slide in order to pick up the object, so he would slide down on his abdomen. Within a short time he acquired a technique of releasing his grasp on the edge of the slide in order to pick up the lure. However, Jimmy went through this initial incomplete act every time the elevation of the slide was increased.

The changes in Jimmy's performance which have so far been reported occurred during the first two weeks of his practice period when no direction or urging was given by the experimenter. It is rather interesting that during those two weeks he never once successfully *walked* up and down even the lowest slide. He would start up and then stoop to creep the last two thirds of the distance. For practically ten months Jimmy had preferred erect locomotion to creeping, yet when he was confronted with only a slight slope there occurred a reversion to an earlier phase of the behavior-pattern. To activate his walking up the incline required a longer time as well as assistance from the experimenter.

At the end of the first two weeks of Jimmy's practice period the experimenter not only arranged the situations but called the child's attention to the lures and encouraged him to engage in motor activities necessary to obtain the object. He was urged to walk up the low inclines rather than to creep. Although Jimmy had refused consistently to walk up the low incline, when the experimenter allowed him to hold her hand he willingly walked up and down the slide at 11°. This occurred when he was 683 days old. Immediately following this achievement he accomplished the task without assistance. The following day he walked up and down the incline of 18° and half way up the one of 24° without assistance. But it was not until he was 697 days old that he walked the entire distance up the incline of 24°. Walking up and down slopes of 11° and 18° was largely a matter of reëducating his attitude. When the slope was increased to 24°, he had also to improve his motor performance, and as a result it required a greater amount of exercise to show comparable improvement. Furthermore, walking up these slides of steeper grade evoked initial reversions to immature walking patterns. The upper extremities became extended and abducted to aid in balancing. The lower extremities were flexed at the knees and pelvis, and in descending he would often break into uncontrolled running steps as he neared the end. At first he seldom tried to walk down. His customary reaction was to stoop, turn around, and slide down on the abdomen, feet downward. It was, as a matter of fact, necessary to give him assistance in walking down on the first few occasions.

The extent to which the slightest help, or even a suggestion of help, will facilitate a child's performances is often amazing.

If the child can merely hold on to the distal phalanx of the little finger of an adult he will walk up and down inclines even though he has consistently refused to do so alone. The hold he has upon the adult is of no actual aid in the motor act of walking. The same effect may be obtained even if the adult does not so much as touch the child. One may merely stand near with a protecting hand back of the child in order to facilitate his walking down, although he cannot be induced to make one step while the experimenter stands a few feet away. If the experimenter gives him such assistance once or twice, often he will walk readily up and down the low inclines alone. The question of how much assistance should be given to a child, and how and when it should be given, in order to expedite learning is one that needs a great deal of study. It has been the writer's experience that the slightest help at one stage measurably improves the child's performance. At another time, if help is offered, the child gives up and depends upon the adult.

It is interesting that Jimmy acquired facility in walking up and down the incline of 24° before he succeeded in climbing up or creeping up an incline of 32° or more. This is in direct contrast with Johnny, who was creeping up an acclivity of 61° long before he was able to walk up even the mildest slide. The method Jimmy used at first in ascending these steeper acclivities showed a variation from that usually taken by the infant whose slide-climbing behavior is grafted on to the early creeping pattern. Jimmy usually tried to ascend in the hand-knee position. His first obvious move toward ascension consisted of placing his hands on the ridges of the slide, raising first one foot and then the other but failing to get both feet on the slide at once. Later he would go so far as to get his body completely off the floor on to the slide, but as his knees could not grip the surface he would slide back to the floor. He had much more difficulty in acquiring the technique of using his toes for gripping than does the baby who begins to acquire the activity when he is just beginning to creep.

It is easy to see the gradual steps involved in the motor aspect of Jimmy's learning to ascend the steeper slides. It was only on the acclivities of 32° or more that Jimmy showed progressive variations in motor pattern. His initial actions on slides #5 and #6 were further complicated by a conflict between the impulse to creep and the impulse to walk up particular slopes. For example, when he was 707 days old he started to creep up slide #5. He got both hands and feet on the slide, stood up, took two steps, then dropped to a prone position and slid back to the floor. The following day he made a similar attempt on slide #6. Subsequently he succeeded in creeping up slide #6 before he crept up slide #5. This difference was probably due to the fact that the conflict in impulses to creep and to walk up slide #5 was more pronounced than it was on slide #6, which was so steep that the urge to walk up it was soon abandoned.

When he was 722 days old he successfully crept up an incline of 48°. But never once during the two and a half months of special exercise did Jimmy succeed in getting more than two-thirds the way up on slide #8, placed at an angle of 61°. He succeeded in ascending this incline when he was 774 days old, a little more than three months after the inception of his exercise period, even though during the last month of that time he had not been given special practice in this activity. On that day he also climbed two-thirds the way up the incline of 70°. An explanation for his striking success, despite the intervening month of no exercise on these two slopes will be offered in connection with a discussion of the influence of attitudes upon motor performances in Chapter VIII.

Jimmy began daily practice in ascending slides fourteen months later than did Johnny. It is hardly fair to compare the length of their learning periods on a particular slope because (1) from the conditions of this experiment we cannot be sure that the time when Johnny manifested ability to ascend and descend a particular incline was the earliest date at which it was possible for him to do so; and (2) because development is indicated more by the *way* the child ascends the slide than by the fact of his reaching the top. Nevertheless, a comparison in terms of the interval of time which elapsed from the day exercise was begun on the lowest slide until the child had successfully ascended slopes of a given steepness is not without value.

Both children ascended the lowest incline of 11° within one day from the time special exercise began, but it was twenty-one days before Johnny crept up the incline of 24°, whereas Jimmy did this successfully on the ninth day of his practice period. This difference in learning time would indicate that Jimmy's maturity in general motor activities at the inception of special exercise lessened his learning period on this slope. On the other hand it required Jimmy practically the same length of time to ascend the incline of 32° as it had required for Johnny to attain that performance fourteen months younger. Also, on the incline of 61° Johnny made a successful ascent 119 days after his first experience on the lowest incline and Jimmy did not do so until 102 days after his practice in slide-climbing was begun. As a matter of fact, Johnny might have achieved this performance earlier had it been presented to him. He succeeded in going up this particular slope unassisted four days after it had first been presented to him, whereas Jimmy did not go entirely up it until forty-nine days after he made his first attempt on it.

The fact that Johnny acquired an ability to climb or creep up the slide before he began to walk erect indicates that this behavior was an expansion of his creeping development. Jimmy, in contrast, had attained a well-controlled erect gait when his practice in slide climbing was initiated. Jimmy succeeded in creeping up the lower inclines about a week before he succeeded in walking up them. Once he began to walk up and down the inclines of 11° and 18°, he did so very easily without at the time extending and abducting the upper extremities to aid in balancing. The fact that he did not have to make these particular postural adjustments to the situation indicates that his growth in this activity was essentially a matter of acquiring a more coöperative attitude instead of increased precision in motor performances. Steeper inclines of 24° or 32° demanded of Jimmy improvement in the motor as well as the attitudinal aspect of the behavior. It was twenty-five days after his practice period began before he walked up the incline of 24° and fifty-seven days before he walked up the one of 32°. In comparison, Johnny walked up both of these slopes sixty days after the inception of his daily exercise in walking up low inclines. Johnny was only thirteen months old when he first walked up the incline of 32°, whereas Jimmy was twenty-four, yet Jimmy required approximately the same amount of time in total practice before walking up this particular incline as did Johnny—a negligible difference of three days. However, Jimmy began to walk up this slide practically as soon as he began to creep or climb up it, there being a difference of only seven days in his acquisition of the two performances. There was,

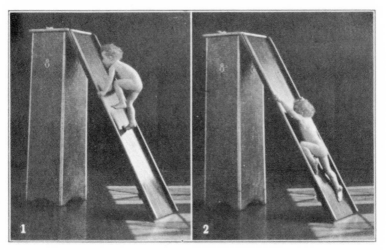

PLATE IX. BEHAVIOR ON SLIDES (JIMMY, TWENTY-SIX MONTHS)
1. Ascends slide placed at an angle of 61°. 2. Descends the same slide.

in contrast, three and a half months between the times Johnny learned to creep and to walk up this incline.

An analysis of the steps of development involved in the acquisition of the same performance by these two children when there was a difference of fourteen months at the time practice began lends emphasis to the assertion that there appear to be critical periods in the growth cycle when certain activities are most economically acquired. Creeping up the inclines was an activity completely new to Johnny at the time practice began. Since his interests were, at that age, comparatively limited, there were fewer interferences to prevent concentrated effort on the expansion of the creeping pattern into slide-climbing. His learning problem was essentially a matter of gaining control over the motor performance involved. The same was true of his walking up and down the inclines at a slightly later age.

Jimmy, on the other hand, had acquired adequate motor abilities for creeping or walking up the lowest inclines at the time practice was initiated. Since the motor equipment necessary to ascend the lowest inclines was mature in him at the time practice was begun, it would not be expected that exercise of the act would materially alter the motor aspect of his performance. Jimmy's failure to ascend the low inclines can be attributed only to his uncoöperative attitude. Therefore his learning problem on the lower slides was largely a matter of reëducating his attitude toward the situation. In this instance repetition of the activity or familiarity with the situation quickly modified his attitude. As soon as he had gained a venturesome mood his methods of creeping and walking up the inclines of 11° and 18° were mature and well controlled.

But in ascending slides of greater slope the story is a little different. Here the problem of developing greater motor control and coördination also entered into the learning situation. Then it was that there appeared regressions to less mature phases in the manner of behavior. Then it was that the learning time expanded.

Thus it seems that Johnny experienced an advantage in this type of performance by having acquired it before other types of development, such as height discrimination and distractibility, entered in as interfering factors.

Turning Off Stools

Before the inception of Jimmy's special exercise in getting off pedestals he had acquired a negative attitude toward the situation to such an extent that he had never once accomplished the performance or even made much effort to get off the lowest stool, which was only 7½ in. high. During the first two weeks of his practice period he climbed up several times on stool #2 just enough to get his hands and knees upon the top surface of the stool, though he did not during this time actually stand up on any of the stools. However, after getting both hands and knees upon the top surface of the stool 14¼ in. high he could easily lower his feet until they reached the floor.

His failure to get off these low stools during the period of restriction is justly attributed to his uncoöperative attitude, since eleven days after his exercise period began, when he was stood upon stool #2, he immediately and without hesitation or complaining succeeded in getting off. The motor aspect of the performance was at that time fully developed. The increased familiarity in the laboratory gained through his daily experience in the room, even though the experimenter did not definitely direct his activity, had been sufficient to establish an acquiescent attitude. Since he had adequately developed motor technique to get off this low stool, he succeeded in doing so the first time he was placed upon it after his practice period began, although he had not once during his period of limited activity successfully performed this act. He showed no difficulty in getting from a standing to a squatting or hand-knee position when on top of the stool, and he manifested no difficulty in getting his lower extremities over the edge. It will be recalled that these were aspects in the learning situation which were of great trouble to Johnny in achieving this feat. Jimmy in contrast, once his attitude had been altered, could get off a stool from a standing position just about as easily as he could from a sitting position. He did not on this first occasion go through the round about method of sitting on the stool, then edging forward, next rotating his body into a prone position, and finally holding on to the edge and lowering his body. Instead he merely stooped into a hand-knee position, grasped opposite edges of the top of the stool with each hand and dropped both lower extremities over the edge of the stool surface, so as to place him in the prone position with his trunk flexed at the waist-line over one top edge of the stool. If the stool was so low that his feet could touch the floor, then he had no trouble getting into a standing position on the floor.

But when the height of the stool was too great for Jimmy to touch the floor as his trunk was flexed over the top edge, a new element was introduced into his behavior-situation. He then experienced greater difficulty in both somatic and attitudinal aspects of the behavior. It required a longer time for him to get control of the activity and the several aspects of the behavior-course revealed reversion to immature phases. A more diffuse type of behavior occurred when he discovered his inability to touch the floor. He would draw himself again to the hand-knee position on top of the stool, turn around several times, and then drop his lower extremities over the adjoining edge. Sometimes he would thus try all four edges. If he carried his effort to reach the floor with his feet a little too far, he would sometimes lower his body so much that he could not regain the hand-knee position on the stool. In that case he would lose all control over his movements. He would hang, grasping the opposite edges of the stool until from fatigue he dropped to the mat below. There was nothing deliberate in his method of dropping, and he showed no skill in protecting himself as he dropped. This type of behavior is an excellent illustration of the error involved in judging developmental performances in terms of the end results rather than in terms of the process of attainment. If the comparison of Johnny's and Jimmy's achievements were limited to objective ratings in terms of the frequencies of success in getting off stools of certain heights, it is obvious how grossly misrepresentative of growth the data would be. It is not so much the *fact* that he gets off a stool of a particular height as it is the *way* he does it which is of import to the study of growth.

Johnny acquired early in his practice period certain adaptations in dropping from the high pedestals which took an inordinately long time for Jimmy to achieve. For example, when a child is getting off a pedestal higher than the length of his body, it is necessary that he should change the position of his hands so that they do not grasp opposite edges of the stool but that both hands grasp the same edge. In this way his body is lowered the utmost before he releases his grip on the top edge. It was not until 108 days after his training period began that Jimmy first made this adjustment. Johnny in contrast had acquired this technique at the age of thirteen months, in only twenty days after his training period in getting off pedestals from a standing position had begun.

When Johnny first began to drop himself off the highest stools it was observed that he struck his face against the side of the stool as he dropped; but in a few days it was further observed that he spontaneously kicked with one foot against the perpendicular surface of the pedestal so that as he fell his body would be thrown out sufficiently to avoid striking the side of the stool. While Jimmy succeeded in getting himself off pedestals 46½ and 54¼ in. high within twenty-five days from the start of his practice period, he did so by getting himself so fatigued that he could not hang on any longer nor could he regain the top of the stool. It was not until he was 780 days old, or 108 days after the inception of his exercise period, that he deliberately moved his hands forward so that both would grasp the same top edge of the stool, that he deliberately released his grasp so that he would drop to the mat, and that in dropping he kicked his body out so as to protect his face from striking the side of the stool as he fell. Furthermore it was 108 days after his training period began before he succeeded in getting off the stool of 63¼ in. in height. If time is reckoned from the first occasion Johnny was stood upon a stool until he had achieved a deliberate quality of getting off the 63¼-in. pedestal, and if for Jimmy the time is calculated from the day his practice period began until he succeeded in getting off the 63¼-in. stool independently then it required Jimmy twenty-five days longer to achieve this performance at the age of twenty-six months than it did Johnny when only thirteen and a half months old.

As a matter of fact there is no way in which such a comparison is justifiable. Before Johnny had his first experience of standing upon a stool he had already acquired the ability of getting off from a sitting position a stool considerably higher than his body length. He had therefore acquired the technique of holding on to one edge of the stool before allowing himself to drop to the mat below. When first placed in a standing position, his problem was to learn to sit or stoop on top of the stool in order to get his feet suspended over the edge. Jimmy, on the other hand, had no difficulty in getting his feet suspended over the edge. The extent to which experience in getting off chairs might have modified Jimmy's behavior in this aspect of the performance is beyond the control of the present study. However, the chief problem for him was to develop a favorable attitude and adequate technique for lowering his body and releasing his grasp so as deliberately to drop to the mat.

Johnny undoubtedly experienced a decided advantage in having daily exercise in this type of activity while the behavior-course was in a state of comparative plasticity, before discrimination and other conflicting and interfering traits developed.

Skating Behavior

Jimmy had already gained considerable control over the maintenance of equilibrium when his practice on roller-skates began. Practice in this performance began when he was 687 days old. So far as the experimental conditions are concerned he had not previously had experience in this activity. However, when the experimenter approached him with skates, he not only held up his foot to have the skates placed on him, but his general attitude indicated a familiarity with them. It is possible that this familiarity was gained in play with his older sisters and brothers at home. It was impossible for the experimenter to determine the extent of his experience with skates. Furthermore, since this investigation does not afford adequate data for comparing his behavior with that of other children of corresponding chronological age when they first experience skates, it is impossible to know if his behavior was atypical.

He was on the first occasion not only able to maintain an erect posture but to take short steps forward. He showed no tendency to roll his feet on the floor but raised his feet for stepping. When he lost his balance and fell to a sitting position, he could not regain the erect position without aid. Jimmy could from the beginning rise from a squatting position when he was wearing skates and could regain the erect posture after bending over to pick up toys on the floor. His attitude from the first was one of cooperation and enjoyment in the situation.

Within fifteen days Jimmy had learned to get from a recumbent to a standing position with his skates on. It will be recalled that it required more than two months of skating experience before

Johnny attained this aspect of the performance. Jimmy's method of rising was essentially the same as that of Johnny. He rolled into a prone position and supported himself on hands and feet before raising the upper part of the body.

Notwithstanding his apparent excellent start, his actual skating movements were extremely slow in developing. There was a long period immediately following his initial experience when no lures or urging were adequate to stimulate him to move. He would stand on the skates as long as twenty minutes at a time, without taking one step forward. Often if the experimenter attempted to give assistance by holding his hand he not only would put forth no effort himself but would become limp. When he did move, his mode of action consisted of rigid slides of first one foot slightly forward and then the other. There was no rhythmical swing, and the upper part of the body was not greatly involved in the movement. After thirty-five days of experience on the skates Jimmy showed some improvement in speed and was using his right foot slightly rotated externally as a pusher. However, it cannot be said that Jimmy had really accomplished the performance of skating. After experience on skates extending over a period of two and a half months he was still pushing with his right foot, showing no indication of an alternating rhythm as involved in the skating movement. His attitude was always more acquiescent in this situation than in others. Although his attitude continued to improve during the practice period, his actual performance was only slightly improved. Jimmy had the advantage of observing Johnny on skates. Despite his favorable attitude and other advantages, Jimmy's skating performance at the end of his practice period was not superior in method to that of Johnny at the age of fourteen and a half months, when he too had experienced practice for a period of two and a half months.

Jimmy's behavior in the coasting situation is a convincing illustration of the impeding effects other types of development may have upon the acquisition of a particular performance. When first presented to the slope of 3.6° for coasting on skates, his lower extremities became abducted but he did not appreciate the necessity of adducting them in order to maintain the standing position. His feet kept spreading until he fell into a sitting position. Since Jimmy had already learned to sit down easily, he would deliberately sit down as soon as he started to move on the decline.

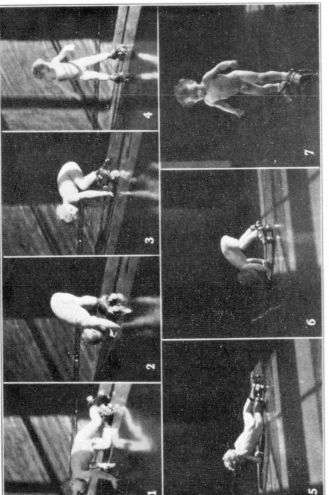

PLATE X. SKATING

1, 2, 3. Johnny at twenty-one months in the assumption of an erect position when on skates. 4. Johnny has developed a rhythmical skating movement. 5 and 6. Jimmy at twenty-six months in the assumption of an erect posture on skates. 7. Jimmy uses his right foot as a pusher.

It was therefore impossible to induce him to stand up long enough to coast. By the time his practice period terminated about the most he could be induced to coast down the low grade before sitting down was approximately four feet. At one time the experimenter was able to get him to coast eight or ten feet before sitting. This was accomplished by the experimenter's walking behind him with arms outstretched as if to catch him if he fell. Actually the experimenter did not touch him.

In skating behavior Johnny undoubtedly enjoyed an advantage because of having acquired the activity earlier in the course of development. It appears that the most economical time to learn skating is when the baby is just beginning to gain equilibratory control. If he gets a fall at the early age he is so accustomed to falls that he does not become negatively adapted. For the older child the same type of fall is more painful; his powers of recalling the effects of the fall are better developed, and the greater understanding of a likelihood of falling interferes with his putting forth utmost effort to gain the abandonment essential to a good skating movement.

Jumping

From Chapter IV, it will be recalled that there were two situations in which jumping behavior was studied in this investigation. In the first situation the child was stood upon a high pedestal and told to jump into the receiving arms of an adult; in the second he was stood upon lower stools and directed to jump on a mat placed on the floor beside the stool. In neither of these situations had Jimmy ever made the slightest attempt to jump during his period of restriction. On the high pedestal he would squat, cling to the experimenter, and cry. On the low stool he would stand extending his arms toward the experimenter, crying and otherwise beseeching help.

After the two first weeks of his practice period, during which time he had gained a more acquiescent attitude, he was directed to jump from the low stool, $7\frac{1}{2}$ in. high. On this occasion he did not stand crying as he had customarily done during his restricted period. He smiled, shifted his weight from one foot to the other, slightly flexed his lower extremities, then extended them as if preparatory to jumping, but finally raised himself to step off with the right foot in the lead. The flexion and extension constituted a partial movement of the initial aspect of the jumping pattern, but the movements were so isolated that they appeared to belong more with the diffused, generalized shifting of his weight than actually with a jumping pattern. They represent the inchoate initial phase. Height discrimination in this situation was evidenced from the beginning of his practice period. Although he willingly stepped off the 7½-in. stool, and his attitude on the higher stool was more favorable than earlier, he would not attempt to step off the stool 14¼ in. in height. He did not cry or show the disturbance on this stool which characterized his behavior before the practice period. But when placed on the 14¼-in. stool, he would squat and reach toward the experimenter. When the height of the stool was slightly increased, the exaggerated flexion of the lower extremities resulted in squatting, a less mature reaction than that observed on the 7½-in. stool. Even when the experimenter held him under the arms he did not make the accommodation of flexing and extending the lower extremities or the spine in preparation for jumping. This mode of behavior appeared a week later. Twenty-three days after his practice period began, the flexion and extension of his lower extremities at the knees and the pelvis had become sufficiently developed to denote a definite preparatory set to jumping. The movement was not carried through to completion, and he straightened himself to an erect position as he *stepped* off the stool. He had achieved the two essential movements in jumping, but they were exaggerated and isolated. Although the two movements were successive, they were not sufficiently integrated to constitute a jump. This was the first occasion when Jimmy ever stepped off the pedestal 14¼-in. high. These isolated stepping movements continued to be the characteristic features of his jumping behavior during the remainder of his practice period. There were days, of course, when he would not even step off stool #2, but certainly he never once actually *jumped* off any of them.

When placed on the high stools for jumping into the extended arms of an adult his discrimination of varying heights was further indicated. Although he was less tense and appeared quite content on a pedestal 38¼ in. high, on a stool 54¼ in. high he would complain and reach for the adult. On the 38¼-in. stool his characteristic mode of behavior was squatting. One month of his practice period had elapsed before he was observed to thrust his body forward slightly. He made that movement then only when the adult was standing near and when he was placed upon a stool of such height that the arms of the adult were in practically the same plane as his shoulders. There followed a period of about eight days when his mode of activity consisted of standing on the stool, shifting his weight from one foot to another, extending his arms toward the experimenter, flexing the lower extremities and finally thrusting his body forward slightly with the right shoulder in the lead. After fifty-one days of his practice period had elapsed he behaved in a similar manner when placed on a slightly higher pedestal. Although in time he became less tense and more contented when placed upon the stool 63¼ in. high, the experimenter never succeeded in getting him to jump off this stool during his entire practice period.

There is no doubt that Johnny experienced an advantage in learning this activity early. It is ordinarily past the second year before children have developed a good jumping technique. Johnny had developed both an adequate motor performance and a cooperative attitude before height discrimination and other inhibiting factors entered into the situation to impede his optimum development. The experimenter is convinced that Jimmy would have begun jumping off the higher pedestals if the practice period had been continued longer. During his exercise period he not only had daily opportunity to exercise this activity but he had observed Johnny engage in the performance as well as adults who jumped off the lower pedestals. It appears that Jimmy had every advantage except the younger age, and yet his performance at twenty-six months was not comparable to the jumping behavior of Johnny at fifteen and a half months.

Since Jimmy, despite the fact that his practice period was longer than the time Johnny spent in achieving this performance, had not successfully achieved a well-developed method of jumping, it is safe to conclude that Jimmy's advanced age gave him no advantages. Within eighty-three days after his exercise period began in jumping from a standing position off the high stools Johnny was leaping off the highest pedestals with great delight. After 108 days of his practice period Jimmy still had not accomplished this act, although Jimmy was nine months older than Johnny at the time their respective periods of daily exercise in this performance were begun.

There was a similar difference shown in the comparative development of the two children in jumping off the lower stools on to the floor. After 108 days of his practice period Jimmy was still stepping off the lowest stools and was squatting and dawdling when placed on stools of twenty-four inches or higher. Only seventy-two days of his special exercise had elapsed before Johnny was doing a fairly creditable jump off the lower pedestals.

It is a little difficult to determine just why the experimenter was unable to get Jimmy to jump off pedestals. Certainly he had built up a dominant negative attitude toward the situation during his restricted period. This attitude did not persist through his practice period. Toward the end of his training period he would ask to be placed upon the stools for jumping. Once there he did not object to the situation, as was indicated by his smiling and other evidences of being pleased with the conditions. But he simply could not be induced to thrust his body forward. Height and distance discrimination apparently develop later than does the act of thrusting the body forward. During his inactive period Jimmy had spent more time during which the act of thrusting the body forward had received no exercise than had been spent in building up his rejection of high positions. Therefore, the aspect of this performance that was first subject to modification during his practice period was his attitude toward high places. With increased experience in the situation Jimmy's negative attitude to high places was converted into a more coöperative one. But the acquiescent attitude to heights was not sufficient to activate his throwing himself off the pedestal. For Jimmy the process of learning in this situation was just the reverse of what it had earlier been for Johnny. It seems reasonable that those older aspects of the behavior-pattern which had been first acquired by Johnny should be the ones most difficult to modify through the exercise of Jimmy later.

Manipulation of Graded Stools

When Jimmy was 665 days old he was observed to make use of a familiar piece of furniture in climbing to secure an objective. He spontaneously pushed a chair up against the wall and climbed up to press a button for turning on a light. Under laboratory conditions, however, until the time his practice period began at the age of 672 days, he had progressed no further in this type of behavior than to make a transitory association between the available piece of furniture, namely stools, and the object out of reach. After standing beneath the object for some minutes, he had on several occasions glanced at the stool, then immediately run to it. However, he apparently lost sight of the object by the time he reached the stool and so started pushing it in various directions about the room.

After the inception of his practice period, he not only pushed the low stool about the room but climbed up on it after he had pushed it a short distance, though it was not necessarily placed under the object when he climbed up. His sense of position and differences in height of stools had not as yet become integrated. A few days later he pushed the low stool directly beneath the high one on which was located the object. If he could reach the object from the stool selected, all was well, but if he could not, there occurred a reversion in behavior-mode to the level characterized by pushing the stool aimlessly about the room. Sometimes the purposive aspect of his activity was carried to the extent of placing the lowest stool on another side of the tall one and again climbing up to reach.

Twenty days after his practice period began he started to make use of two lower stools. That is, being unable to reach when standing on the first stool he pushed another one beside it. However, he apparently had no appreciation of height differences, since he placed the lowest stool adjacent to the tall one on which the object was located and then from the middle one climbed up on the stool most removed from the tall one. Having gotten the idea of using more than one stool, he began to group around the tall stool more low stools than was necessary. He made no pretenses of using them in climbing up to reach the object even after he had gone to the trouble of collecting them. If he perchance got two stools in the right order so that he could climb from a lower one to a slightly higher one and successfully reach the object, then all was well. If, however, he failed to get them in the right order, he would not, at this stage of development, interchange their positions so as to get the higher stool next to the tallest one on which was the lure.

The first evidence of his substituting for a low stool a higher one occurred forty-six days after the beginning of his practice period. On that occasion he moved a low stool away and put a chair in its place. From the chair he successfully reached the object. But this interchange of furniture was a transitory phase of the pattern which did not occur until 108 days of his exercise period had elapsed. At that time he was definitely discriminating in the selection and placement of the low stools, the object being located on the stool 63¼ in. high. The following account of his behavior reveals the way in which discrimination was developing in this situation. He first placed stool #1 beside stool #8, on which the object was. Then he removed #1 and put #2 in its place without previously carrying the act through to the extent of climbing up on #1 to make sure that he could not reach the object. Then he looked the situation over, pushed #2 aside and put stool #4 in its place. Immediately he placed #2 and #1 beside #4 in succession and climbed up to reach the object. On a later occasion he did not go so far as to push stool #1 beside the tallest stool. He started toward #2, pushed it about one foot, paused, and looked at the other stools; then, dropping #2, he went for #4, which he placed beside #8. Then he lined #2 and #1 up in order beside stool #4.

The way in which the excess movements were gradually eliminated is obvious. It is also easily detected that the sequence of phases in the development of this behavior-pattern were the same for Johnny and Jimmy despite the difference in chronological age at which they began practice in this activity. Although Jimmy at the end of his practice period had solved this problem adequately in the case where the lure was on a tall stool, he had not done so for the case in which the object was suspended from the ceiling, eight feet above the floor. This situation, being more difficult, stimulated a regression to more immature phases of the pattern as indicated by his climbing upon stools which were not placed immediately beneath the object.

Comparison of the time required in their respective accomplishments by Johnny and by Jimmy reveals greater achievements for Johnny within a given period of practice time than was shown by Jimmy during an equal interval of time. The practice period was initiated with Jimmy five and a half months after Johnny's first experience in the situation. In forty-three days after Johnny's training period began he was rather consistently discriminating in the selection and placement of two stools of different heights beside a tall one on which the lure was placed. Jimmy made

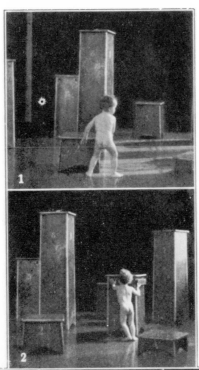

PLATE XI. JIMMY MANIPULATING STOOLS (TWENTY-SIX MONTHS)

He actively discriminates in selection of stools of the proper height in order to obtain the lure without going to the extent of placing the lowest stool beside the tall one.

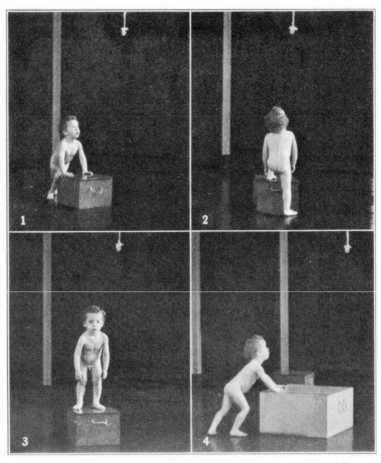

PLATE XII. JIMMY MANIPULATING BOXES (TWENTY-SIX MONTHS)

He successfully places one box beneath a suspended object. When he cannot reach the object from that one, he tries another box, but he has not gotten the idea of placing one box on top of the other.

his first substitution forty-six days after the inception of his practice period, and discrimination and selection were not permanent aspects of Jimmy's behavior-pattern even after two and a half months of exercise in this situation. This difference is all the more interesting since Jimmy had before the onset of practice no pronounced negative attitude toward the situation such as he had shown in the climbing and jumping situations. Therefore the problem of training him in this situation was not essentially a matter of building a more coöperative attitude. Once he had overcome his resistance to the laboratory in general, this particular situation was appealing to him.

One factor which accounted for the difference between the performances of Johnny and those of Jimmy was the amount of time they would at a given occasion devote to this problem. Jimmy would try an arrangement of one or two stools. These failing, he would quickly give up and direct his attention to other activities. Johnny would work persistently even as long as forty minutes at a time, arranging and rearranging the series of graded stools. Apparently Johnny had learned from previous experience that if he worked hard enough he would gain the object. Therefore he was loath to give it up as unattainable. At the inception of their respective practice periods, Johnny and Jimmy were more approximately in the same stage of maturation in this particular behavior-course than in others discussed earlier. Therefore their behavior disclosed eventually the same sequential phases. But, due primarily to attitudes which were transferred in part from previous experiences in other activities, Johnny's performances under these particular laboratory conditions expanded beyond those of Jimmy. He was able to manipulate more stools for objects suspended in higher places. In the process of developing an understanding of spatial and height relations, however, the two children showed the same developmental steps or learning processes.

Manipulation of Graded Boxes

Jimmy was twenty-one months old before he was observed in the act of picking up a portable piece of furniture, such as a chair, and carrying it about the room. In this instance he did not do so with the obvious purpose of making use of the chair in achieving an objective. About this time, whenever he was presented with the situation involving a suspended object with only the graded boxes available for his use in obtaining it, his initial mode of behavior consisted of standing beneath the object and reaching vainly toward it. Soon, however, he began to show a partial or inchoate association of the box with the suspended object. Unable to reach the object, he made a fleeting connection with the box; that is, he went to it and began pushing it about the room. Since he showed no intention of using the box purposively, the experimenter placed one box immediately under the object, but with the object suspended so far above that it would be necessary for Jimmy to place another box on top of the one which the experimenter had put in position under the lure. Jimmy climbed upon the box placed by the experimenter. He was extremely cautious as he rose to a standing position on the box and tilted his head back in order to see the suspended object. He was reluctant even to raise his arms above his head as he stood on the box. Upon finding that he could not reach the object, he got down but straightway became interested in other activities without indicating any connection between a second box and his dilemma.

However, this situation gave him the idea of using the boxes in climbing. Subsequently he would first stand under the object and reach vainly, then he would push one box directly under the object and climb up. When he could not reach he would get down, push the original box away, and put another in its place. Unable to reach the lure, he would again start pushing the boxes helter-skelter about the room or engaging in irrelevant activities. That is, the next progressive move proving ineffectual there was a regression to a less mature phase of the behavior-pattern. The idea of placing the box under the object continued to expand until it became exaggerated. He would often try all four boxes, one by one, under the object.

Seventy-one days after his practice period began he apparently was getting the idea of using more than one box at a time, but he made no attempt to lift one upon the other. Instead he pushed them side by side, stepped from one to the other and then became interested in the activity rather than in the lure. It was 102 days after the beginning of his practice period that he not only went a step further than placing one box directly under the object, but also ran for the second box and lifted it. But that, too, was only a partial appearance of an emerging aspect or new phase of this behavior-pattern. He merely *carried* the second box about the room and did not complete the act of placing it on the first box. It is indicated that he had gone beyond the stage of merely pushing it *beside* the first one as he had previously done, although he had not developed to the stage of placing it on top of the other one. Jimmy was in this stage of his development when his practice period was terminated.

Johnny's behavior in this situation is convincing evidence that he experienced a definite advantage in having had experience in the situation at a younger age. Long before 102 days of practice had elapsed, Johnny was able to stack three boxes one upon the other in order to obtain his objective. It was apparently a general attitude of persistence toward laboratory work which was of chief benefit to Johnny in expanding his performances of this type. In so far as Jimmy's development had progressed, he was manifesting the same phases in the growth of this behavior-pattern as had been observed in Johnny earlier.

Tricycling

Of all the types of behavior which were under observation during this investigation that of tricycling, which appears to be so simple, is one of the most interesting. Motivated by Dr. Raven's (*48*) method in teaching Meshie, a young female chimpanzee, to ride a tricycle, the writer placed Johnny on a small tricycle when he was 350 days old. Dr. Raven's own account of the method used in training Meshie to ride a tricycle and the steps involved in her learning performance are as follows:

"When Meshie first arrived from Africa, our children carried her on the handlebars of their tricycles as they rode about the yard. She seemed to enjoy this and often ran up to a tricycle, mounted it, and turned the handles from side to side as she sat with her feet on the saddle. Her legs were so short that her feet could not reach the pedals. Later I bought Meshie a kiddie-car with pedals well adapted to her, but even then, when she first got on it she sat with her legs flexed and her feet drawn up. I took hold of her feet and pulled them down to the pedals, which she grasped just as she does the handles with her hands. It was not easy for her to understand how to push with her feet; she would forget about holding the pedals and would draw her feet up to the seat. To overcome this, I finally fastened her feet to the pedals with strips of cheesecloth. If I did not watch closely, she would immediately reach down with her long arms and untie the cheesecloth, but if I spoke to her she would let it alone. It took only a short time for her to learn to push the pedals, but sometimes she made a mistake and pushed the wrong way, so that the machine ran backward. When she was seated in the proper position, I held a peach or grape or other food she considered choice before her, calling her to come to me and reprimanding her if she attempted to dismount. At first I gave her the reward when she succeeded in propelling the kiddie-car only a few feet, but I increased the distance as she became more proficient. It was clear after a very few lessons that she understood how to hold the pedals, and the cheesecloth fastenings were no longer necessary.

"Thus far, I had always stood directly before her. When I stood somewhat to one side, she pedaled right past me, for her hands on the handle-bars remained passive. When she passed in this manner she grew very much excited, stuck out her lips, and talked at a great rate. Then I pushed her arm to turn the machine. A few more lessons and she had learned to steer. When she ran into the wall or a chair, she reached out with her foot and pushed herself away, turned the handles, and went forward again, repeating this until she cleared the obstacle. Soon she learned that when the machine was in a corner or between objects where she could not turn it, or when the wheels were caught on the edge of a rug, she must dismount and pull it free. It was very comical to see her quickly dismount, impatiently jerk her kiddie-car clear of the obstacle, then mount and hurry on.

"After several lessons indoors I took her out on the sidewalk. There she at first ran into the fence that bounded the walk on one side, or rode off the curb on the other side. Some of my friends thought I was cruel to let her ride off the edge and take a tumble, then make her pick up the car and pull it back on the sidewalk only to repeat the performance within a few seconds, but it soon taught her to keep away from the fence and the curb. Sometimes our small children and their friends had a parade, each one on some sort of tricycle or bicycle, with Meshie as the leader. She seemed to enjoy it as much as any of them." (P. 612.)

This description of Meshie's learning to ride a tricycle exposes not only Dr. Raven's technique in handling her but some of the fundamental principles of behavioral development which have received attention and emphasis in this discourse.

A similar method was tried with Johnny, though he was much younger at the inception of his practice period than was Meshie, who was three and a half years old when she began to learn tricycling. Johnny was barely beginning to stand erect and walk alone when his feet were tied to the pedals of a small tricycle while lures were held in front of him to stimulate his movement forward. But he did not attempt to move his feet forward. Instead he engaged in a generalized activity of shaking the vehicle. In order to give him the idea of movement, the experimenter pushed the vehicle forward, but still all Johnny did was to reach for the object, shake the tricycle, and vocally complain. This type of behavior continued as characteristic of his activity on the tricycle for more than three months, though the experimenter continued to put him on the tricycle daily five days a week.

When he was about 420 days old he began to develop what is termed colloquially a philosophical attitude. Since he could do nothing about getting the lure which was held in front of him, he ceased complaining and appeared to accept the whole performance as a daily disagreeable task. He sat peaceably on the tricycle but would put forth little effort. Less than a month later, his efforts were both pathetic and humorous. As long as the writer continues to experiment with infants, she never expects to see again a child want more to do something, struggle more desperately to comply in a situation which for some reason was completely beyond him, than Johnny obviously wanted to move the tricycle forward. Seemingly he got the idea that his feet had something to do with the motion, for he would push hard with both feet on the pedals simultaneously. This action merely raised him up in his seat. Finally, when he was 476 days old his feet were no longer tied on the pedals. He would give great attention to keeping them there even though it was difficult for him to do so when the experimenter pushed the tricycle forward a few feet. Then, obviously imitating the experimenter, who gave the vehicle a shove occasionally, he would turn toward the back wheels and try to push them around with his hands. In an effort to give him the idea that it was pressure first with one foot and then the other which made the tricycle go the experimenter started the vehicle by pressing down first upon one of Johnny's knees and then the other. But alas! when left to his own devices, he, again imitating the experimenter, put his own hand upon his knee, pressed down, then looked wonderingly to the experimenter, since naturally he did not move the tricycle despite his great effort.

When he was eighteen months old the experimenter, with the hope that the momentum gathered in going down a slope would give him the feeling of going forward without having the experimenter near to start the tricycle moving, started him on the tricycle down a low grade of 3.6°. He was much interested in this activity, but when the tricycle stopped he would again stand upon both pedals and shake the vehicle. This type of practice was continued for thirty-five days longer until he was 583 days old to be exact, before he was giving unequivocal evidence of making two or three cycles by pushing alternately with his feet on the pedals at the end of the coasting. Within five days he could push alternately on the pedals through several cycles provided the experimenter started him and provided he kept the rhythm up without getting the tricycle thrown into reverse. He could not unaided start the tricycle, and if he got it started backwards he could not reverse the order. He could merely keep up the movement which had been set for him. Although he would keep his hands on the handle-bars, he was not able to steer. Then there came a period of regression during which time he showed scarcely more progress than during all those dismal months previously.

By the time he was 618 days old he could start the tricycle alone, though more frequently he needed some help in so doing. He was also at this time beginning to show some steering ability by turning the handle-bars when he saw himself heading toward the wall. If, however, he bumped into the wall he did not know how to back up and start over again. Sometimes he would reach out with his hands and push against the wall. When 636 days old he demonstrated his ability to avoid the wall, but for a period he overemphasized the steering aspect of the performance. Though he would avoid the wall, he turned the handle-bars frequently from left to right so that his course was ridiculously zigzag. It was not until he was 678 days old, or fifty-seven days after he had shown the first glimmer of real understanding, that it might be said he had developed an accomplished performance on the small tricycle.

When 678 days old his practice was begun upon a larger tricycle equipped with a bicycle chain so that the pedals were located between the front and rear wheels. On this new vehicle he reverted to earlier phases or modes of action. He had difficulty in starting the tricycle and began shaking it. Even this shaking, which in the beginning seemed to be only a generalized response indicative of an inadequacy, in this instance soon began to take on a rhythmical forward and backward motion as if in that way he were trying to set the tricycle going. He was from the beginning able to pedal. Therefore, learning on this larger vehicle was not a matter of developing a new behavior technique but was rather a matter of putting forth more physical effort, more force in essentially the same type of action. In this respect his development showed such rapid progress that in less than three weeks he was practically as efficient on the larger tricycle as he was on the smaller one.

Jimmy had had experience on a kiddy-kar at home before the age of 672 days, when his practice period on the tricycle began. At that time his general behavior in this situation was to stand astride the tricycle and move it by walking on the floor. Before his practice period began he had advanced beyond the stage of diffuse general behavior expressed in shaking the vehicle. He had also acquired some idea of steering before the beginning of his practice period. He was observed on this first occasion to put his feet several times on the pedals, although he did not push the pedals as he did so. It was necessary for the experimenter to direct him to keep his feet upon the pedals. Even from the beginning Jimmy enjoyed tricycling. His attention span was longer for this than for any other experimental item in this investigation. When he kept his feet on the pedals, his reactions at first were somewhat diffuse, although they were better organized than the initial movements of Johnny in this situation. Jimmy would shake the handlebars and move the upper part of his body backward and forward in an effort to start the tricycle moving. There was not the totally undirected shaking of the vehicle which characterized Johnny's early responses.

At the end of the first month Jimmy was pushing alternately for two or three cycles after the experimenter had given him a start, and within another week he was starting, steering, and controlling the vehicle with considerable skill as it moved forward. If, however, he ran into a wall or other object, he did not appreciate the technique involved in backing up and starting over or in steering to one side in order to avoid running into the object again. If he ran into pieces of furniture, he would try to push them aside with his hands. Jimmy developed in a short while a method of reversing the tricycle provided it got started backwards.

After one month and a half of Jimmy's practice period he was quite proficient on the small tricycle and was thereupon introduced to the larger one. Like Johnny he had trouble starting the larger tricycle, although he was able to pedal after it had been started for him. Within two weeks Jimmy was equally proficient on the small and larger tricycle, and he was showing greater skill at times in starting the tricycle than was Johnny, although Johnny moved more rapidly. At this stage of their development they manifested equal difficulty in backing up and starting over after they had run into a wall. They showed a tendency to do so because the experimenter had instructed them in this aspect of the performance. Later when left more to their own devices, both dismounted and pulled the vehicle aside in order to get out of the dilemma.

Discounting the long period when Johnny showed no overt improvement or comprehension of the necessary method involved in tricycling and dating his learning period from the time when he first showed unquestionable appreciation of pressing alternately with his feet on the pedals, it might be said that Johnny's learning time on the small tricycle consisted of fifty-seven days and Jimmy's of forty-eight days. There was also a difference of five days in favor of Jimmy in their learning period on the larger tricycle.

There are several explanations for Johnny's delayed development in tricycling. In the first place it was not possible to get the *conditioned* reaction such as Dr. Raven (48) did with Meshie because the pedals of a tricycle which are placed in the center of the front wheel are badly adapted to the walking step of the infant. The acquisition of tricycling would be facilitated if the pedals were placed more in line with the seat so that the child would not need to operate his feet through a cycle several inches in front of the pelvic girdle.

Secondly, in all the situations wherein the experimenter has succeeded in expanding the development of Johnny beyond that ordinarily expected of children of corresponding chronological age, it was possible to break the performance up into steps or gradations of difficulty. It was not so with tricycling, which demands

that the child be able to integrate several complicated performances in order to move the vehicle at all. It would probably be a
better learning situation to start the infant on some vehicle such
as a kiddy-kar before placing him upon a tricycle. In this way
he would not only get the idea of using his feet to make the
vehicle move but also would learn the technique of steering.
Therefore, by the time he was placed on a tricycle he would
have gained command of certain aspects of the performance.
These aspects he learns to integrate with the new elements he is
at the time acquiring. It is the conviction of the writer that
Johnny not only was not benefited by his earlier experiences in
tricycling, but that these earlier experiences actually hindered his
learning even after it was possible for him to grasp the idea of
alternately pushing with his feet on the pedals to move the
vehicle. He had become tolerant of a task which was too complicated for him, and hence it lost the lure which it would have had
provided it had been presented to him as a new situation later.
The comparison of the twins in their acquisition of tricycling
lends additional support to the contention that there are ad-
ventitious periods during which time the acquisition of a particular
performance may be most economically accomplished.

Associated Activities

In comparing the development of Johnny and of Jimmy during
the latter part of the second year, it must be borne in mind that
in the activities which were developing most rapidly at that time
Jimmy was much less completely isolated than he was with respect to the motor activities which were developing earlier. Also,
there was in time units less of a gap between the inception of
Johnny's exercise period and the beginning of Jimmy's exercise
period in these later activities than there was in the earlier motor
performances. Furthermore, it was not feasible under the laboratory conditions which obtained either to restrict or to stimulate
the experiences of Jimmy or Johnny to any great extent in activities of this sort.

For these reasons it would not be expected that as great divergence would be shown in their respective attainments of the
higher-order activities. Nevertheless, under the controlled laboratory conditions Jimmy, even during his practice period, did not

approach the performances of Johnny in recall and location of hidden objects or in the selection of unfamiliar objects by elimination. But in their general behavior, as expressed in non-laboratory situations, such differences in the associational development of the two children were not apparent.

It was not until one month of Jimmy's practice period had passed that he began to locate the objects which were hidden immediately before he engaged in activities such as getting off stools and climbing slides. Before that he not only did not locate the object, but he seemingly did not appreciate that he was expected to look for it. As soon as he climbed down or was taken off the stools, he would direct his attention to activities of his own choosing. A most salient factor in recalling the location of particular objects is the realization at the time they are hidden that they will sometime later be called for. Johnny's greater familiarity with laboratory conditions gave him an advantage in this respect. After Jimmy was 704 days old, however, he ordinarily recalled, immediately after engaging in some diverting activity, the hiding place of one object. A month later he would recall the location of three or four objects hidden earlier during the practice hour.

But Jimmy's ability to recall the location of objects which had been hidden the night before never during his practice period approached the attainments of Johnny. During the first three weeks of his practice period, when on his arrival each morning at the clinic he was requested to find the hidden object, he not only failed to recall its whereabouts but gave not the slightest indication that he understood he was expected to look for something. He would patiently listen while the request was being made, then go scampering off about his own business. In about three weeks, however, he was indicating his appreciation of the fact that he was expected to find something as revealed by a pause or delay for a few moments after the request had been made as well as by his looking about him and questioningly to the experimenter. He did not, however, recall the direction or the location of the object. When he was 729 days old the movement of another person in the direction of the hidden object apparently gave him the necessary clue, for he turned and walked directly to the hiding place. Never during his entire practice period of two and a half months did he consistently respond by recalling and locating the position of an object which had been hidden about fifteen hours earlier.

Language Development

It can hardly be claimed that Jimmy's language experience either during his period of restriction or during exercise was remarkably less than Johnny's. It will be recalled that during Jimmy's isolation he was kept in a clinic nursery where during the day he was exposed to the spoken words of adults as well as the chatter of the young children. While such isolation curtailed his motor experiences, the arrangement did not lessen his language experience. Moreover, it is quite conceivable that, having his motor activities lessened, he gave more attention to linguistic stimuli going on about him although they were not directed specifically toward him.

At the time Jimmy's practice period began, Johnny was showing a superiority in language comprehension and also a greater tendency to link his words up with meaningful situations. Jimmy, on the other hand, enunciated more clearly and manifested a distinct superiority in the use of sentences and phrases rather than single words. He had a noticeable proclivity for repetition of the same phrases or sentences irrespective of the situation. For example, he would repeat by the hour "Opie de door" whether a door was in view or not and regardless of the prevailing conditions. These were, in a sense, vocal gymnastics.

Unfortunately in regard to their language development the writer is dependent upon observational notes rather than objective measures. On Jimmy these notes are too fragmentary to reveal distinct steps of development, since it was not possible to keep adequate notes while he was comparatively isolated. By the time his practice period began he was already able to express himself in many ways by the use of language accompanied by gesture. Certainly it appeared that during the period of practice and the months immediately following Jimmy showed a noticeable superiority to Johnny in language usage. It is possible that Jimmy's superiority in language usage may have been something of an illusion, since as the children grew it became apparent that Jimmy had a stronger tendency to make a verbal response whereas in a similar situation Johnny was more inclined to make a motor response. In quantity alone the sounds Jimmy emitted during twenty-four hours would be many times the verbalizations of Johnny in an equal amount of time. However, allowing for the possibility of illusion, the writer is still inclined to believe that during Jimmy's practice period, that is, between the ages of twenty-two and twenty-five and a half months, he was advanced beyond Johnnny in his language usage.

There were no outstanding differences in their language comprehension during these months when observed under non-experimental conditions. It will be recalled that some months earlier Johnny's language comprehension both in and out of the laboratory appeared to be somewhat advanced beyond that of Jimmy.

Reference to Chapter V will recall the status of Jimmy's language comprehension at the end of his control period as revealed under laboratory conditions. At that time he had begun to recognize certain objects by name and also to appreciate when an unfamiliar object had been referred to, though he did not complete the act of selecting the unfamiliar one by a process of elimination. During Jimmy's practice period fifty-two days had elapsed before he was consistently selecting the unfamiliar object by eliminating five or six familiar ones. It will be recalled that Johnny was selecting the unfamiliar object forty-six days after his practice period in this activity began. While this difference is not sufficient to conclude that Johnny enjoyed a learning advantage by having begun his practice 106 days earlier than did Jimmy, it is adequate evidence against Jimmy's having any great advantage due to his increase in chronological age at the onset of the practice period. It is possible that the differences in attainment would have been more marked if the interval between the inception of training periods for the two children had been greater than 106 days. That question must, however, remain a matter of conjecture until additional experimental evidence is brought to bear upon it.

Jimmy after one month of his practice period was unquestionably discriminating differences in size in concrete situations, though he had not done so in response to language directions. For example, when placed upon stool #4, from which he did not like to get off, he would point to a lower stool and repeat "dat stoo," indicating that he preferred to get off the lower one. Also he would object when a cracker was broken if the smaller piece was handed to him. However, never during his practice period did he unequivocally select on the basis of size when confronted with two objects alike in every way except size, provided he was given no clue other than the verbal directions.

Jimmy showed no evidence whatever of color discrimination during his practice period. When an object was hidden in one of four drawers alike except in color, and when the drawer containing the object was interchanged with one of another color, Jimmy invariably selected on a positional basis. Not finding the object in the drawer of the correct position, he would most likely begin opening any drawer which happened to be adjacent. When the exercise periods were terminated, neither Johnny nor Jimmy had profited fundamentally by their experiences in color discrimination.

Summary and Interpretation

We have seen that the effect a particular external factor or influence might have upon the growth of an organism or the growth of a behavior-pattern is contingent upon the *time* at which the activating agent is introduced as well as the fact or nature of its introduction. In emphasizing the critical periods of susceptibility to modification in the behavorial development of an individual we should avoid the implication that during the lifetime of an individual any one chronological period can be designated as the age when learning proceeds most rapidly and easily. It is not, in so far as this investigation can determine, the chronological age of the individual *per se* which denotes the "critical periods" of modifiability. It is instead the stage of plasticity or immaturity of the behavior-pattern which determines the degree of susceptibility to alteration. Although too broad generalizations are at this time dangerous, it appears that if the external influence is brought to bear upon a behavior-pattern or an aspect of a pattern at the time of inchoation, then the optimum effect upon development of that particular pattern is effected. While there are opportune periods for influencing the growth of a behavior-pattern through extrinsic factors, the permanence of the effect of repetition or restriction of an activity is dependent not only upon the time the experimental factor is introduced but also upon the duration of its influence. As long as an organism or a behavior-pattern continues growing, so long does it have powers of restoration. Unless the period of deprivation has extended unduly, the restorative powers of the young child are enormous; hence the performances of a child whose activities have been restricted can at a later date, under the proper conditions, be brought to approximate the activities of the child whose opportunities for action have been stimulated. Since, however, the performances given the longest period of restriction were in the case of Jimmy the ones which were most difficult to reëstablish, there is reason to believe that if the period of deprivation had been continued sufficiently long powers of resoration as well as the performance *per se* would have suffered impairment. In the development of those behavior-patterns where the gap between the inception of Johnny's practice period and the inception of Jimmy's exercise in the same activity was wide there occurred differences in the developmental phases of the pattern to a degree which was not apparent in the development of patterns wherein the boys had attained more comparable performance levels at the time practice was initiated.

Chapter VII

THE EFFECT OF EARLY EXERCISE UPON SUBSE-
QUENT EXPERIENCE DURING INFANCY

(In collaboration with Dr. Harriett Fjeld)

IN the foregoing chapters we have shown that repetition of an activity will in many instances advance the performance of infants to a level of complexity far beyond that which is ordinarily attained by a child of corresponding years provided the repetitive factor of exercise occurs at a favorable time. We have also been concerned with the comparative effect exercise of a performance may have upon the development of the behavior-pattern *per se* when exercise of the activity was introduced into the growth process at different stages of its development.

It is a well-known fact that the learning of one performance may facilitate or inhibit the learning of another. The degree to which the knowledge of one activity enhances or curtails the acquisition of another is dependent upon the degree to which the two performances are kindred or at cross-currents. In the present investigation we essayed to determine not the extent to which the knowledge of one performance would influence the acquirement of another but the extent to which the acquisition of one perform-ance at an earlier chronological age may or may not affect the learning of another performance at a later date.

Since Johnny and Jimmy received practice in the same type of activities but at different chronological periods, it was possible to study the comparative effect practice in certain performances would exert upon the learning of other performances when the practice in the earlier activities had been instigated at different developmental states of the action-pattern. Therefore, when Johnny and Jimmy were twenty-four and a half months old, after Jimmy had received two and a half months of intensive exercise in activities in which Johnny had begun training as much as fourteen months earlier, both babies were subjected to a period of exercise in activities equally new to them and under the direction of an experimenter equally unfamiliar to them. These experiments were conducted by Dr. Harriett Fjeld. Whenever the writer observed the children's behavior it was through one-way vision mirror glass, so the writer could not be seen by them. Their practice period extended for one month. Daily records were kept by Dr. Fjeld, and analysis of behavior-patterns in these situations is primarily her work.

Since Johnny had displayed a superiority in gross motor performances, an effort was made to devise learning situations which would not involve a great deal of gross motor activity and thereby favor the child advanced in this respect. The learning situations selected were primarily matters of perceptive and manual dexterity rather than gross body performances. Many of the experimental situations in this series were adaptations of problem situations used by Dr. Theodore Jackson * in his studies with chimpanzees. A detailed description of each situation and the learning process as revealed in the reactions of the twins follows.

Multiple Sticks

A small pen or cage was constructed with perpendicular bars spaced 3⅝ in. apart, thus forming a grill through which the child could work on problems set in front of the cage. In general a small piece of fruit was used as the incentive. The fruit was placed upon a little, shallow tray just in front of the cage, beyond the child's arm length. On the first occasion a seventeen-inch stick was placed at an oblique angle between the tray and the grill, thus suggesting to the child the use of the stick for raking in the object. When first confronted with this situation, both Johnny and Jimmy immediately picked up the stick and started to rake in the small tray.

In his raking movements with the left hand Johnny knocked the tray away from him and thereupon shifted the stick to the right hand. Again he touched the tray, but his coördinations were poorly controlled and he pushed it a little to one side instead of drawing it toward him. This movement apparently indicated to him that he was going to push it away from him again, for he dropped the stick and made an incomplete reaching movement

* Unpublished data.

with his hand. The reaching movement constituted a partial regression to a less mature phase of the behavior-course, but apparently his perceptive development inhibited his persisting with the reaching act. After the tray had been readjusted within reach with the stick, he again picked up the stick with his right hand and drew the tray directly toward him.

Jimmy also responded immediately by picking up the stick in his left hand and succeeded in touching the tray with it. But when the stick slipped off the edge, so as not to draw the tray toward him, he dropped the stick and began reaching with his arms through the bars. He vainly reached as far as he could, but when he found that he could not touch the tray with his hand he again picked up the stick, this time with the right hand, and tried again to rake the tray in. Failing to do so, he stood up and put his right leg through the bars, in this way essaying to get himself out of the cage in order to get the object. Having failed at that he returned to the stick. Each time he grasped the stick a little too near the center to enable him to reach the object successfully. He apparently did not perceive the possibility of grasping the stick near the end in order to give him greater reaching length. Failing with the stick the third time, he stood up and tried to push open the side door through which he had entered the cage. On this occasion he did not succeed in getting the object.

It is easy to see that the initial move of both Johnny and Jimmy was in the right direction. When, for different reasons, they did not succeed in their first move toward the goal both regressed to a more immature reaction, viz., reaching with only the arm through the bars. It is a less mature response for the child to move his body toward the object than to manipulate the means provided by his environment to draw the object to him. Both boys had progressed beyond the initial phase of this pattern at the inception of their practice period in this activity. Most children who are not schooled in laboratory procedure when they first confront this situation display a diffuse mode of behavior consisting of shaking the bars, jumping up and down, and trying to get their bodies through the bars.

After the boys had succeeded in drawing in the tray with the seventeen-inch stick, the situation was set so that it was necessary for them to make use of both a seventeen-inch and a twenty-four-inch stick in order to obtain the lure. The tray was placed too far away to be reached with the seventeen-inch stick. It was necessary for the child to use the shorter stick to rake in the twenty-four-inch stick and then to use the second stick for raking in the object.

Although Johnny had successfully used the single stick in raking in the object, when confronted with this more difficult situation his initial action represented a reversion to a less mature mode of behavior. He put his right leg through as if to reach with his foot, then tried to push his body through the space between the perpendicular bars. Failing to get through the first one, he tried several spaces. Then he picked up the shortest stick and reached as far as he could toward the tray with it, overlooking the longer stick which lay horizontally between him and the object. Unable to reach the object with the short stick, he quickly dropped it and again tried to push himself through the bars until finally he had to be extricated by the experimenter. It is possible that if Johnny had not come so near getting himself through the bars his ultimate performance on this occasion would have been different. If a child can almost succeed in a false move, then he is less likely to correct himself. Johnny could get himself through the space between the bars except for the cephalic diameter. Therefore, being so near success by this method, he put forth greater effort to succeed on this basis rather than make a new attack. In any event, when the situation became more difficult, his urge to move his body rather than manipulate his environment was much more persistent.

Jimmy's actions when confronted with the two-stick situation also showed a reversion to more generalized behavior as soon as he became blocked in the purposeful act of obtaining the lure. His first move was to reach with the shortest stick toward the tray containing the food. In so doing he touched the longer stick and drew it toward him with the shorter one. But this was only a partial act which was not carried through to completion. As a matter of fact, the writer would be inclined to label it an accidental rather than an inchoate move, since it obviously was not his original purpose to reach the second stick, but instead to reach the food. Furthermore, he made no attempt to use the longer stick once he had drawn it near him* For a while he persisted in

---

* The difference, in the writer's opinion, between an accidental and an inchoate response is that the child has either a different purpose or no purpose

PLATE XIII. MULTIPLE STICKS

At twenty-six months Johnny has mastered manipulation of multiple sticks.

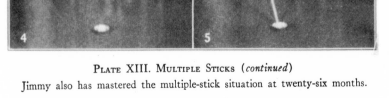

PLATE XIII. MULTIPLE STICKS (*continued*)

Jimmy also has mastered the multiple-stick situation at twenty-six months.

trying to reach the tray with the shorter one. Unable to reach the object he then began to shake the bars of the cage and to chatter to the experimenter about irrelevant things.

On the sixth day of their practice period both Johnny and Jimmy were successfully using the short stick to rake in a longer one, dropping the shorter one in order to use the longer one for reaching the food. But when there were three sticks of various lengths placed horizontally in front of the cage and the food was placed so far that it could be reached with only the longest stick, there resulted again a regression to a more diffuse type of behavior. It was necessary in this situation for the child to pick up the first stick and rake in the second one; drop the first stick and pick up the second one to use in raking in the third stick, then drop the second stick in order to use the third one for raking in the food. The behavior of both boys when the three-stick situation was first presented is illustrative of an initial loss in proficiency when the situation was made more difficult.

Johnny at first did not even pick up the second stick after he had raked it in with the shortest one, although he had been consistently doing so when there were only two sticks. He continued trying to reach the longest stick with the shortest one, which was in his hand at the time. Unable to do so, he became engaged in generalized behavior, viz., kicking with his feet against the floor for a while. A little later, although he picked up the second stick, he did not attempt to use it in raking in the third one. He engaged in general play with it inside the cage; dropped it in the cage, then again picked up the shortest stick and began hitting the floor with it in anger, complaining because he could not successfully reach the food or the longest stick with it.

Jimmy on the same occasion carefully raked in the tray when only two sticks were necessary to reach it, but when three sticks were required he, like Johnny, drew the second stick toward the cage and then, failing to pick it up, continued trying to reach the food or longest stick with the shortest one. When he could not do that, he put his left leg through the bars and tried to reach with his foot. Unable to do that he again tried to open the door through which he had entered the cage.

which results in the accidental response; whereas an inchoate response is incomplete and merely suggestive, but the purpose which initiated the move is the identical purpose which leads to the culmination of the movement.

After three trials in the triple-stick situation Johnny was successful. Jimmy was successful in the use of the three sticks on the fifth trial. In general, Johnny showed much less dexterity in the raking process due in a large measure to a broken right index finger, which was at the time supported in splints. Jimmy was more cautious in his movements and less likely to push the object off to one side or out of reach. The experimenter is inclined to believe that the fractured finger was not the sole explanation for the differences in dexterity between the two children as displayed in their raking movements. Johnny, having a tendency to move more hurriedly, made broad sweeping movements which were likely to push the object off to one side and out of reach; Jimmy was inclined to draw the object in slowly and directly. It is possible that Johnny's greater experience in gross motor movements was influential in determining the character of his motor movements in this situation. To the extent that this is true his early experience was a handicap in his acquisition of this performance. Furthermore, Johnny was more persistent and willing to keep on working than was Jimmy, even if he was not at the time succeeding in getting the object. In perception and comprehension of the problem situation the performances of the two children were closely parallel. In general, it is a safe conclusion that the earlier intensive exercise of Johnny did not serve to accelerate his acquisition of this activity.

The necessity of studying each behavorial situation as a *movement* rather than as a stimulus-response unit can hardly be overemphasized. For example, in the above situation, Johnny's motor incoördinations were such that he knocked the incentive hopelessly beyond his reach even if he used all the means at his command. From that moment it was a different situation for him. That movement determined the next one.

Tool Construction

The conditions of this experimental situation involved the child's learning to work with an L-shaped rod for drawing a box toward the cage. Once he had learned to make proper use of the rod, the situation was arranged so that he would have to combine two pieces of rod in order to construct the hook or make it into an L shape. The child was placed in the cage as in the previous

experiment. A metal rod consisting of two pieces, joined at right
angles so as to form an L, was placed in front of the cage. This
metal rod could be used to draw in a box in which was placed
the fruit or objective. A wooden ring measuring 1¾ in. in diameter
was attached vertically to the box, and the simplest method of

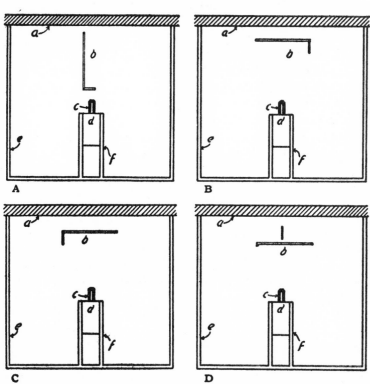

FIG. 15. TOOL CONSTRUCTION

a, Base of cage; *b*, L rod; *c*, ring attached to box wherein the metal L
end of the rod is inserted; *d*, box containing lure; *e*, 2-in. rail to one side of
which the box track is attached; *f*, wooden track. A, position 1, rod complete
with L end toward box; B, position 2, rod complete with handle end toward
child's right; C, position 3, rod complete with handle end toward child's left;
D, position 4, disjointed rod.

getting the fruit was to insert the L-end of the rod through the
wooden ring, then pull the box toward the cage. The box was
placed on a short wooden track in order to avoid its being turned
to one side in which case the straight end of the rod could be
inserted in the ring sufficiently to pull the box forward. Every

effort was made to make it impossible for the child to succeed in getting the object unless he used the hooked or L end of the rod in doing so.

At the beginning of the training period the rod was placed at right angles to the cage with the L end toward the box. The position was used to suggest the possible use of the L end of the rod. Since the children had had previous experience in using a straight stick to draw in a tray with fruit, it was not surprising that they immediately picked up the L rod and tried to get it hooked in the ring attached to the box. The association of an instrument in front of the cage as a means of obtaining the incentive had become an established pattern. The initial aspect, viz., overlooking the stick and merely trying to get themselves through the bars, had been eliminated by the time the children first experienced this particular situation. Since they associated the rod and the lure, it was subsequently placed parallel to the base of the cage with the L end of the rod on some occasions turned to the child's left and on other occasions to his right.

It was observed that when the L end of the rod was placed to the child's right, both Johnny and Jimmy picked the rod up by that end and attempted to draw in the box with the straight end. Jimmy's greater caution and dexterity enabled him to do this on four different occasions. In general Johnny was inclined to be less careful in his movements but to exert more force and work with greater persistence even when his efforts were ineffectual. It seems to the writer that this noticeable persistence might reasonably be a transfer from his practice in more gross motor performances where force and persistence were often effective in solving the problem for him. Johnny's coördinations in the insertion of the L through the ring and in drawing the box toward him were less well controlled than were those of Jimmy; but the two children were equally proficient in learning to shift the rod so as to grasp it with the straight end and insert the L end through the ring on the box.

After thirty trials with the two pieces of the rod properly joined, the situation was presented with the short and long pieces of the rod disconnected, i.e., with the short piece placed at right angles to the base of the cage and the longer rod lying beyond the short one, but parallel to the base of the cage. The various positions of the L rod are illustrated in Figure 15. Wher the rod was disjointed, both children immediately picked up the pieces of the rod and inserted the short one into the opening of the long one so as to make an L on the end. They then shifted the position of the hand on the rod in order to hold it at the opposite end as they put the L end between the bars to draw in the box. There was considerable correspondence in their performances. Putting the two pieces of rod together did not appear to be done for the specific purpose of constructing a tool for use in obtaining the incentive. They had become accustomed to the rod with the L end attached, and their initial motive appeared to be that of mending the rod. In the case of both boys it was after the two pieces of rod had been put together that attention fell upon the fruit, which became a stimulus for the next move involving reaching through the bars with the rod. There is no reason to believe from the comparative performances of the twins that the earlier and more extensive experience in other activities which Johnny had sustained exerted any outstanding influence upon his learning in this situation.

Suspended Basket, Hook, and Ring Situation

The situation described in the heading above contained one element with which the boys had had previous experience, namely an object suspended from the ceiling. Johnny had had more extensive experience in working with objects suspended from the ceiling than had Jimmy. However, on previous occasions there were stools or boxes in the room which they could manipulate in order to obtain the suspended object. In this instance, the object or fruit was placed in a basket; the basket was attached to a string which ran through a small ring near the ceiling, while another ring was attached to the opposite end of the string. The ring at the end of the string was placed on a hook in the wall which was located within easy reach of the child. No furniture was available in the room of which the child might make use in trying to get the basket. Of course, the necessary operation in order to obtain the lure involved lifting the ring off the hook in order to release it so that the basket would fall to the floor.

The reactions of the two children on the first day they were confronted with this situation reveal the influence of their previous experience involving an object suspended from the ceiling. Although all furniture had been removed from the room, Johnny's first action was to go running about calling for a "stool." Then in a far corner he saw a cardboard box placed behind a cabinet so that it was hardly visible, but which the experimenter had neglected to remove from the room because of its apparent insignificance as a climbing device. Johnny saw it and ran toward it, obviously with the intention of trying to use it. When the experimenter interfered, he ran beneath the basket and looked toward it, half-way extending his arms in the direction of the object. He was not really straining or vainly reaching in a manner characteristic of children when they are first confronted with a suspended-object situation. Completely thwarted, there was a momentary regression in Johnny's behavior to a less mature phase of the pattern. The reversion was only a rudiment of the early phase, since Johnny obviously did not expect to *reach* the object in this way. Presently his gaze moved from the basket to the long string attached to the hook on the wall. He straightway ran to the hook and jiggled the ring off it. He kept his eye on the basket as he first pulled down on the string and then raised his arm up again until it was above his head, all the while watching the basket drop down as his arm went up. Then he deliberately released his grasp on the string and the basket fell to the floor.

Jimmy's behavior when first confronted with this situation consisted of standing beneath the object for a brief moment, straining and reaching vainly toward it. Due to his less extensive experience, Jimmy appeared less convinced of the futility of the reaching act in this situation. Presently he saw the hook and ring on the wall. He ran immediately to it and by jiggling succeeded in getting the ring off the hook. He first pulled down upon the string, then raised his arms above his head, watching the basket go up and down as he did so. He became so engrossed in this activity, which he did repeatedly, that it was necessary for the experimenter to remind him of the fruit. Jimmy showed no evidence on this occasion of understanding the connection between releasing his hold on the string and the drop of the basket. As a matter of fact, he continued to hold on to the end of the string as he walked toward the basket.

These primary modes of action clearly indicate that Johnny's more extensive experience with an object suspended from a ceiling worked as an interference in his first move in this new situation.

PLATE XIV. HOOK, RING, AND BASKET SITUATION

Above, Johnny; below, Jimmy. At twenty-six months Johnny and Jimmy release the ring on the hook in order to obtain an object suspended in a basket.

PLATE XV. BALANCED-WEIGHTS SITUATION

Jimmy's initial act of standing beneath the object and reaching vainly was typical of the early phase of the behavior-course as observed in other children. He did not persist in this futile reaching very long. During a period of twelve practice days neither Johnny nor Jimmy completely mastered the mechanics of lifting the ring off the hook. Since they invariably succeeded in ultimately getting it off by engaging in sufficient jiggling of the ring back and forth, that aspect of the learning situation was not well devised. There was really no incentive for improving their methods, since the one they utilized ultimately worked. There was no occasion when either of them failed completely to get the ring off the hook. As a matter of fact, Johnny usually kept his eye on the basket even as he fingered the ring and hook. He appeared to understand the connection between the release of his hold on the string and the drop of the basket from the ceiling from the beginning. Jimmy showed evidence of understanding that particular relation during his third practice period. Jimmy appeared to have greater skill in taking the ring off the hook, since he looked at his manipulation rather than at the basket. The time consumed in getting the ring off the hook was less for Jimmy than for Johnny, but it is doubtful that his actual understanding of the mechanism was much greater, since he too moved the ring back and forth until it came off. He moved it with greater caution, and it therefore slipped off the hook a little more readily.

One week after their practice period in this situation was terminated, the experimenter arranged the basket and string connected with the hook and also scattered the graded stools about the room in order to see if the children would exercise any choice on their methods of getting the object. Both children ignored the stools, went directly to the hook and ring, released the hook, and let the basket drop.

Balanced Box and Double Pulley Situation

In this situation equally weighted objects were attached to different ends of a small rope. At one end there was a box containing the desired food and at the other a block of comparable weight. The rope was run through two pulleys placed fifty-six inches apart. When the child entered the room the box containing the fruit was placed fifty-four inches from the floor, whereas the weight was only eleven inches from the floor. It was necessary, therefore, for the child to push the weight up, thus lowering the box, in order to get the incentive.

On the first day that Johnny faced this situation he paused, looking the situation over as he approached the apparatus. Then he grasped the weight and began handling it, turning it over and looking on all sides. In doing so he raised it slightly so that the food box was lowered although Johnny did not perceive this relationship or observe the box as it was lowered. Presently he noticed that the food box was slightly lower. Dropping the weight, he stood beneath the food box, standing on tiptoes and trying to reach it. He could almost touch the bottom of the box with the tips of his fingers. Since he could not actually grasp it, he went back to the weight and pulled down on it as far as it would go. He observed the food box go up as he pulled on the weight, but he did not even then get the idea of raising the weight in order to bring the food box down. He had gotten a partial understanding of the situation, viz., movement of the weight brought about movement of the food box, but this idea was not advanced to the realization that a down movement of one meant an up movement of the other and vice versa. Failing to achieve the object on this occasion, he directed his attention to other activities.

Jimmy's behavior on the initial trial appeared to be more purposeful. He picked up the weight and moved it down and then up. Then he observed that the food box had been lowered. He started toward the food box but noticed that it was still too high to be reached. He then returned to the weight and pulled down and then up on it with greater force—in fact, sufficiently to lower the food box within his reach. Jimmy's first performance looked as if he had greater comprehension of the situation than was substantiated by his subsequent modes of behavior. On the second day he apparently became a little confused with his practice in the basket-hook situation, for he ran to the hook on the wall and pulled at it, although there was no string attached to it leading to the object. After he had handled the hook for a little while he then returned to the weight, pulled it down, and pushed it up, but not sufficiently high to lower the food box within his reach. On subsequent occasions he usually moved the weight up and down several times until he observed the food box within his reach. Then he would release the weight and run to the food box.

Pulling the weight up and down repeatedly was an act in itself which Jimmy relinquished only when he saw the food box within reach. There was no indication that Jimmy understood the relationship between the two. He would hold on to the weight as he moved his arms up and down with great excitement. In this way he ordinarily achieved the object, and hence there was no incentive to stimulate his understanding of the mechanism of the situation. At the end of his practice period Jimmy's understanding seemed not to have developed beyond the stage of realizing that the down and up movement of the weight brought the object within reach.

Although Johnny failed to obtain the object on the first day, he was, during his following experiences in this situation, more interested than was Jimmy in the *modus operandi* by which the food was obtained. On the fourth day he picked up the weight to examine it, but he observed the food box move as he did so. He then slowly pulled the weight down as far as it would go, keeping his eye on the food box as it was raised to the top. Immediately he pushed the weight up slowly, watching the food box drop as he pushed the weight up. This experience apparently gave him the idea that pushing up on the weight lowered the box, but it was not a completely matured idea, as will be seen from his behavior of the following day. On that day with one movement he pushed the weight up slightly. He then started toward the food but could just touch the bottom of the box. When he could not get the food box, he went back to the weight, but since his initial move was inadequate, there appeared a regression in his behavior to a less mature level, indicated by moving the weight up and down several times in succession. Suddenly he noticed that the food box was low enough to be reached. He got the banana out of the food box, but stood for several seconds looking at the apparatus as if puzzled over its mechanism before beginning to eat the piece of fruit. By the end of their practice periods, which consisted of eleven days in this activity, all excess activity had been eliminated in Johnny's performance. He went directly to the weight and with one gross movement pushed it sufficiently high to lower the food box well within reach.

Although in terms of success, as it might be expressed in attaining an objective, Johnny's performance in this situation was not superior to that of Jimmy, yet the quality of his behavior manifested a superior comprehension of the situation. In this instance the writer is inclined to believe that Johnny's proclivity to pause and study the situation acquired during his manipulation of stools and boxes was definitely transferred to his activity in this situation.

String Situations

There were several situations involving an arrangement of two or more strings. A tray with a small piece of food was attached on the end of one string in each situation. The child was placed in the cage used in the experiments described earlier, and the strings were arranged in various configurations on the floor just in front of the grill. The child was told to get the food. If he selected the wrong string for the purpose of drawing in the food, the experimenter closed the door in front of the grill so that he could not make a second selection on that particular arrangement at a given trial. The arrangement of the strings consisted (1) of detour patterns involving a long string to which was attached the object together with a short unattached string and (2) of cross strings involving two or more strings of the same length crossing each other at the mid-point with the object attached at the end of one. Figure 16 illustrates the various string configurations.

The performances of Johnny and Jimmy in these situations were strikingly parallel. On the first occasion when the strings were arranged according to (a) of Figure 16 Johnny selected the correct string. When the configuration was changed to (b), he apparently paid very little attention to the configuration but stopped to pick up the string which was on his right. This string, of course, was the short, unattached one. The situation, appearing simple, had failed to exact adequate attention from Johnny as he made the move to pick up the string. It was only when he saw the door beginning to close that he really glanced at the string arrangement. His failure to select the right string was not due to an inability to discriminate but to a lack of attention to the situation.

Jimmy likewise on this first occasion selected correctly the long string on his right at the first trial. At the second trial he started to reach for the short string on his right, but he glanced toward the string, paused, and deliberately shifted his position in order to take the long string on his left. Subsequently neither child in

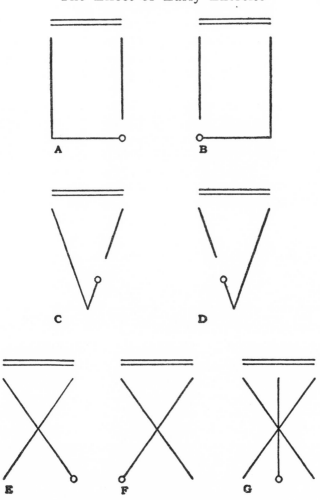

Fig. 16. String Configurations

A, B, C, and D represent the detour arrangement of two strings, with the end of the correct string placed first on child's right and then on his left. E and F illustrate the arrangement of two strings of equal length. G shows three strings of equal length in cross-arrangement.

eight different trials made an error, when two strings were arranged in detour fashion, in selecting the string to which the lure was attached. This situation was obviously too simple to constitute a problem for them. Change in configuration of the detour pattern as illustrated by C and D of Figure 16 introduced no disturbing element to them. They were equally successful on all detour arrangements.

The cross strings were more difficult for them, but the performances of the two boys were almost equivalent on these also. Out of seventeen trials extending over a period of six days, both children failed to choose the correct string ten times. By the end of the training period both boys were consistently selecting the correct string. Although their total records in errors and successes were equivalent, Jimmy showed slightly less variability from day to day in his selection during the last four days of the practice period than did Johnny.

So far as learning and discrimination in these string situations are concerned, it is obvious that Johnny's earlier and more extensive practice involving gross motor activities was of no advantage to him in solving problems of this sort.

Size Discrimination

It will be recalled that at the end of their practice periods neither Johnny nor Jimmy was showing consistent discrimination of size differences in response to verbal directions. Their learning in size discrimination was undertaken by Dr. Fjeld under somewhat different laboratory conditions. The child was placed in the cage as in the previous situations. When the door opened he was presented with two boxes of different size. One was 4 in. square and 2 in. deep, the other one was 1½ in. square and ¾ in. deep. To each of these boxes was attached a string which extended within reach of the child near the base of the cage. During the first few trials the child could see the food placed in the big box, and all he had to do was to pick up the right string and draw the box toward him. As he did so the experimenter, who was observing through a one-way vision mirror glass from an observation room said: "It is the big one." These preliminary trials with the food visible to the child were for the purpose of familiarizing him with the experimental conditions. After several trials with the food in evidence, a piece of gray cardboard was attached to the front side of each box. The cardboard front to the bix box measured 8 in. square in comparison with the 3-in. square on the front of the small box. It was the difference in the size of these two cardboards that the child should learn to discriminate in response to "big" or "little." The training method consisted of placing the food consistently in the big box, but changing the left-right position of the boxes with reference to the child who was in the cage. The experimenter, who operated from an obscure position, said: "It's the big one" each time the door of the cage was opened.

After thirteen trials Johnny began consistently to select the big box irrespective of its left-right position. After eighteen trials Jimmy began to make this selection regularly. While they were at this time selecting on a size basis, the selection was not in response to the language direction. It took them thirteen and eighteen trials respectively to get the idea that the object was always in the big box. Once they got the idea, they selected the big one by making a concrete perceptive distinction, rather than associating it with the symbolic verbal sound, that is, the language of the experimenter which accompanied the selection.

After they had begun to select the big box consistently, there followed a similar practice period when the object was always placed in the small box. After fourteen and eight trials respectively, Johnny and Jimmy were consistent in selecting the small box regardless of its position. It was then that the real test of size discrimination in response to verbal directions began, since the experimenter now would not only change the position of the boxes but would alternate placement of the fruit in the big and the little box.

After sixty-eight and seventy-two trials respectively when the food might have been in either box, both Johnny and Jimmy were still failing to distinguish size difference in response to verbal directions. Johnny would often imitate the experimenter by repeating the words "big one," but even then he showed no appreciation of the meaning of the words in relation to his performance. Since the boys were incapable of discriminating on a language level, both during this practice period showed a regression to a less mature phase of the pattern by selecting on the basis of position, that is, they began invariably selecting the box on the right. It is interesting that the children showed this position-habit after the same amount of experience in the situation, specifically after thirty-three trials for Jimmy and thirty-four for Johnny. When their practice periods were terminated, neither was really manifesting size discrimination in response to language directions. Certainly Johnny's earlier and more extensive experience was of no notable benefit to him in his behavior in this situation, even though he had had more extensive experience than Jimmy in size discrimination under other conditions. It appears that their symbolic associations had not developed so that they could grasp adjectival differences of this sort.

There was a high degree of correspondence in the attainments of the twins in situations wherein the amount of their experience was equivalent. Qualitatively there frequently occurred considerable differences in their attitude and manner of activity. These qualitative differences were of such a nature as to attribute them to the earlier and more extensive practice Johnny received in other types of activities.

Comparative Ratings on Standardized Intelligence Tests

The writer has previously asserted that at birth Jimmy appeared superior in development to Johnny. In so far as developmental level is an indication of endowment he appeared to be superior in that respect. Ratings by means of standardized tests were not made of the children until the end of Jimmy's control period. Such ratings were postponed until that date for several reasons. In the first place the reliability and validity of the tests at the younger age levels is highly questionable; secondly, the experimenter and coworkers preferred not to have their opinion of the children biased in any way during the longer practice period; and thirdly, ratings of this type are not pertinent to the main objective of this investigation, which was to study processes of development under differing conditions. This study has been more concerned with the sequential phases of development of infants who received different amounts of external stimulation than it has been with the levels of achievement.

However, since Johnny's performance during practice in many ways transcended the performances of other babies of corresponding chronological age, the question frequently arose as to the possibility of his being exceptionally endowed. Also, the experimenter has been repeatedly asked to express an opinion as to the possible effect the early practice which Johnny received would have upon his general intelligence. Therefore, ratings on standardized tests were made of the two children at two different periods,

The Effect of Early Exercise

namely, when they were twenty-two months old, just prior to
Jimmy's period of special exercise, and when they were twenty-
five months old, which was near the end of his practice period.
The ratings were made by Dr. Metta Rust, a disinterested person
who was equally unfamiliar to the two children.

At the first examination on the Merrill-Palmer Scale of Mental
Tests, Johnny earned a mental age of twenty-one months, sigma
value — 0.5, and percentile rank of 30. Jimmy on the same test
series scored a mental age of twenty months, sigma value — 1.0
and percentile rank of 20. The ratings on the Minnesota Pre-
School Scale when the babies were twenty-two months old yielded
a combined total score of 54 for forms A and B for Johnny. The
intelligence quotient equivalent to this score was 85. Jimmy's
combined total score on forms A and B at the same time was 51,
which was equivalent to an I. Q. of 82.

On the Merrill-Palmer Scale at the second examination Johnny's
mental age was twenty-nine months, or four months beyond his
chronological age, in contrast to the first testing when his mental
age had been one month less than his chronological age. Sigma
value of the second rating was 1.5 and his score placed him in the
90 percentile. Jimmy, whose mental age at the first testing was two
months less than his chronological age, now earned a mental age
of twenty-eight months on this series, with a sigma value of 1.0
and a percentile rank of 80. During the three-months' interval the
performance of each child had jumped the equivalent of eight
months on this scale. The second rating on the Minnesota Scale
yielded a combined score of 67 on forms A and B for Johnny, the
I. Q. equivalent for this score being 94; rating on the same test
for Jimmy showed a combined score of 65, the I. Q. equivalent for
which is 91. On this scale the I. Q. rating of both children increased 9 points during the three-months' interval. These figures
indicate that at both examination periods Johnny consistently
earned a higher rating on the two scales than did Jimmy, but the
difference between the scores was small. The relative position of
the children from one period to the other remained constant. It
was obvious, according to the examiner, throughout the testing
series at both periods that Johnny was much more persistent in
a task at hand than was Jimmy, who was inclined to abandon the
task if it proved a little difficult. It was this persistence which
enabled Johnny to fit all the pieces into the Mare and Foal test

of the Merrill-Palmer series, though he continued to work at the task beyond the time limit and therefore did not score on it. These data lend supporting evidence to the writer's contention that the children were not more than normal in endowment, and for that reason Johnny's learning potentialities during the period of infancy gain greater significance.

The writer does not propose to enter into a discussion of the validity and reliability of standardized measures of intelligence for young children,* nor into the flagrant controversies over the nature and organization of general intelligence. It is the conviction of the writer that when dealing with infants measures of intelligence expressed in terms of end result or in terms of frequency and time involved in a performance are inadequate means of revealing either individual differences or the extent to which experience in one type of activity may influence or alter the acquisition of another.

Discussion

Although Johnny had enjoyed earlier and more extensive practice in certain activities, he apparently was not greatly benefited thereby in the acquisition of performances of a different order. When achievement is measured by end results, his performances in most of the situations reported in this chapter were not superior to those of Jimmy. When achievement is indicated in terms of time consumed in completing a performance, he showed no definite superiority which could be attributed to the influence of his earlier experience.

On the other hand, there were certain distinct qualitative differences which characterized the behavior of Johnny as compared with that of Jimmy when they were confronted with equally new situations. Some of these qualitative differences can be explained adequately only on the basis of Johnny's more extensive early experience in other activities. Differences in manner of behavior cannot be determined by end result. When attainments are expressed in terms of frequency of success in obtaining the lure or in terms of the amount of time consumed in securing it, important differences in method of procedure are obscured. For example, consider Johnny's behavior in the weight-box-and-dual-pulley situation in contrast to Jimmy's. Actually, Jimmy secured

* See *24* for discussion of this subject.

the lure as frequently as did Johnny and in about as short a time. But Johnny was more inclined to pause and look the situation over before acting; he appeared more persistent and less willing to quit when he met with difficulty. Even at that early age Johnny was obviously more concerned with the *modus operandi* than with end result. These were differences in attitude which may or may not improve the end-result of a performance. On the Mare and Foal test Johnny's increased persistence enabled him to finish the task, though not within sufficient time to make a score. On size discrimination his greater persistence stimulated his continued pulling on the wrong string, thereby delaying his efforts at discrimination of the difference in size of the boxes.

Attitudes of receptivity, coöperation, persistence, resistance, and inhibition are often transferred from learning one performance to learning another. But an attitude of receptivity or persistence, which in one situation may promote a solution of the problem, may in another situation prove to be a stumbling block to the desired attainment. The fundamental principles of behavior are often clouded both in experimental and in standardized test situations because of the current tendency among psychologists to disregard all the behavorial movements which do not have direct reference to the specific objective which the experimenter sets for the child. Experimental studies of behavior will not attain their utmost significance until it is possible to record behavior as a movement, accounting for all the factors entering into a given act and not limiting reports to the specific movements which have reference to the incentive arranged by the experimenter. The subject's incentive may be totally different from the one set by the experimenter in a particular situation.

A mode of behavior that appears stupid when considered merely in terms of the immediate task may, when *all* factors are considered, appear to be a highly intelligent act. For example, the infant or young child who sits rather listlessly trying to fit pieces into a form board, increasing his time and his score in errors, may appear dull to the experimenter when as a matter of fact he needs to urinate and has not adequate language equipment for conveying the idea. He may not even have sufficiently differentiated perceptive development to understand exactly what his need is. The impulse to urinate is just enough to interfere with concentration of activity upon the line arranged by the experimenter. If the impulse to urinate is more forceful, the subject's behavior in the same situation may be quite different. He may refuse to sit contentedly at the examining table, may chatter incessantly and incoherently about irrelevant things, go frequently toward the door, and throw blocks around the room. He may not even once during the examination mention the need to urinate, and he may not wet his pants. Confining his attention to the child's achievement in a particular performance, the experimenter would ignore the pressure which was most forceful in governing the subject's behavior at the moment.

All aspects of behavior (splanchnic, somatic, cognitive, and conative) must be taken into account in each activity at any moment. They should be considered not merely as parts of the individual, but as different aspects or factors in each behavior-pattern. Some aspects of a behavior-pattern are more plastic and more variable than others. The total number of somatic or cognitive aspects involved in any action-pattern are limited by the conditions of the situation. For example, if a child is placed in a cage, there are only a limited number of motor activities available to him. But the possibility of attitudes which he may have in that particular situation are boundless. The attitude is perhaps the most pervading yet fluctuating aspect of any behavior-pattern. Since it is the most variable aspect of a behavior-pattern, it is subject to greater modifiability than are either the somatic or cognitive factors in any one situation. Furthermore, there is greater possibility of transferring an attitude from one situation to another than there is in transferring motor skills or techniques or perceptive acumen. Since the influence of an attitude is of such moment in determining the type and extent of the overt behavior-pattern, we feel impelled to discuss it in greater detail as it is observed in the development of the infant and young child.

Chapter VIII

THE DEVELOPMENT AND INFLUENCE OF ATTITUDES

SINCE the influence of attitudes has been greatly emphasized in the preceding chapters, it would be merely begging the question to attribute as much weight to their influence as we have done without at the same time concerning ourselves with the constitution and development of attitudes. It is well enough to admit that a particular attitude of an individual exercises enormous influence in directing and organizing his performance at the moment, but that does not answer the question, Whence comes the attitude? Certainly attitudes are not created out of the blue for the sole purpose of facilitating or inhibiting somatic activity.

The writer is using the term *attitude* broadly to indicate all those diffuse or specific feeling tones which accompany a motor action or state of being. It is a more inclusive term than *emotion* but also one which has not been subjected to so much abuse and is therefore less liable to misinterpretation. Except for purposes of convenience in discourse it is impossible in ordinary behavior to separate motor activity from mental or attitudinal activity. They are merely different aspects of the same performance. As such they should not be considered as entities apart from the total performance, yet in analyzing the factors which enter into the formation of a behavior-pattern it is possible to see the interrelation of all aspects of a performance only when the nature of each is given consideration.

Both structurally and functionally an attitude seems to be a pervading activity of the total organism, more pervading than are other aspects of an action-pattern. One thinks of digestive activity as being a function primarily of the alimentary tract and motor activity as a chief concern of the muscular system. Mental activity is considered to be a fundamental function of the central nervous system, especially the brain. But when one thinks of attitudinal activity there come to mind not merely the autonomic and central nervous systems but the glandular systems and other factors. There is no one organic system which seems to localize the major functions of attitudinal development as the special organic systems just mentioned localize other developments. In making this statement we speak, of course, in a broad general sense, for when it comes to actuality the total organism is concerned in all aspects of activity and the differences here mentioned are differences only in degree. Although merely differences in degree, they are none the less significant. It is customary to speak of an "attitude of repose," of "attention," of "flight," of "receptivity" or "rejection." These phrases suggest a definite bodily adjustment, an expression of readiness to act, or a predisposition on the part of the organism to respond in a given manner. But the bodily adjustment is an indication or expression of the attitude and does not constitute the attitude as such. Moreover, the attitude is not merely a readiness to respond in a given manner but, acting somewhat as a catalyzer, it gives direction, force, and quality to the somatic action.

That a prevailing attitude is a cardinal factor in the organization of a performance at a given moment is so obvious as to constitute a truism. In fact an attitude is more rightly considered always as a catalyzer, giving strength to the motor or mental aspect of the performance. It is only when behavior is considered in terms of end results that an attitude can be described as an inhibiting factor. A particular attitude may be *inhibiting* one type of activity which the conditions of the situation make possible and perhaps it is the desired type—desirable from the viewpoint of both observer and subject—but at the same time the same attitude is *facilitating* another type of action. An uncoöperative attitude may interfere with a child's walking up an incline, but at the same time it will facilitate the act of sitting down and crying. It must be kept in mind that inertia is just as much a behavior-pattern as is violent activity, and that an attitude which is at the one moment checking or counteracting the impulse to move forward is at the same time reinforcing inertia.

Furthermore, it is highly fallacious to conclude that an attitude of coöperation, receptivity, or acquiescence is always effective in promoting the desired somatic response. As a matter of fact the converse is only too often true. A most receptive and coöperative attitude may become a stumbling block to optimum performance. A common remark on the performance of a tyro is that "He is too eager." When there is an undue attitude of receptivity and co-operation, the somatic performance is likely to become diffuse and generalized. This principle is well illustrated in the behavior of the baby who is just beginning to extend his arms to reach for an object in the visual field. If the sight of the object is excessively stimulating, the energy which should be directed toward extension of the arm in the direction of the object becomes converted into disorganized general body activity. It is desirable that the individual should be interested in the object just enough to elicit a well-controlled motor act. Too little interest would fail to stimulate a movement in the direction of the object, and too much interest would interfere with the individual's control over the motor activity involved.

It is speculative but highly reasonable to suppose that one important factor making it possible for the growing baby to eliminate the excess motion in the reaching-prehensile act is greater familiarity with objects in his environment. That is, as his sensory experience with various objects becomes wider, his anxiety to touch and investigate the immediate object is lessened, and the excess or overflow of activity is greatly reduced, thereby making it possible for him to direct and control the act of reaching toward the object. It might be said then that it was not so much exercise or use of the somatic extensor movement or even repetition of the integration of visual and motor acts as it was increased sensory experience with objects and things which promoted the development of the reaching-prehensile act. In other words, it was not merely exercise of the reaching-prehensile pattern which perfected this activity but more expansive sensory experience as well. Nor was it in this instance mere satisfaction of attaining and possessing the object which established and fixed the discrete reaching pattern. The development of a kind of sophisticated attitude, curtailing excessive eagerness, would apparently be influential in eliminating excess motion. If this surmise should be true, and to the writer it seems highly plausible, then it is of extreme significance in formulating a theory of development. The value of repeated exercise of a function is shown in a new light.

Ordinarily an intense attitude, whether coöperative or negative, tends to interfere with well-directed, purposeful motor activities. Intensity of attitude does not, however, invariably interfere with the purposeful aspect of behavior. The writer is reminded of many instances where infants have succeeded in certain motor performances made under intense strain whereas, when experiencing less tension, the same child would have given the impression of being quite incapable of the motor act. For example, most of the clinic children who have succeeded in getting off the higher pedestals mentioned in the earlier chapters have done so along with an obvious display of perturbation. When less disturbed they became cautious, would turn first to one side of the stool and then another, and would finally refuse to get off unassisted. Usually, however, a perturbed state even in this situation does not facilitate the desired somatic response. More frequently an attitude of perturbation interferes with the child's making an effort to get off the pedestal at all but rather stimulates him further to sit on the stool, crying and reaching toward an adult for help.

Every adult has had similar experiences when in fits of anger he has been able to lift loads or move objects which were otherwise completely beyond his strength. It is the impression of the writer that an intense attitude is likely to interfere with the *initiation* of the movement toward the goal. Once the organism has been set into motor action of a given type, the intensity of the attitude may reinforce the activity. If we consider an attitude as a facilitating and not an inhibiting agent, then the intensity of the attitude promotes the purposeful act provided the action has become directed by the time the attitude grew intense. But if the intense feeling develops while the movement is in an initial diffuse state then the intensity of the attitude increases the diffuseness of behavior, thereby interfering with its becoming purposeful and directional. In other words, if the initial act is already directed, the intensity of the attitude adds to its completion, but if the initial movement is in a purposeless direction then the ineffectuality of the activity enhances the intensity of the attitude and a vicious circle is set up leading to diffuse and disorganized activity.

Development of Attitudes

It has been more or less tacitly assumed that an attitude on the part of an individual at any moment is the product of his previous experience in that and similar situations. The early Behaviorists claimed that an infant is born equipped with only limited attitudinal or emotional action-patterns, but by the process of conditioning or associative shifting an attitude is transferred from one situation to another. These primary patterns are thus greatly expanded and increased in complexity. The number and variety of stimuli which will stimulate a particular attitude are thereby increased, so that the attitude *per se* becomes more and more complex until the feeling tones at a given moment and in a particular situation are no longer pure and simple. It is beyond the scope of this investigation to contribute to the already voluminous polemic writings on the subject of emotional or attitudinal development. Notwithstanding the available discourse on the subject, knowledge of this aspect of behavior is still more a matter of controversy than of fact. Certainly no one would question for a moment that previous experiences of an individual, and the attitudinal feelings which accompanied those experiences, are highly influential in determining the attitude and behavior of the individual in subsequent situations.

It is, however, questionable in the mind of the writer whether attitudes at all times can be explained adequately on a purely associational basis. There is some reason to believe that an attitude may originate in an imbalance of two or more growing behavior-patterns which are developing at different rates. For illustration let us return to the familiar example of the infant who is developmentally at the threshold of the reaching-prehensile action. Visual perception has proceeded more rapidly than the motor mechanism necessary for the tactile perception, and hence when the baby sees the object he develops an attitude of anxiety which is expressed in the diffuse movement of the arms. The feeling of anxiety arises from the fact that visual perception has developed beyond the means of tactile and other sensory experiences involved in the situation.

It is conceivable that the origin of an attitude is a product of pure physiological growth rather than of associational experience as that term is ordinarily used. Consider the development of an attitude of resistance as seen in the behavior of the infant. It has previously been pointed out that in the newborn infant flexor activities are developed beyond those of extensors. When extensor activities begin to develop during the early months there is a tendency to exaggerate or overdo the extensor aspect of behavior. But, since the extension is not at that time well differentiated, there results a state of general muscular tension rather than any purposeful extensor movement. It is no uncommon experience of those who handle infants to pick up a baby and have him respond by a general condition of tension, notably hyperextension of the spine, which makes it practically impossible to get him in a sitting position. The adults who observe him then say that he is angry or that he objects to being picked up or to sitting down. If the adult happens to be offering him a bottle she is likely to contend that he does not want his food. Actually the baby *objects* to nothing except flexion. The adult endows the baby with a feeling or attitude which has not at the time become entirely integrated with the extensor pattern. The hyperextension is merely a manifestation of a lack of control over and a tendency to exaggerate a newly developing function.

A few months later the attitude of resistance may be expressed in quite a different somatic pattern. Instead of hyperextending the infant becomes limp and cannot be induced to stand on his feet; if one picks him up he slips elusively, eel-like, out of the hands. This pattern constitutes a counter-reaction to the hyperextension phase. It is itself exaggerated for a time, but it more frequently occurs concurrently with a purposeful attitude of resistance. In the later stages of development the hyperextension or hyperflexion becomes associated and integrated with the attitude so that it actually constitutes an expression of the attitude. But in the initial phase the flexor-extensor development appears to be independent and not directly connected with the attitude it seems to connote. Ultimately the child will use both flexion and extension discriminately in manifesting resistance.

Furthermore, the origin of even more complex feeling tones or attitudes can be explained adequately on a developmental rather than a purely associational basis. For example, a young infant, of less than six or eight months, will indicate no feeling of insecurity when placed upon a high pedestal. But twelve months later if the same child is placed upon a high pedestal he will become tense and in other ways indicate an attitude of insecurity. Something has happened in the interim which makes his behavior in this situation distinctly different at eighteen months from his behavior at eight months. The general theory would be that he had at some time experienced disagreeable feelings (as from a fall, for instance) which he associated with that situation. These past experiences contributed to his attitude of insecurity at eighteen months. Although the conditions of the experiment would be difficult to carry out, the writer is willing to gamble the prediction that if it were possible to prevent a child's being placed in positions of height and to prevent his falling even the slightest distance during the first two years of life, he would, if placed upon a high pedestal at that time, manifest a more intense attitude of insecurity than he would if he had experienced innumerable falls from the pedestal, provided the falls had been treated by adults in a matter-of-fact way. The fact of the fall *per se* or the discomfort associated with it does not alone account for the origin of the attitude.

There is a reasonable explanation for the feeling of insecurity of the older child other than disagreeable associations with the particular situation or similar ones. The attitude arises from a normal growth imbalance due to different rates of development in several aspects of the behavior-pattern. The younger infant shows no attitude of insecurity because he has inadequate powers of discrimination in height differences. The older child manifests the muscular tensions and other signs of insecurity in the situation not because he has had falls and disagreeable associations with the situation necessarily but because his perceptive equipment for distinguishing differences in height has reached a stage of rapid development and hence there is, for the time being, an imbalance in his perceptive ability and his motor adjustments for meeting the situation.

The account of Johnny's development in jumping (page 171, Chapter IV) illustrates this point. Notwithstanding the fact that the motor aspect of jumping off high pedestals had been expanded through experience before he began to show signs of discrimination in height differences, when his perception in this respect became more acute there occurred a period of insecurity characterized by muscular tension, especially when he looked over the edge of the stool on which he was standing. With continued experience he soon recovered his former abandon. As soon as a child's perceptive and motor equipment becomes integrated, his attitude of insecurity may be eliminated if rightly handled. Of course other factors may enter the situation to perpetuate the attitude of insecurity even after the growth imbalance has been adjusted. We are here discussing the inception of attitudes rather than their mode of development. In the course of development experience is highly important during the integrative phase. Once an action-pattern has become fully matured, individual experiences in the situation are of prime importance in determining the attitude. Once height discrimination, motor equipment, and discriminative powers are well integrated, it is the child's individual associations which govern his attitude when he is placed on high pedestals. It is not claimed that particular attitudes never arise from purely associational experiences. It is merely contended that the *conditioning* theory does not offer adequate explanation for the origin of all attitudes.

It seems that the origin of many childhood "fears" may be attributed not necessarily to some unpleasant experience and resultant associations but to a natural growth imbalance or lack of integration between several aspects of development. A child walking in the dark will show muscular tensions if his perceptive development is at such a stage that it does not integrate smoothly with the motor adjustments involved. This attitude may persist until it constitutes a "fear" of the dark if the child's experiences are not treated in a matter-of-fact way. If the child's experiences are treated casually, the tension resulting from a normal growth imbalance will soon fade except to the extent that a degree of tension may be needed for handling the situation.

One reason students of behavior have not advanced further in their analysis of attitudinal behavior is due to the tendency to regard attitudes and emotional adaptations as entities rather than *aspects only* of a performance. It is fallacious to speak of *an attitude* in a particular situation, for there are many attitudes in a constant state of flux in all situations. Nevertheless, the immediate conditions, both intrinsic and extrinsic, are as important as, if not more important than, past experiences in determining the attitude of the subject at the moment.

A profitable analogy would be to consider a single performance as similar to a chemical compound. Energies intrinsic and extrinsic are in a constant state of interaction. A little more or a little less of this or that alters the behavioral compound. It makes an enormous difference whether a particular behavior ingredient is introduced into the growth compound at one time or another. The same ingredient which, if introduced at one time, will assimilate may, at another, produce a precipitate, while at still another time the result may be an explosion. Likewise in an interplay of behavior forces it cannot be said that associational experiences, past or present, make the attitude; nor can it be said that the prevailing attitudes as such determine the somatic performance. Success or failure in a type of activity may be instrumental in fixating a general attitude of persistence. An attitude of persistence may be an asset or a liability in achieving a particular goal. The fact that attitudes are less specific in their organic structure means that they are more plastic and subject to greater modification through experience than any other aspect of behavioral development.

Attitudes of Johnny and Jimmy

The intimate interrelation between attitude and performance as well as the transfer of attitude from one situation to another is illustrated in the comparative behavior of Johnny and Jimmy after a month's emancipation from the experimental situations in which they had previously been exercised. From the time the twins were 743 days old until they were 773 days, they were being practised by Dr. Fjeld in situations equally new to them. During that time they were not allowed to see the apparatus consisting of stools, boxes, slides, skates, tricycle, and so forth on which they had previously been exercised in certain activities. They were, however, during that month getting their daily exercise in new situations in the same room, though with different equipment and with a different experimenter. At the end of the month their activities were observed in those situations in which they had received earlier experience in order to see what effect the month of abstinence would show on their retention of previously acquired performances.

At the end of that month Jimmy made his best performances in practically every situation wherein he had previously been exercised, while Johnny showed an obvious though temporary deterioration in practically every performance. This deterioration can be attributed to nothing other than his lack of practice in those performances during the intervening month. As was pointed out earlier, in many of the situations it was not Jimmy's performance *per se* but a more coöperative attitude which was being cultivated during his practice period. He continued developing a more coöperative attitude during the month that followed, although his actual activities were quite different. An improvement in his performance after a period of abstinence is therefore understandable. There must have been a transfer of the more acquiescent attitude acquired during the interval to the performance or activities in which he had been exercised previously. Johnny, in contrast, had already acquired a completely coöperative attitude during his practice period, and hence his motor performances at the end represented his maximum ability. For that reason he suffered an actual loss in performance by virtue of the month's lack of specific experience. The loss, however, was not permanent, for with two or three days' practice he had regained his customary proficiency in these activities.

When the children were twenty-six months old their period of special exercise was definitely terminated. Subsequently their days were spent at home, although they were returned to the laboratory at biweekly intervals for follow-up examinations. Six months have passed since, and the children are thirty-two months old at this writing. During these months when they have not been getting daily practice in any special activities, since nothing specifically has been done to promote more coöperative attitudes, there has been an outstanding comparative change in the activities in which they received varying amounts of practice at different chronological ages. Jimmy has in many ways shown a regression to former behavior-patterns—that is, action-patterns which obtained during his control period. For example, although he had during his practice period deliberately been climbing off high pedestals, now he cries and clings to the edge until from fatigue he drops to the floor. Although he had never, even during his practice period, actually jumped off the pedestals, he had become quite affable when placed on the stools for jumping, whereas now crying terrifically he clutches the experimenter. Not only in attitude but in method of motor performance Jimmy has shown a reversion in those activities wherein there was the greatest temporal gap between his and Johnny's achievement of the activity. Although Jimmy, quite coöperative now, attempts to ascend the steeper slides, he often uses the hand-knee method, instead of using his toes for gripping, and despite his effort he has been unable to ascend the two steepest slopes.

In contrast Johnny has maintained his acquiescent attitude in all those activities which he acquired early and in most instances has improved in skill. There has been no permanent loss of skill in his climbing and jumping performances. On the skates there is usually shown at each monthly examination an initial loss in skill, but by the time he has gone about 500 feet he is showing a steady gain toward his former proficiency. On the other hand, in those activities toward which Jimmy never during his control period developed such a strong negativistic attitude, e.g., manipulation of stools and boxes, activities wherein the time interval between the inception of Jimmy and Johnny's respective practice periods was much less, the differences in their levels of performance remain comparatively constant. While in actual attainment Johnny's performance in these situations is still considerably beyond that of Jimmy, both children show an initial temporary loss when their performances are compared with their own previous performances. But before terminating a particular performance the activity of each child is likely to show a gradual improvement, sometimes advancing beyond the actual achievement at the previous examination period. In those activities wherein their practice periods were equivalent both in time of inception and in duration, their retention of these performances has been quite similar. In these situations both have been acquiescent and coöperative during their post-practice periods. Thus it would appear that while we succeeded during his practice period in altering Jimmy's attitude toward many performances, the period of alteration was in every instance of insufficient duration to make the coöperative attitude a permanent one.

In the present discourse the importance of an attitude as a guiding and forceful agent in any behavioral act has been recognized. Since an attitude is more plastic and pervading than other aspects of a performance, it is also more modifiable and transferable. We are of the opinion that the origin of all attitudes cannot be adequately explained on an associational basis. There is reason to believe that they may arise from a normal growth imbalance in two or more aspects of a developing behavioral pattern.

Chapter IX

THE PHYSICAL DEVELOPMENT OF JOHNNY AND JIMMY

THE conditions of this investigation invariably arouse certain questions with respect to the physical development of the twins. Some of the most frequent of these questions are: (1) What effect did the intensive and increased amount of daily exercise have upon the physical development of the children? (2) Since the twins were kept indoors during a large share of their waking hours at the hospital and, therefore, probably were not given the amount of exposure to direct sunlight a good pediatric schedule would call for, what effect did the indoor life have upon their general physical well-being?

The writer makes no pretense of being able to answer these questions adequately. The limitations of the clinic staff did not permit a well-controlled experimental study of physical development. However, routine physical examinations were made of each infant who has figured in this investigation. Customarily the physical examination occurred on the same day that the behavioral development of the child was recorded. This arrangement made it possible to avoid an accumulation of records on infants a large percentage of whom may not have been performing at par because of some temporary physical ailment.

It will be recalled that at birth Jimmy weighed slightly more than Johnny. From Figure 17 showing their respective increments in body weight it is easily seen that Jimmy continued to hold his relative superiority in weight during the first three months. There followed a period of approximately five months when neither Johnny nor Jimmy was consistently in the lead in so far as body weight was concerned. However, between the seventh and eighth month Johnny began to gain more rapidly, and subsequently his weight has consistently been greater than Jimmy's. Not only did he weigh more than Jimmy, but the percentage of increase from month to month also showed a steady and consistent rise. It is observed that this difference in weight increments became apparent just about the time Johnny started swimming, ascending and descending inclines, and other gross muscular activity. Johnny's gain in relative weight closely parallels the time he began to engage in those activities in which he has shown definite superiority in behavioral performances. Whether his increased activities contributed to his gain in weight is a question beyond the province of this investigation.

Not only in weight but in body length also Johnny's development during the first two years of life has been more rapid than Jimmy's. Unfortunately it was not possible to obtain accurate anthropometric measurements of the twins until they were fifteen months old. By that time Johnny was already beginning to show considerable superiority in motor performances. At the time of birth both infants measured 505 mm. in body length. Additional measurements were not made until fifteen months later, when Dr. C. B. Davenport began to make regular periodic anthropometric measurement of the twins as well as of other infants studied at the clinic. At that time Jimmy measured 8 mm. taller than Johnny, but during the next ten months Johnny gained to the extent of 33 mm. beyond Jimmy in body length. Dr. Davenport customarily recorded forty-three different measurements on the children at each examination. On the basis of these observations, which extended over a period of ten months, he reports that in July, 1933, Johnny was behind Jimmy in development, while in May, 1934, Johnny had advanced markedly beyond Jimmy.

It would be unwise to infer from these data that the noticeable increase in body size which Johnny developed during the latter part of his practice period had any direct relationship to his greater amount of motor activity. It may be true, but this investigation makes no such claim. On the other hand, these data are significant in a negative way. At least so far as this experiment is concerned, it cannot be said that the excessive daily exercise was harmful to the physical growth of the subject.

No attempt was made to keep a record of the daily food intake of the babies. Although they were given the same type and quantity of food, so far as their clinic diet was concerned, the impression nevertheless was gained that toward the latter part of the practice period Johnny ate noticeably more than Jimmy. It was always he who would call for second helpings. The difference in food consumption is no doubt responsible to a considerable extent for his increase in weight. Had it been experimentally essential to keep the food intake constant for the two children, it would have been physically impossible without recourse to forced feeding, which would have been both unwise and unnecessary for the present study. The old adage applied to horses is equally true for children. Neither child in his clinic eating has shown eccentricities or marked food dislikes during the time of this investigation. It may be that Johnny's increased motor activity stimulated his appetite. If that were the sole explanation, it would be expected that the difference in food intake would have been minimized when Jimmy also began to engage in more motor activity. On the contrary, Johnny's tendency to eat not only more in quantity but more rapidly persisted during Jimmy's practice period, when the amount of daily motor activity for the two was fairly comparable. There is another plausible explanation for these differences. It so happens that during the control period Jimmy was spoon-fed by a nurse for his midday meal at the clinic. Johnny, on the other hand, from the time he could handle a spoon was allowed and encouraged as much as possible to feed himself. It is the writer's opinion, though it is an opinion based upon observation without experimental evidence to substantiate it, that during the many months when Jimmy was being spoon-fed he developed lazy eating habits from which he has not been completely cured. Johnny, in contrast, especially during the early stage of his feeding training when his motor coördinations were poorly controlled, found it necessary to put forth a great deal of effort in order to get enough food. As his motor coördinations became more efficient he could consume a greater amount of food by expending the same amount of energy to which he had already become accustomed.

One aspect of physical development in which Johnny was outstandingly different from Jimmy and other clinic babies seems to be directly related either to the type or amount of gross motor activity which he was daily experiencing. This was general muscular relaxation. The writer has never observed an infant or young child who could be so completely relaxed. This difference was sufficiently great to be noted by the casual observer who merely walked into the nursery and lifted several children.

In other types of growth there was a high degree of correspondence in the physical development of the two children. Anterior fontanelles were recorded as closed for both children during the same week, when they were fifteen months old. Development in the eruption of teeth was strikingly close. Both erupted two lower incisors when they were 225 days old and by the time they were 757 days each had twenty deciduous teeth fully erupted.

During the first twenty-four months of life Johnny and Jimmy spent relatively few of their waking hours in the out-of-doors or exposed to the direct rays of the sun. Keeping infants under such conditions inevitably arouses the question of possible rickets. Actually, the only occasion when signs of rickets were noted occurred in the medical report when the twins were 350 days old. At that time a rachitic rosary was reported for Jimmy and a slight case of Harrison's groove for Johnny. For that reason, when the twins were fifteen months old the clinic staff assumed the responsibility for their daily intake of cod-liver oil. The amount was increased from two to four teaspoons a day for both. Subsequently no mention of rachitic signs has occurred in their regular medical records, and indeed it is true that such manifestations as they may have had at any time were mild.

However, there was a period of four or five months when Jimmy's lower extremities were noticeably more bowed than were Johnny's. Of course, there is a normal degree of bowing in the lower extremities of all growing infants, but from general observation the writer is convinced that Jimmy's recovery from the infantile bowing was much slower not only than Johnny's but slower than that of other infants of corresponding locomotor development who have come under the observation of the experimenters. Whether or not Jimmy's lack of activity was contributory to his slower rate of development in this respect is a matter of conjecture. It is obvious that he spent more of his waking hours in a sitting posture than would the average child of twelve to eighteen months. If he spent more time in a sitting position, it follows that certain bones were subject to greater stress than would normally have occurred in a more active environment. All infants who are just beginning to sit customarily sit with their legs flexed at the knees and their thighs abducted at the pelvis. In the beginning they also use their upper extremities for support. Now if the child is suffering from rickets at this age the bones are unable to resist the stress put upon them, and hence both arms and legs become bowed and deformed, sometimes permanently. If the child is not suffering from rickets it will require a greater amount of stress upon particular bones to effect the same degree or permanency of deformity. If the stress is relieved on certain bones there may be a correction even if the patient is rachitic. Dr. Park (47) states that bends in the radius and ulna have been observed to disappear entirely within a year after the patient had ceased using the arms for supporting the body in the sitting posture. Whether or not Johnny and Jimmy might have suffered a mild degree of rickets when they were from a year to fifteen months of age was never unequivocally determined, since roentgenograms were not made; but the fact remains that Johnny's long bones lost their bowed appearance several months earlier than did Jimmy's. This difference is at least suggestive of the idea that the strain placed upon Jimmy's long bones through the longer periods of sitting which were inevitable during his period of restricted action were possible contributing factors to his delayed development in this respect. While these data are significant as suggestions, generalizations or conclusions are entirely unwarranted.

Roentgenograms of wrists and long bones were made when the twins were thirty-two months old. At that time the skeletal maturation of both was normal. These roentgenograms clearly indicate that the different experimental rôles of the two children had had no permanent effect upon their skeletal growth.

It is also interesting that, although the twins were not exposed to a customary amount of direct sunlight for the growing infant and although their diets were not as carefully controlled as is desirable, both present perhaps better than average health records for the child of two years of comparable socio-economic level. Neither seems to have suffered any gross or permanent impairment as a result of the divergence of their experimental rôles.

Aside from the chronic respiratory infection which was common to both children, the following outline is a fair indication of the frequency and nature of their illness which called for clinic or hospital treatment.

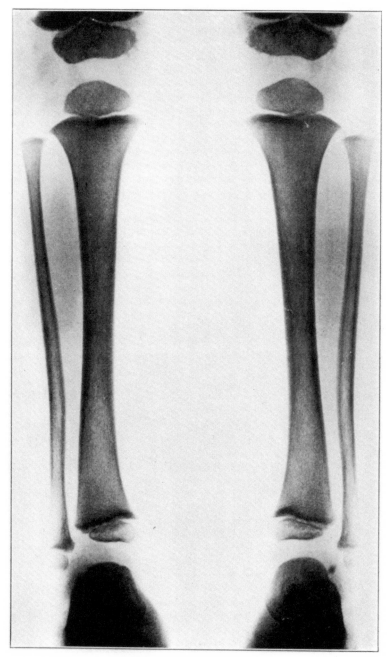

PLATE XVI. SKELETAL GROWTH

This x-ray of Johnny's legs shows normal growth at thirty-two months.

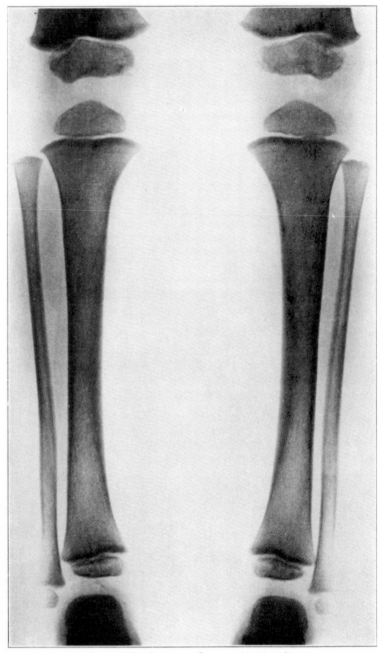

PLATE XVI. SKELETAL GROWTH (*continued*)
Jimmy's growth at thirty-two months was normal.

Johnny	Age in Months	Jimmy
Acute bronchitis	3	....
Measles	12	Measles
Common cold } Acute nasopharyngitis }	18	....
Acute nasopharyngitis	19	....
....	23	Laceration of ring finger and contusion of middle and ring fingers on right hand. No fracture
Fracture of middle phalanx of index finger on right hand	24	....
Successful vaccination	26	Successful vaccination
....	26	Suppurative cervical lymphadenitis
Circumcision	27	Circumcision
Tonsillectomy and adenoidectomy	29	Tonsillectomy and adenoidectomy

It is easily seen from the above outline that there was nothing strikingly different in the health records of the twins beyond Johnny's slightly greater proclivity for acute respiratory infections. Furthermore, notwithstanding their respective rôles as subjects in a protracted experiment, there is nothing of outstanding significance in their health records during the first two years as compared with other children. The only definite conclusion the writer would feel disposed to make on the basis of these records is that the sort of existence these children were called upon to live during their first two years had no obviously deleterious effect upon their physical development. It is certainly safe to say that the health records of Johnny and Jimmy were, during the time of the investigation, equal to and probably superior to those of other infants of similar socio-economic level who have served as subjects periodically in this study and who spent most of their days in their home environment.

Chapter X

GENERAL PRINCIPLES OF GROWTH

SINCE development is a factor common to all living matter, it is not unreasonable to assume that there are fundamental principles of development inherent in the process of growth despite the nature or character of the growing organism. We speak of the growth of a cell, a plant, a tumor, a disease, a culture, a society, an idea, or a behavior-pattern. Do we mean the same thing when we speak of growth in such diverse connections? If development is a process having general identifying characteristics which transcend the particulars wherein the growth occurs, then an adequate theory of development must embrace the process involved in cellular cleavage, organ differentiation, and simple and complex behavior activities.

The psychologists have failed to arrive at an all-embracing theory of development in behavior because too often their subjects, whether plants, lower animals, or humans, have been adults, or, if the subjects were not adults, then the particular trait under observation was mature or well determined at the time study of it was initiated. The limitations of the conditioning theory, for example, lie in the fact that it is constructed out of reaction patterns which are mature. Under such conditions growth would be a matter of associations or rearrangements of patterns already developed, whereas development really involves the *emergence* of something new—a way of behaving in which that particular individual has never behaved before. The ability to secrete saliva is a fully developed reaction pattern in the dog. By conditioning he learns to secrete saliva at the ringing of a bell as well as at sight of food. One type of stimulus has been substituted for another, but the dog's manner of reaction is the same as it was before the conditioning.

The baby can be conditioned to cry at the sight of a rabbit, though it is presupposed that he had the ability to cry long before he saw the rabbit. Again, a newborn baby is equipped with a well-developed sucking mechanism. By ringing a buzzer every time a bottle is presented to the infant it is possible to condition him so that the mere ringing of the buzzer will set up the sucking response, though there is no nipple to suck on. So far as the infant's overt response is concerned, nothing new has been created in his behavior-repertoire. But one could ring a buzzer a thousand times over simultaneously with the presentation of the bottle and yet not get a three or four months old infant so *conditioned* that he would take the initiative of deliberately ringing the buzzer in order to have the bottle brought to him. The problem in development is to ascertain what has occurred to make it possible for the older child to take such initiative, whereas no amount of conditioning was sufficient to develop it in the growing baby.

When the inseminated egg begins to divide, it is behaving in a way that particular egg has never behaved before; and when the baby first pulls himself up and stands alone, he is behaving in a way that that particular baby has never behaved before. These changes in behavior are the phenomena characteristic of development.

The sort of development that means a mere *substitution* of stimulus or response is different from that type of growth which involves the creation or emergence of a new type of behavior; new, that is, in so far as the particular individual is concerned. It is, therefore, necessary to distinguish between situations which involve merely a substitution of stimuli or responses and those which actually create a new pattern in the overt-action-system. An adequate theory of behavior development will embrace the process of cellular cleavage; the infant's learning to walk, the ten-year-old's learning to ride a bicycle, and the college student's solving a problem in calculus. An adequate theory of development must embrace the emergence of new behavior-patterns. But one does not study development as such, one studies the development of something. One may study the development of a plant, of ossification, of a social order, or of an infant.

In the present investigation we have chosen to study the development of a few select behavior-patterns as they are manifest in the growing infant and young child. Of course a behavior-pattern cannot for purposes of study be dissected from the infant of which it is an integral part, nor does it function as an isolated unit distinct from and uninfluenced by other sections of the child.

Nevertheless, we have shown, we believe, that it is possible to focus attention upon the development of a particular behavior-pattern, as it is seen within the individual, in the same way in which one might focus attention upon an individual child as a specialized nodal point of the environment in which he lives. In fact it is scarcely more difficult to establish the origin and continuity of a behavior-pattern within an individual than it is to establish the origin and continuity of an individual within a society. The individual represents a nodal point of specialization within an environment; correspondingly, behavior-patterns are nodal points of concentration of activity within the total action-system of the individual's behavior.

In any investigation it is necessary for the purposes of analysis to set arbitrary bounds and restrictions to the material upon which attention will be focused. Therefore in studying the development of behavior-patterns we have deliberately limited our analysis to those growth changes which can be observed in the somatic movements of the subject. Of course, morphological changes of the nerve cells, cellular lamination, and myelinization of nerve fibers are just as much a matter of behavior development as are the sequential changes in the achievement of walking, fighting, or learning to read. But unfortunately we are not able to analyze all the factors which enter into the development of an action-system. Since, however, the development of behavior as indicated merely in the overt-behavior patterns herein described enhances the advancing information on the nature of growth *per se,* as well as pointing out the phases of growth in these particulars, this detailed account of the development of select behavior-patterns gains a significance beyond the factual details.

When the course of a behavior-pattern is followed systematically, the appropriateness of the term *pattern* becomes more evident. The growing of a behavior-pattern is likened to a design in the process of being woven, composed as it is of various colored threads. All of the threads do not move forward at the same time nor at the same rate. The weaver picks up the gold thread and weaves it back and forth, though at the same time steadily forward. Then he drops it in order to bring the blue thread forward a distance, until finally the two become united to make the pattern complete. The design is contingent upon the interrelation of the various threads. It is not the summation of the blue and gold threads but their position with respect to each other and to the piece as a whole which determines the design. To unravel one of the threads would mean destruction of the design. Fortunately it is not necessary to unravel the threads in order to analyze the structure of the design. The course of each thread can be followed in detail. Likewise one may trace the movements of a behavior-pattern and follow the phases of its development from the origin to the consummation without isolating it from the conditions in which it thrives.

Any activity is composed of many ingredients, some of which may for convenience be considered as external and others as internal with respect to the organism, *but none of these factors can be considered as external to the behavior.* It is their relationship to each other which gives the activity pattern and form. A watch in the visual field is just as much an integral part of the activity of reaching and prehension as is the flexor-extensor movement of the arm. Although retaining their own identity, these factors unite in the formation of a behavioral pattern which is distinct from the summation of its parts. While the watch, the eyes, and the arms may remain as constant ingredients in the activity, as the behavior-pattern matures it becomes apparent that the interrelation has materially altered. The form and design of that interrelation have changed. These changes are the signs of development.

In order to ascertain these changes in a pattern of behavior, it is desirable to follow its course of development from the moment of origin until it attains functional maturity or fixity. Unfortunately when studying behavior-patterns in the human infant it is not possible always to realize this ideal. It is not possible because the human infant is a complex animal, born into the world with a long phylogenetic history plus a good start toward ontogenetic growth. Ordinarily the human infant is not available to the experimenter until after birth. All behavior-patterns do not, in ontogeny, begin developing at the same time. By the time the infant is born, some have not only started growing but have attained a high degree of fixity. It is therefore obviously impossible to start analysis of these action-patterns at their inception. Instead, one must calculate maturational level of the behavior-pattern at the time it becomes available for observation.

The maturational level of each behavior-pattern should be calculated in terms of its phylogenetic history and of the neuro-structural level at which in ontogeny it is controlled. Phyletic behavior-patterns have been considered here solely in terms of their ontogenetic manifestation. Since the cortex of the newborn infant is not functioning to any appreciable degree, all of the activities of the newborn infant are presumably controlled at an infracortical level. Some infracortical activities have not only attained fixity at the time of birth but continue to function at an infracortical level throughout ontogeny. Other behavior-patterns of the newborn infant may be in the late stage of development as infracortical activities and may soon appear in new forms as patterns of higher order. Such phylogenetic behavior-patterns are seen in the newborn baby merely as rudiments. These rudiments are controlled at an infracortical level, and in the human subject they never attain functional maturity as infracortical activities. Although these rudimentary patterns never attain maturity at an infracortical level, they are succeeded by activities of functional similarity controlled at a higher structural level. Ontogenetic manifestation of still another order of phyletic behavior-patterns occurs in the human subject during post-natal development. It is possible therefore to study the ontogenetic manifestation of these patterns from their inception, although they are rooted in the phylum.

While it is not possible to initiate study of all behavior-patterns of the infant at the time of their inception, it is possible to calculate the particular phase of development in which the action-pattern happens to be at the time the baby becomes available to the experimenter and to continue study of its course of growth until it achieves fixity. The stage of development a particular pattern may have achieved can be estimated in terms of the degree of fixity it manifests and the degree of individual control over the performance.

Having used the growth of behavior-patterns as a means of studying the process of development, we have become convinced that the principles of growth are fundamental as to the process, regardless of the particulars of the growing organism. This analysis of growth in behavior-patterns is quite in line with observations which have frequently been made upon organic development.

Wherever there is development or growth there is also a period of inception, incubation, consummation, and decline. Nothing springs forth full-grown. Development is extremely gradual. There are spurts and rhythms in development, but it can safely be said that nothing is created without preparation. "Growth is not a straight line affair nor is it a smooth curve, but it increases by steps, sometimes by leaps and bounds; at times it is slow and then again it is rapid. This is true not only for the body as a whole but also for its parts and organs, or functional systems. The cells themselves do not all divide and multiply at the same time, but first one and then another becomes active, and those that divide consecutively are not usually the adjacent ones." Bean (*I*, p. 45) was speaking of organic growth, but the statement could easily be used to describe the growth of a culture, an idea, or a behavior-pattern if the appropriate words were substituted. There are rhythms, spurts, fluctuations, pauses, and regressions preceding fixity or functional maturity. The secret of a full understanding of the meaning and process of development lies hidden in the factors which determine these rhythms and fluctuations of growth.

A more detailed study of the development of particular action-patterns than this investigation has afforded is essential if the nature of rhythmical fluctuations is to be ascertained. A behavior-course is not an isolated unit growing in every direction all at once. It is comprised of many aspects, each of which has its own growth rate and rhythm. While each aspect of a growing action-pattern has its identifying way of developing, it is at the same time an integral part of the total behavior-pattern, in the same fashion that the behavior-pattern in question is an integral part of the total action-system of the individual. One aspect of a behavior-pattern goes through a period of rapid development, then pauses as another aspect moves rapidly forward. But the growth of each aspect of development influences and determines the growth of the other. The development of one aspect overlaps with the development of another so that there are no sharp lines of demarcation separating the phases of a developing pattern, but the connection of one phase or one pattern with another is more than a mere overlapping. There is a close interdependence in the growth of the various aspects of a pattern. Development works back and forth, yet steadily forward; here and there it strikes rapids, in other spots it pauses or regresses. The appearance of a new movement or aspect of a pattern facilitates or inhibits the growth of a previously developing movement and also determines the emergence and organization of a succeeding one. It is the gradual twining and interweaving of movements and phases of developing patterns which make it difficult to allocate the rhythms and spurts of growth.

In his discussion of an experience Dr. Dewey (*13*) has given an accurate description of the process of development in behavior. It is natural this should be so, since any activity which he would call *an* experience must constitute for the experiencer development also.

"An experience," he says (Ch. III), "has pattern and structure because it is not just doing and undoing in alternation, but consists of them in relationship. . . . In such experiences every successive part flows freely, without seam and without unfilled blanks, into what ensues. At the same time there is no sacrifice of the self-identity of the parts. . . . As one part leads into another and as some part carries on what went before, each gains distinctness in itself. . . . Because of continuous merging, there are no holes, mechanical junctions, and dead centers when we have *an* experience. There are pauses, places of rest, but they punctuate and define the quality of movement. They sum up what has been undergone and prevent its dissipation and idle evaporation. Continued acceleration is breathless and prevents parts from gaining distinction. . . . Experience like breathing is a rhythm of intakings and outgivings. Their succession is punctuated and made a rhythm by the existence of intervals, periods in which one phase is ceasing and the other is inchoate and preparing."

While we have not in this investigation been able to ascertain the definition of these rhythms and spurts of development, our findings, though tentative, suggest that the following phases or alterations can be expected in the growth of any behavior-pattern, despite the complexity of the activity or the structural level at which it is controlled.

(1) Since we made observations only on overt manifestation of behavior, the initial phase in the development of a particular behavior-course would be that period just prior to the first emergence of a somatic movement indicating the appearance of the growing action-pattern. Whatever may be the nature of the growth prior to the overt manifestation of the action, it would have to be

analyzed through some other method than direct observation. It is, for example, conceivable that a growth is in progress which will later make it possible for the baby to respond overtly to a bell held before his face, but the nature of the development cannot be observed in the actions of the newborn infant. This is true because there is a period following birth when his movements have no perceptible reference to objects within the visual field. The initial phase in the development of an activity is that period which occurs just prior to the first identifiable movements of the behavior-pattern.

(2) The second phase is indicated by the first somatic movement which can be recognized as a developing aspect of the behavior-course. This movement is inchoate and ephemeral and is coupled with, if not obscured by, diffuse general activities. It can be observed only infrequently, and then it is not carried through to completion.

(3) Little by little this partial, incomplete movement can be seen to become more definite and expansive. In fact it often becomes so expansive as to appear excessive or exaggerated. There is a tendency to overwork a newly developing activity. This tendency to exaggeration is expressed both in time and in extent of the movement. As the child begins to get control over a pattern or an aspect of a pattern, the activity itself becomes the incentive for repetition.

(4) In due process of growth, however, the exaggeration of this particular movement becomes checked or inhibited by the emergence of another movement. The conflict of the two is likely to evoke greater diffuse activity for a time, but gradually the second movement reaches the period of rapid development until it too becomes overemphasized, often to the extent of being excessive. Often the second aspect or movement develops so rapidly that it temporarily excludes the earlier one. Ultimately the excess activity is eliminated until the movement becomes restricted to its most specific and economical form—usually somewhere between the two extremes. We so often think of growth as an expansion or accumulation of something. In reality elimination and regression are as essential to development as accumulation and expansion.

(5) Once a pattern or an aspect of a pattern has attained a certain degree of fixity or definiteness it may unite or integrate

with another aspect of the pattern or another action-pattern in order to form a new, more complex behavior-pattern. The process of development may therefore be quite different when the behavior-pattern is in different stages of maturation. At an early phase the process may be a matter of eliminating excess motion, growth progressing from a general diffuse state to one of greater specificity, whereas in the later stages of development the process may be primarily that of constructing patterns of greater complexity. Within a given individual both processes are going on at all times, since different action-patterns are in different stages of development.

In the development of a behavior-pattern the outstanding fluctuations or spurts appear to occur in connection with conspicuous changes in the growth cycle. That is, when one aspect of the action is declining there often occurs an increase in the activity before it finally fades out. This feature of development has become familiar in colloquial speech as the "second wind" or "end spurt." On the other hand a newly developing aspect of the pattern may herald its forthcoming. There sometimes appears sporadic evidence of a new aspect of the pattern before it definitely manifests itself as a newly developing part of the pattern. Often these sporadic occurrences are followed by long pauses or regression just before the movement appears as a characteristic aspect of the behavior-course. This feature of development has become proverbial in the familiar adages, "A new broom sweeps clean," "Beginner's luck," etc. When the same spurts and variations occur in the development of primitive behavior-patterns one becomes convinced that the principle is fundamental.

The Modification of Infant Behavior

In fact and in principle the underlying processes which obtain in the *development* of behavior also apply to the *modification* of behavior. Development is a process of modification, and it is really impossible to draw a distinction between the two; but when we speak of modified behavior we usually mean that it has been modified in such a way as to change it from a course of development which occurs under the usual circumstances. It is in this sense that we have used the term *modified behavior*. Behavior-patterns can be modified by (1) speeding up the growth process,

(2) prolonging or reducing the rate of development, or (3) in some way altering the form or sequence of the pattern which ordinarily occurs during development. Changes in any of these ways may be brought about through deliberate manipulation of the factors involved in the growth process. In so doing, it is not the principles of development which are altered but merely the relationship between the ingredients which make up the growth compound. There are many ways of artificially or deliberately altering the relationship of the factors which activate the growth process. One very obvious method is to increase or restrict the amount of exercise or use the growing behavior-pattern is allowed. In this way it is possible to estimate the effect repetition of a function may have upon its development.

The extent to which exercise of an activity may alter the development of a particular behavior-course in infancy is contingent upon the following conditions: (1) the neuro-structural level at which the activity is controlled; (2) the state of plasticity or fixity of the behavior-course at the time increased exercise or use is introduced; (3) the state of fixity attained by the behavior-pattern at the time the factor of special exercise is withdrawn, and (4) the phylogenetic origin and importance of the behavior-pattern.

Those behavior-patterns which have achieved a high degree of fixity and are controlled at an infracortical level are subject to no appreciable alteration through mere repetition of the activity during the post-natal development of the subject. Also phyletic rudiments of behavior-patterns controlled at an infracortical level are resistant to influence or alteration of any significance by increased exercise of the activity. Those phylogenetic activities which succeed these infracortical rudiments, that is, the kindred activities which are governed at a higher structural level, can be modified in minor details through individual exercise of the function. But the essential form and nature of the behavior-course is resistant to alteration through repetition of the function within the lifetime of a single individual. The degree to which the activities of this second order are modifiable in this manner appears to be in direct ratio to the temporal gap between the two types of activity. That is, the gap between reflex swimming movements and voluntary swimming movements is greater than is the corresponding relation between reflex stepping movements and voluntary walking. Therefore voluntary swimming is subject to greater modification through exercise of the action than is voluntary walking.

Activities of ontogenetic origin can be greatly accelerated through exercise of the performance, but the degree to which they can be modified is dependent upon the state of maturation or plasticity of the behavior-pattern at the time the factor of exercise is introduced. In géneral it appears that the period of greatest susceptibility occurs when the behavior-pattern is at its threshold of rapid development. In this connection it must be recalled that behavior-patterns do not grow all at once but that each aspect has its own period of rapid development. Therefore if maximum profit is to be gained by exercise of a growing behavior-pattern, the exercise should occur in connection with the particular aspect of the pattern which is in a state of rapid growth.

Since growth is gradual, first one aspect and then another gaining ascendancy, the exercise of the activity should be introduced in a similar way if optimum results are to be obtained. Since a child does not acquire all aspects of an action-pattern at once, it would seem reasonable that a gradual, step-by-step presentation of the activating agents should facilitate the development of new activities.

While there are critical periods in the development of any behavior-pattern when it is most susceptible to modification, it must not be inferred that behavior-patterns can be modified through exercise only during these critical periods of susceptibility. It means merely that these are the most economical periods of achievement. To delay beyond the period of greatest susceptibility means that other factors which have begun to grow will act as interferences and distractions, thereby rendering the achievement of the particular pattern more difficult.

The permanency of the expansion which an action-pattern gains through additional exercise is contingent upon the degree of fixity the behavior-pattern had achieved at the time the modifying agent, i.e., the factor of special exercise, was withdrawn. It does not necessarily follow that a performance which has been developed under special conditions will be retained after those conditions are removed. Unless the behavior-pattern has become fixed, it is only reasonable to expect that there will be a loss in performance unless the conditions which brought it about are continued.

Correspondingly, if the growth of a behavior-pattern has been hindered through restriction, it is to be expected that recovery will be evident when the restrictions are removed. In physiological development this aspect of growth is called regeneration and in behavior it is often referred to as reëduction. Great improvement in the development of behavior can be effected provided the cycles and rhythms functioning in the growth of particular behavior-courses can be disclosed, and provided the proper activating influences can be brought to bear upon the growth process at the most opportune time.

Not only in regard to the practical means and methods of modifying behavior development, but also in understanding theories of development themselves, we have often been confused because of the tendency to disregard the different degrees of plasticity or maturity of the growing organism in interpreting and formulating theories of growth. For example, the apparent controversy over individuation versus integration is clarified if the different stages of development of particular action-patterns are taken into account. From the descriptions of behavior development contained in the preceding chapters it is easily seen that at one stage of development the process of growth is predominantly a matter of eliminating waste motion, development being from an undifferentiated state to a more specific one, or a process of individuation. But once a pattern, or an aspect of a pattern, has attained an appropriate degree of specificity, further development is indicated by an integration of two or more action-patterns, or aspects of an action-pattern, into another of greater complexity. It is not therefore a question of one theory being correct and the other wrong. The two processes are by no means mutually exclusive. Actually, both processes can be observed in the actions of the same individual at the same time, but the processes represent different stages of maturation in the growth cycle.

This attempt of the writer to describe and interpret the course of behavior development is an excellent illustration of the stage of incubation represented by an inordinate amount of excess motion, a tendency to overlook the obvious and to overemphasize some particular aspect just because it is a slightly new point of view to the author. Somewhere in the diffusion there is recognized a deliberate and conscious movement which, though inchoate, is nevertheless in the direction of a goal. In a descriptive analysis of development one is beset by difficulties, among them the most obvious being the fact that development is *movement,* dynamic movement. The static bounds of language concepts are too limiting to allow a precise definition of development. Perhaps the time will come when the movements of growth can be expressed in mathematical formulas as precisely as the movements of celestial bodies, but until that time arrives we shall have to be content with cumbersome descriptive analyses.

References

1. Bean, R. B., "The Pulse of Growth in Man," *Anatomical Record*, 1924, V. 28, #1, pp. 45-61.
2. Bonnevie, K., "Studies in Papillary Patterns of Human Fingers," *Journal of Genetics*, Nov., 1924, V. 15, #1, pp. 1-113.
3. Bridges, Calvin B., "Salivary Chromosome Maps," *Journal of Heredity*, Feb., 1935, V. 26, #2, pp. 60-64.
4. Carmichael, Leonard, "Origin and Prenatal Growth of Behavior," in *Handbook of Psychology*, Carl Murchison, Editor (Clark University Press, 1933), pp. 31-159.
5. ——————, "Heredity and Environment: Are They Antithetical?" *Journal of Abnormal Psychology*, 1925, V. 20, #10, p. 245.
6. Castle, W. E., *Genetics and Eugenics* (Harvard University Press, 1921).
7. Coghill, G. E., "Neuro-embryonic Study of Behavior: Principles, Perspective and Aim," *Science*, Aug. 18, 1933, V. 78, #2016, pp. 131-138.
8. ——————, "Structural Basis for Integration of Behavior," *National Academy of Science*, Oct., 1930, V. 16, #10, pp. 637-643.
9. ——————, "Individuation versus Integration in the Development of Behavior," *Journal of General Psychology*, 1930, V. 3, #3, pp. 431-435.
10. ——————, "Genetic Interrelation of Instinctive Behavior and Reflexes," *Psychological Review*, May, 1930, V. 37, #3, pp. 264-266.
11. Cummins, Harold, "Dermatoglyphics in Twins of Known Chorionic History with Reference to Diagnosis of the Twins Varieties," *Anatomical Record*, July, 1930, V. 46, #2, pp. 179-198.
12. Dewey, John, *Philosophy and Civilization* (Minton, Balch & Company, New York, 1931): "Unit of Behavior," pp. 233-248; "Conduct and Experience," pp. 249-270.
13. ——————, *Art as Experience* (Minton, Balch & Company, New York, 1934).
14. Driver, Ernest C., "Temperature and Gene Expression in Drosophila," *Journal of Experimental Zoölogy*, Feb. 5, 1931, V. 59, #1, pp. 1-28.
15. Dürken, Bernhard, *Experimental Analysis of Development*,

tr. H. G. and A. M. Newth (W. W. Norton and Company, New York, 1932).

16. Frank, Lawrence K., "Causation: An Episode in the History of Thought," *Journal of Philosophy*, Aug. 2, 1934, V. 31, #16, pp. 421-428.

17. Frank, Lawrence K., "Locus of Experience" *Journal of Philosophy*, June 7, 1923, V. 22, #12, pp. 327-329.

18. Freud, Anna, "Psychoanalysis of the Child," in *Handbook of Child Psychology*, First Edition, Carl Murchison, Editor (Clark University Press, 1931), pp. 555-567.

19. Furfey, P. H., and Muehlenbein, J., "Validity of Infant Intelligence Tests," *Journal of Genetic Psychology*, 1932, V. 40, #3, pp. 219-223.

20. Gesell, Arnold, *Infancy and Human Growth* (The Macmillan Company, New York, 1925).

21. ——————, "Maturation and the Patterning of Behavior," in *Handbook of Psychology*, Second Edition, Carl Murchison, Editor (Clark University Press, 1933), pp. 209-235.

22. ——————, *Mental Growth of the Pre-school Child* (The Macmillan Company, New York, 1925).

23. Gesell, Arnold, and Thompson, Helen, "Learning and Growth in Identical Twin Infants," *Genetic Psychology Monographs*, July, 1929, V. 6, #1, pp. 1-124.

24. Goodenough, F. L., "Measurement of Mental Growth," in *Handbook of Psychology*, Second Edition, Carl Murchison, Editor (Clark University Press, 1933), pp. 303-328.

25. Herrick, C. Judson, "The Evolution of Cerebral Localization Patterns," *Science*, Nov. 10, 1933, V. 78, #2028, pp. 439-444.

26. Irwin, O. C., "Organismic Hypothesis and Differentiation of Behavior," *Psychological Review*, July, 1932, V. 39, #4, pp. 128-146.

27. Jackson, C. M., "On the Prenatal Growth of the Human Body and the Relative Growth of the Various Organs and Parts," *American Journal of Anatomy*, 1909, V. 9, #9, pp. 119-165.

28. James, William, *Principles of Psychology*, V. 1 (Henry Holt and Company, New York, 1902).

29. Jordan, H. E., and Kindred, J. E., *Textbook of Embryology* (D. Appleton and Company, New York, 1926).

30. Keibel, F., and Mall, F. P., *Manual of Human Embryology*, V. 1 (J. B. Lippincott Company, Philadelphia, 1910).

31. Kohler, Wolfgang, *Gestalt* (Horace Liveright, New York, 1929).

32. Komai, Taku, and Fukuoko, Goro, "A Set of Dichorionic Identical Triplets," *Journal of Heredity*, Aug., 1931, V. 22, #8, p. 233.

33. Lashley, K. S., "Mass Action in Cerebral Function," *Science*, March 6, 1931, V. 73, #1888, pp. 245-254.

34. Levin, Max, "Can Single-Ovum Twins Be of Opposite Sexes?" *Journal of Heredity*, Jan., 1931, V. 22, #1, pp. 17-19.

35. Lewin, Kurt, "Environmental Forces," in *Handbook of Child Psychology*, Second Revised Edition, Carl Murchison, Editor (Clark University Press, 1930), pp. 590-625.

36. Lovejoy, Arthur O., "Meaning of 'Emergence' and Its Modes," *Proceedings of the International Congress of Philosophy*, #6, 1927, pp. 20-33.

37. Marquis, Dorothy G., "Criterion of Innate Behavior," *Psychological Review*, 1930, V. 37, #7, pp. 334-348.

38. —————, "Can Conditioned Responses Be Established in Newborn Infants?" *Pedagogical Seminary Journal of Genetic Psychology*, 1931, V. 39, #4, pp. 479-492.

39. Morgan, Thomas H., *Embryology and Genetics* (Columbia University Press, 1934).

40. Newman, H. H., "Differences Between Conjoined Twins," *Journal of Heredity*, July, 1931, V. 22, #7, p. 201.

41. —————, *Biology of Twins* (The University of Chicago Press, 1917).

42. —————, "Brief Reply to Reichle Article 'Diagnosis of Monozygotic Twinning,'" *Journal of Heredity*, Jan., 1934, V. 25, #1, p. 37.

43. —————, "Palm-print Patterns in Twins," *Journal of Heredity*, Feb., 1931, V. 22, #2, pp. 41-49.

44. —————, *The Physiology of Twinning* (The University of Chicago Press, 1923).

45. —————, "Studies on Human Twins: 1. Methods of Diagnosing Monozygotic and Dizygotic Twins; 2. Asymmetry Reversal of Mirror Image in Identical Twins," *Biological Bulletin*, 1928, V. 55, #10, pp. 283 and 298.

46. Painter, Theophilus S., "Salivary Chromosomes and the Attack of the Gene," *Journal of Heredity*, Dec., 1934, V. 25, #12, pp. 467-476.

47. Park, Edwards A., "On Some Aspects of Rickets," First Blackader Lecture—1931, *Canadian Medical Association Journal*, 1932, V. 26, #3, pp. 3-15.

48. Raven, H. C., "The Further Adventures of Meshie," *The Journal of the American Museum of Natural History*, Nov. and Dec., 1933, V. 33, #6, pp. 607-617.

49. Reichle, H. S., "Diagnosis of Mono-ovular Twinning," *Biological Bulletin*, May, 1929, V. 56, #5, pp. 313-326.

50. —————, "Diagnosis of Monozygotic Twinning," *Journal of Heredity*, Jan., 1934, V. 25, #1, pp. 33-37.

51. —————, "Diagnosis of the Type of Twinning," *Biological Bulletin*, March, 1929, V. 56, #3, pp. 164-176.

52. Rife, D. Cecil, "Genetic Studies of Monozygotic Twins," *Journal of Heredity*, Oct., 1933, V. 24, #10, p. 407.

53. Ritter, William E., and Bailey, Edna W., "The Organismal Conception," *University of California Publications in Zoölogy*, 1929, V. 31, #14, pp. 307-358.
54. Science News Letter: "Chromosome Structure Details Described By Russian," Oct. 13, 1934, p. 236. (Dr. Nicolai Koltzoff, Dr. Calvin B. Bridges, Prof. T. S. Painter.)
55. Science News Letter: "Genes Traced to Individual Chromomeres in New Research," Nov. 10, 1934, p. 302. (Prof. H. H. Muller and Dr. A. A. Prokofyeva.)
56. Shirley, Mary M., *First Two Years*, V. 1 (University of Minnesota Press, 1923).
57. ——————, "Locomotor and Visual-manual Functions in the First Two Years," *Handbook of Psychology*, Second Edition (Clark University Press, 1933), pp. 236-270.
58. Siemans, H. W., "Diagnosis of Identity in Twins," *Journal of Heredity*, May, 1927, V. 18, #5, p. 201.
59. Stockard, C. R., "Developmental Rate and Structural Expression," *American Journal of Anatomy*, Jan., 1921, V. 28, #1, pp. 115-278.
60. ——————, *Physical Basis of Personality* (W. W. Norton and Company, New York, 1931).
61. Tilney, Frederick, and Kubie, Lawrence S., "Behavior in Relation to the Development of the Brain," *Bulletin of the Neurological Institute of New York*, June, 1931, V. 1, #2, pp. 229-313.
62. Tilney, Frederick, "Behavior in Its Relation to the Development of the Brain: Part II. Correlation Between the Development of the Brain and Behavior in the Albino Rat from Embryonic States to Maturity," *Bulletin of the Neurological Institute of New York*, June, 1933, V. III, #1 and 2, pp. 252-357.
63. Watson, John B., *Behaviorism*, Revised Edition (W. W. Norton and Company, New York, 1930).
64. Wheeler, R. H., and Perkins, F. T., *Principles of Mental Development* (Thomas Y. Crowell Company, New York, 1932).
65. Wheeler, W. M., "Emergent Evolution of the Social," *Proceedings of the International Congress of Philosophy*, #6, 1927, pp. 33-46.
66. Wickes, Francis G., *Inner World of Childhood* (D. Appleton and Company, New York, 1927).
67. Woodworth, Robert S., *Contemporary Schools of Psychology* (The Ronald Press Company, New York, 1931).
68. ——————, "Dynamic Psychology," in *Psychologies of 1930* (Clark University Press, 1930), pp. 327-336.

Index

A

Anticipatory reactions, 222
Associational relations, 200
  development of, 201
Atavisms, 19
  crawling movements, 20
  Moro reflex, 20
  stepping movements, 20
  suspension-grasp reflex, 20
  swimming movements, 20
Attitudes:
  definition of, 283
  development of, 286
  influence of, 286
  modification of, 291, 293
  of receptivity or coöperation, 284
  of resistance, 288
  transfer of, 291, 293

B

Bean, R. B., 305
Behavior:
  adult coercion or freedom of, 205
  atavisms, 19
  classification of, 19
  effect of repeated exercise on, 24, 224
  extrinsic factors in, 17
  intrinsic factors in, 17
  management or guidance of, 204
  modification of, 16; assistance, 231;
    critical periods for, 227, 235, 259;
    effect of chronological age upon,
    234, 235; influence of attitudes
    upon, 227, 230
  ontogenetic, 42
  phylogenetic, 42
  theories of, 6
  time factor in, 259
Behavior-course:
  definition of, 15
Behaviorism, 7
Behaviorists, 286
Behavior-patterns:
  definition of, 15
  growth phases in, 306
  origin of, 302
Bridges, Calvin B., 27

C

Coghill, G. E., 8, 9
Color discrimination, 220, 259
  practice effect in, 221
Conditional relations, 205
Conditioning, 7, 121, 290
  theory of, 300
Crawling:
  analysis of, 66
  effect of exercise on, 69, 72
Creeping:
  definition of, 69
  See also Crawling
Cutaneous irritation:
  analysis of, 111

D

Development, *see* Growth
Dewey, John, 306
Diving, 134
Dürken, Bernhard, 13, 26

E

Eating habits, 296
Embryologists, 10
Embryonic development, 11
Epigenesis, 14
Exercise of activities:
  method of, 121
Experimental method:
  co-twin, 25
  cross-section, 15
  genetic method, 4
Experimental situations:
  balanced boxes, 271
  multiple sticks, 262
  string configurations, 274
  suspended basket, 267
  tool construction, 266
Experimental subjects:
  selection of, 37

F

Fjeld, Harriet, 261

317

$\mathcal{C}$lassics In
$\mathcal{C}$hild $\mathcal{D}$evelopment

An Arno Press Collection

Baldwin, James Mark. **Thought and Things.** Four vols. in two. 1906-1915

Blatz, W[illiam] E[met], et al. **Collected Studies on the Dionne Quintuplets.** 1937

Bühler, Charlotte. **The First Year of Life.** 1930

Bühler, Karl. **The Mental Development of the Child.** 1930

Claparède, Ed[ouard]. **Experimental Pedagogy and the Psychology of the Child.** 1911

Factors Determining Intellectual Attainment. 1975

First Notes by Observant Parents. 1975

Freud, Anna. **Introduction to the Technic of Child Analysis.** 1928

Gesell, Arnold, et al. **Biographies of Child Development.** 1939

Goodenough, Florence L. **Measurement of Intelligence By Drawings.** 1926

Griffiths, Ruth. **A Study of Imagination in Early Childhood and Its Function in Mental Development.** 1918

Hall, G. Stanley and Some of His Pupils. **Aspects of Child Life and Education.** 1907

Hartshorne, Hugh and Mark May. **Studies in the Nature of Character. Vol. I: Studies in Deceit; Book One, General Methods and Results.** 1928

Hogan, Louise E. **A Study of a Child.** 1898

Hollingworth, Leta S. **Children Above 180 IQ, Stanford Binet:** Origins and Development. 1942

Kluver, Heinrich. **An Experimental Study of the Eidetic Type.** 1926

Lamson, Mary Swift. **Life and Education of Laura Dewey Bridgman, the Deaf, Dumb and Blind Girl.** 1881

Lewis, M[orris] M[ichael]. **Infant Speech:** A Study of the Beginnings of Language. 1936

McGraw, Myrtle B. **Growth: A Study of Johnny and Jimmy.** 1935

Monographs on Infancy. 1975

O'Shea, M. V., editor. **The Child: His Nature and His Needs.** 1925

Perez, Bernard. **The First Three Years of Childhood.** 1888

Romanes, George John. **Mental Evolution in Man:** Origin of Human Faculty. 1889

Shinn, Milicent Washburn. **The Biography of a Baby.** 1900

Stern, William. **Psychology of Early Childhood Up to the Sixth Year of Age.** 1924

Studies of Play. 1975

Terman, Lewis M. **Genius and Stupidity:** A Study of Some of the Intellectual Processes of Seven "Bright" and Seven "Stupid" Boys. 1906

Terman, Lewis M. **The Measurement of Intelligence.** 1916

Thorndike, Edward Lee. **Notes on Child Study.** 1901

Wilson, Louis N., compiler. **Bibliography of Child Study.** 1898-1912

[Witte, Karl Heinrich Gottfried]. **The Education of Karl Witte,** Or the Training of the Child. 1914